The Sunnah of Sacred Hatred

By Gregory Heary

Tragically some religious people espouse a contagious doctrine of "hate the sin, but not the sinner". This was not taught by any prophet. It is not taught by Judaism, Christianity, Hinduism, Buddhism or any traditional religion and most certainly it is not taught by Islam. Some Christians may think Christianity teaches this but those who think this don't know the bible adequately. Both the Old and New Testaments teach hatred for others; with Jesus pbuh even making it mandatory.

Psalms 139:21-22 "_Do I not hate those who hate you, Lord_, _and abhor those who are in rebellion against you?_²² **_I have nothing but hatred for them; I count them my enemies_**."

Luke 14:25-26 "²⁵ _Large crowds were traveling with Jesus, and turning to them he said:_ ²⁶ **_"If anyone comes to me and does not hate father and mother, wife and children, brothers and sisters_** _– yes, even their own life –_ **_such a person cannot be my disciple."_**

So the "love everybody no matter how bad they are" doctrine is a modern dogma, recently adopted by the neo-Murjia. This book is about prophetic hatred and how to hate correctly avoiding the extremes. Originally I was going to compose a book proving how all religions teach hatred, but since there is a consensus in the global religious community on the issue of hating I decided to limit myself to the Sunnah of Sacred Hatred to benefit the believers; who unfortunately due to the fashionable catchphrases and philosophies in modern times may have some confusion on the issue. The issue of this book is who to hate and how much. Since this book is meant for English readers, who unfortunately don't have access to many books on walaa wabara which elucidate this subject, I have decided not to include the Arabic of my citations to keep this book a shorter length. First I'll cite translated Quran verses, then hadith, followed by my exposition, and fatwas so Godwilling this issue can be clarified.

Quran Citations Proving Anger For or Hatred Towards Certain beings

1:7

The path of those upon whom You have bestowed favor, not of those who have evoked [Your] anger or of those who are astray.

2:7

Allah has set a seal upon their hearts and upon their hearing, and over their vision is a veil. And for them is a great punishment.

2:8-18

And of the people are some who say, "We believe in Allah and the Last Day," but they are not believers. They [think to] deceive Allah and those who believe, but they deceive not except themselves and perceive [it] not. In their hearts is disease, so Allah has increased their disease; and for them is a painful punishment because they [habitually] used to lie. And when it is said to them, "Do not cause corruption on the earth," they say, "We are but reformers." Unquestionably, it is they who are the corrupters, but they perceive [it] not. And when it is said to them, "Believe as the people have believed," they say, "Should we believe as the foolish have believed?" Unquestionably, it is they who are the foolish, but they know [it] not. And when they meet those who believe, they say, "We believe"; but when they are alone with their evil ones, they say, "Indeed, we are with you; we were only mockers." [But] Allah mocks them and prolongs them in their transgression [while] they wander blindly. Those are the ones who have purchased error [in exchange] for guidance, so their transaction has brought no profit, nor were they guided. Their likeness is as the likeness of one who kindled a fire; then, when it lighted all around him, Allâh took away their light and left them *in darkness. (So) they could not see. They are deaf, dumb, and blind, so they return not (to the Right Path).*

2:26-27

Verily, Allâh is not ashamed to set forth a parable even of a mosquito or so much more when it is bigger (or less when it is smaller) than it. And as for those who believe, they know that it is the Truth from their Lord, but as for those who disbelieve, they say: "What did Allâh intend by this parable?" By it He misleads many, and many He guides thereby. And He misleads thereby only those who are Al-Fâsiqûn (the rebellious, disobedient to Allâh). Those who break Allâh's Covenant after ratifying it, and sever what Allâh has ordered to be joined (as regards Allâh's religion of Islâmic Monotheism, and to practise its legal laws on the earth and also as regards keeping good relations with kith and kin), and do mischief on earth, it is they who are the losers.

2:36

Then the Shaitân (Satan) made them slip therefrom (the Paradise), and got them out from that in which they were. We said: "Get you down, all, with enmity between yourselves. On earth will be a dwelling place for you and an enjoyment for a time."

2:59

But those who did wrong changed the word from that which had been told to them for another, so We sent upon the wrong-doers Rijzan (a punishment) from the heaven because of their rebelling against Allâh's Obedience.

2:61

And (remember) when you said, "O Mûsa (Moses)! We cannot endure one kind of food. So invoke your Lord for us to bring forth for us of what the earth grows, its herbs, its cucumbers, its Fûm (wheat or garlic), its lentils and its onions." He said, "Would you exchange that which is better for that which is lower? Go you down to any town and you shall find what you want!" And they were covered with humiliation and misery, and they drew on themselves the Wrath of Allâh. That was because they used to disbelieve the Ayât (proofs, evidences, verses, lessons, signs, revelations, etc.) of Allâh and killed the Prophets wrongfully. That was because they disobeyed and used to transgress the bounds (in their disobedience to Allâh, i.e. commit crimes and sins).

2:64-66

Then after that you turned away. Had it not been for the Grace and Mercy of Allâh upon you, indeed you would have been among the losers. And indeed you knew those amongst you who transgressed in the matter of the Sabbath. We said to them: "Be you monkeys, despised and rejected." So We made this punishment an example to their own and to succeeding generations and a lesson to those who are Al-Muttaqûn

2:74-79

Then, after that, your hearts were hardened and became as stones or even worse in hardness. And indeed, there are stones out of which rivers gush forth, and indeed, there are of them (stones) which split asunder so that water flows from them, and indeed, there are of them (stones) which fall down for fear of Allâh. And Allâh is not unaware of what you do. (74) Do you (faithful believers) covet that they will believe in your religion inspite of the fact that a party of them used to hear the Word of Allâh ,then they used to change it knowingly after they understood it? (75) And when they meet those who believe (Muslims), they say, "We believe", but when they meet one another in private, they say, "Shall you tell them (Muslims) what Allâh has revealed to you that they (Muslims) may argue with you about it before your Lord?" Have you then no understanding? (76) Know they not that Allâh knows what they conceal and what they reveal? (77) And there are among them unlettered people, who know not the Book, but they trust upon false desires and they but guess. (78) Then woe to those who write the Book with their own hands and then say, "This is from Allâh," to purchase with it a little price! Woe to them for what their hands have written and woe to them for that they earn thereby.

2:85

After this, it is you who kill one another and drive out a party of you from their homes, assist (their enemies) against them, in sin and transgression. And if they come to you as captives, you ransom them, although their expulsion was forbidden to you. Then do you believe in a part of the Scripture and reject the rest? Then what is the recompense of those who do so among you, except disgrace in the life of this world, and on the Day of Resurrection they shall be consigned to the most grievous torment. And Allâh is not unaware of what you do.

2:88-89

And they said, "Our hearts are wrapped." But, [in fact], Allah has cursed them for their disbelief, so little is it that they believe. And when there came to them a Book from Allah confirming that which was with them - although before they used to pray for victory against those who disbelieved - but [then] when there came to them that which they recognized, they disbelieved in it; so the curse of Allah will be upon the disbelievers.

2:97-100

Say "Whoever is an enemy to Jibrael (let him die in his fury), for indeed he has brought it (this Qur'ân) down to your heart by Allâh's Permission, confirming what came before it and guidance and glad tidings for the believers. (97) "Whoever is an enemy to Allâh, His Angels, His Messengers, Jibrael and Mikael , then verily, Allâh is an enemy to the disbelievers." (98) And indeed We have sent down to you manifest Ayât (these Verses of the Qur'ân.), and none disbelieve in them but Fâsiqûn (those who rebel against Allâh's Command). (99) Is it not (the case) that every time they make a covenant, some party among them throw it aside? Nay! (the truth) is most of them believe not.

2:114

And who are more unjust than those who forbid that Allâh's Name be glorified and mentioned much (i.e. prayers and invocations, etc.) in Allâh's mosques and strive for their ruin? It was not fitting that such should themselves enter them (Allâh's Mosques) except in fear. For them there is disgrace in this world, and they will have a great torment in the Hereafter.

2:120-121

Never will the Jews nor the Christians be pleased with you till you follow their religion. Say: "Verily, the Guidance of Allâh (i.e. Islâmic Monotheism) that is the (only) Guidance. And if you were to follow their (Jews and Christians) desires after what you have received of Knowledge (i.e. the Qur'ân), then you would have against Allâh neither any Walî (protector or guardian) nor any helper. (120) Those (who embraced Islâm from Banî Israel) to whom We gave the Book [the Taurât (Torah)] [or those (Muhammad's Peace be upon him companions) to whom We have given the Book (the Qur'ân)] recite it (i.e. obey its orders and follow its teachings) as it should be recited (i.e. followed), they are the ones that believe therein. And whoso disbelieves in it (the Qur'ân), those are they who are the losers.

2:124

And (remember) when the Lord of Ibrâhim (Abraham) [i.e., Allâh] tried him with (certain) Commands, which he fulfilled. He (Allâh) said (to him), "Verily, I am going to make you Imam (a leader) for mankind (to follow you)." [Ibrâhim (Abraham)] said, "And of my *offspring (to make leaders)." (Allâh) said, "My Covenant includes not Zâlimûn (polytheists and wrong-doers)."*

2:130

And who turns away from the religion of Ibrâhim (Abraham) (i.e. Islâmic Monotheism) except him who befools himself? Truly, We chose him in this world and verily, in the Hereafter he will be among the righteous.

2:159-162

Verily, those who conceal the clear proofs, evidences and the guidance, which We have sent down, after We have made it clear for the people in the Book, they are the ones cursed by Allâh and cursed by the cursers. (159) Except those who repent and do righteous deeds, and openly declare (the truth which they concealed). These, I will accept their repentance. And I am the One Who accepts repentance, the Most Merciful. (160) Verily, those who disbelieve, and die while they are disbelievers, it is they on whom is the Curse of Allâh and of the angels and of mankind, combined. (161) They will abide therein (under the curse in Hell), their punishment will neither be lightened, nor will they be reprieved.

2:166-168

When those who were followed, disown (declare themselves innocent of) those who followed (them), and they see the torment, then all their relations will be cut off from them. (166) And those who followed will say: "If only we had one more chance to return (to the worldly life), we would disown (declare ourselves as innocent from) them as they have disowned (declared themselves as innocent from) us." Thus Allâh will show them their deeds as regrets for them. And they will never get out of the Fire. O mankind! Eat of that which is lawful and good on the earth, and follow not the footsteps of Shaitân (Satan). Verily, he is to you an open enemy

2:171

And the example of those who disbelieve, is as that of him who shouts to those (flock of sheep) that hears nothing but calls and cries. (They are) deaf, dumb and blind. So they do not understand.

2:174-176

Verily, those who conceal what Allâh has sent down of the Book, and purchase a small gain therewith (of worldly things), they eat into their bellies nothing but fire. Allâh will not speak to them on the Day of Resurrection, nor purify them, and theirs will be a painful torment. (174) Those are they who have purchased error at the price of Guidance, and torment at the price of Forgiveness. So how bold they are (for evil deeds which will push them) to the Fire. (175) That is because Allâh has sent down the Book (the Qur'ân) in truth. And verily, those who disputed as regards the Book are far away in opposition.

2:190

And fight in the Way of Allâh those who fight you, but transgress not the limits. Truly, Allâh likes not the transgressors.

2:193

And fight them until there is no more Fitnah and (all and every) worship is for Allâh. But if they cease, let there be no transgression except against Az-Zâlimûn (the polytheists, and wrong-doers.)

2:208

O you who believe! Enter perfectly in Islâm (by obeying all the rules and regulations of the Islâmic religion) and follow not the footsteps of Shaitân (Satan). Verily! He is to you a plain enemy.

2:221

And do not marry Al-Mushrikât (idolatresses, etc.) till they believe (worship Allâh Alone). And indeed a slave woman who believes is better than a (free) Mushrikah (idolatress), even though she pleases you. And give not (your daughters) in marriage to Al-Mushrikûn till they believe (in Allâh Alone) and verily, a believing slave is better than a (free) Mushrik (idolater), even though he pleases you. Those invite you to the Fire, but Allâh invites (you) to Paradise and Forgiveness by His Leave, and makes His Ayât (proofs, evidences, verses, lessons, signs, revelations, etc.) clear to mankind that they may remember.

2:276

Allâh will destroy Ribâ (usury) and will give increase for Sadaqât (deeds of charity) And Allâh likes not the disbelievers, sinners.

3:28-32

Let not the believers take the disbelievers as Auliyâ (supporters, helpers, friends) instead of the believers, and whoever does that will never be helped by Allâh in any way, except if you indeed fear a danger from them. And Allâh warns you against Himself (His Punishment), and to Allâh is the final return. (28) Say : "Whether you hide what is in your breasts or reveal it, Allâh knows it, and He knows what is in the heavens and what is in the earth. And Allâh is Able to do all things." (29) On the Day when every person will be confronted with all the good he has done, and all the evil he has done, he will wish that there were a great distance between him and his evil. And Allâh warns you against Himself (His Punishment) and Allâh is full of Kindness to the (His) slaves. (30) Say: "If you (really) love Allâh then follow me (i.e. accept Islâmic

Monotheism, follow the Qur'ân and the Sunnah), Allâh will love you and forgive you your sins. And Allâh is Oft-Forgiving, Most Merciful." (31) Say: "Obey Allâh and the Messenger (Muhammad)." But if they turn away, then Allâh does not like the disbelievers.

3:55-57

And (remember) when Allâh said: "O 'Îsâ (Jesus)! I will take you and raise you to Myself and clear you [of the forged statement that 'Îsâ (Jesus) is Allâh's son] of those who disbelieve, and I will make those who follow you (Monotheists, who worship none but Allâh) superior to those who disbelieve till the Day of Resurrection. Then you will return to Me and I will judge between you in the matters in which you used to dispute." (55) "As to those who disbelieve, I will punish them with a severe torment in this world and in the Hereafter, and they will have no helpers." (56) And as for those who believe (in the Oneness of Allâh) and do righteous good deeds, Allâh will pay them their reward in full. And Allâh does not like the Zâlimûn (polytheists and wrong-doers).

3:61

Then whoever disputes with you concerning him ['Îsâ (Jesus)] after (all this) knowledge that has come to you, [i.e. 'Îsâ (Jesus)] being a slave of Allâh, and having no share in Divinity) say: "Come, let us call our sons and your sons, our women and your women, ourselves and yourselves - then we pray and invoke (sincerely) the Curse of Allâh upon those who lie."

3:85-90

And whoever seeks a religion other than Islâm, it will never be accepted of him, and in the Hereafter he will be one of the losers. (85) How shall Allâh guide a people who disbelieved after their belief and after they bore witness that the Messenger (Muhammad) is true and after clear proofs had come unto them? And Allâh guides not the people who are Zâlimûn (polytheists and wrong-doers). (86) They are those whose recompense is that on them (rests) the Curse of Allâh, of the angels, and of all mankind. (87) They will abide therein (Hell). Neither will their torment be lightened, nor will it be delayed or postponed (for a while). (88) Except for those who repent after that and do righteous deeds. Verily, Allâh is Oft-Forgiving, Most Merciful. (89) Verily, those who disbelieved after their Belief and then went on increasing in their disbelief (i.e. disbelief in the Qur'ân and in Prophet Muhammad) - never will their repentance be accepted [because they repent only by their tongues and not from their hearts]. And they are those who are astray.

3:94-95

Then after that, whosoever shall invent a lie against Allâh, ... such shall indeed be the Zâlimûn (disbelievers). (94) Say: "Allâh has spoken the truth; follow the religion of Ibrâhim (Abraham) Hanifa (Islâmic Monotheism, i.e. he used to worship Allâh Alone), and he was not of Al-Mushrikûn."

3:112

Indignity is put over them wherever they may be, except when under a covenant (of protection) from Allâh, and from men; they have drawn on themselves the Wrath of Allâh, and destruction is put over them. This is because they disbelieved in the Ayât (proofs, evidences, verses, lessons, signs, revelations, etc.) of Allâh and killed the Prophets without right. This is because they disobeyed (Allâh) and used to transgress beyond bounds (in Allâh's disobedience, crimes and sins).

3:118-120

O you who believe! Take not as (your) Bitânah (advisors, consultants, protectors, helpers, friends) those outside your religion (pagans, Jews, Christians, and hypocrites) since they will not fail to do their best to corrupt you. They desire to harm you severely. Hatred has already appeared from their mouths, but what their breasts conceal is far worse. Indeed We have made plain to you the Ayât (proofs, evidences, verses) if you understand. (118) Lo! You are the ones who love them but they love you not, and you believe in all the Scriptures . And when they meet you, they say, "We believe". But when they are alone, they bite the tips of their fingers at you in rage. Say: "Perish in your rage. Certainly, Allâh knows what is in the breasts (all the secrets)." (119) If a good befalls you, it grieves them, but if some evil overtakes you, they rejoice at it. But if you remain patient and become Al-Muttaqûn (the pious) not the least harm will their cunning do to you. Surely, Allâh surrounds all that they do.

3:139-142

So do not become weak (against your enemy), nor be sad, and you will be superior if you are indeed believers. (139) If a wound has touched you, be sure a similar wound has touched the others. And so are the days (good and not so good), We give to men by turns, that Allâh may test those who believe, and that He may take martyrs from among you. And Allâh likes not the Zâlimûn (polytheists and wrong¬doers). (140) And that Allâh may test (or purify) the believers (from sins) and destroy the disbelievers (141) Do you think that you will enter Paradise before Allâh tests those of you who fought (in His Cause) and (also) tests those who are As-Sâbirun (the patient)?

3:151

We shall cast terror into the hearts of those who disbelieve, because they joined others in worship with Allâh, for which He had sent no authority; their abode will be the Fire and how evil is the abode of the Zâlimûn (polytheists and wrong¬doers).

3:162-163

Is then one who follows (seeks) the good Pleasure of Allâh like the one who draws on himself the Wrath of Allah? - his abode is Hell, - and worst, indeed is that destination! They are in varying grades with Allâh, and Allâh is All¬Seer of what they do.

3:176-178

And let not those grieve you who rush with haste to disbelieve; verily, not the least harm will they do to Allâh. It is Allâh's Will to give them no portion in the Hereafter. For them there is a great torment. (176) Verily, those who purchase disbelief at the price of Faith, not the least harm will they do to Allâh. For them, there is a painful torment. (177) And let not the disbelievers think that Our postponing of their punishment is good for them. We postpone the punishment only so that they may increase in sinfulness. And for them is a disgracing torment.

4:44-52

Have you not seen those who were given a portion of the book, purchasing the wrong path, and wish that you should go astray from the Right Path. (44) Allâh has full knowledge of your enemies, and Allâh is Sufficient as a Walî (Protector), and Allâh is Sufficient as a Helper. (45) Among those who are Jews, there are some who displace words from (their) right places and say: "We hear your word (O Muhammad) and disobey," and "Hear and let you (O Muhammad) hear nothing." And Râ'ina with a twist of their tongues and as a mockery of the religion (Islâm). And if only they had said: "We hear and obey", and "Do make us understand," it would have been better for them, and more proper, but Allâh has cursed them for their disbelief, so they believe not except a few. (46) O you who have been given the Scripture (Jews and Christians)! Believe in what We have revealed (to Muhammad) confirming what is (already) with you, before We efface faces (by making them like the back of necks; without nose, mouth, eyes) and turn them hindwards, or curse them as We cursed the Sabbath¬breakers. And the Commandment of

Allâh is always executed. (47) Verily, Allâh forgives not that partners should be set up with Him (in worship), but He forgives except that (anything else) to whom He wills; and whoever sets up partners with Allâh in worship, he has indeed invented a tremendous sin. (48) Have you not seen those (Jews and Christians) who claim sanctity for themselves. Nay, but Allâh sanctifies whom He wills, and they will not be dealt with injustice even equal to the extent of a scalish thread in the long slit of a date-stone. (49) Look, how they invent a lie against Allâh, and enough is that as a manifest sin (50) Have you not seen those who were given a portion of the Scripture? They believe in Jibt and Tâghût and say to the disbelievers that they are better guided as regards the way than the believers. (51) They are those whom Allâh has cursed, and he whom Allâh curses, you will not find for him (any) helper,

4:76

Those who believe, fight in the Cause of Allâh, and those who disbelieve, fight in the cause of Tâghût (Satan,). So fight you against the friends of Shaitân (Satan); Ever feeble indeed is the plot of Shaitân .

4:88-98

Then what is the matter with you that you are divided into two parties about the hypocrites? Allâh has cast them back (to disbelief) because of what they have earned. Do you want to guide him whom Allâh has made to go astray? And he whom Allâh has made to go astray, you will never find for him any way (of guidance). (88) They wish that you reject Faith, as they have rejected (Faith), and thus that you all become equal (like one another). So take not Auliyâ' (protectors or friends) from them, till they emigrate in the Way of Allâh. But if they turn back (from Islâm), take (hold of) them and kill them wherever you find them, and take neither Auliyâ' (protectors or friends) nor helpers from them. (89) Except those who join a group, between you and whom there is a treaty (of peace), or those who approach you with their breasts restraining from fighting you as well as fighting their own people. Had Allâh willed, indeed He would have given them power over you, and they would have fought you. So if they withdraw from you, and fight not against you, and offer you peace, then Allâh has opened no way for you against them. (90) You will find others that wish to have security from you and security from their people. Every time they are sent back to temptation, they yield thereto. If they withdraw not from you, nor offer you peace, nor restrain their hands, take (hold of) them and kill them wherever you find them. In their case, We have provided you with a clear warrant against them. (91) It is not for a believer to kill a believer except (that it be) by mistake, and whosoever kills a believer by mistake, (it is ordained that) he must set free a believing slave and a compensation (blood money, i.e Diya) be given to the deceased's family, unless they remit it. If the deceased belonged to a people at war with you and he was a believer; the freeing of a believing slave (is prescribed), and if he belonged to a people with whom you have a treaty of mutual alliance, compensation (blood money - Diya) must be paid to his family, and a believing slave must be freed. And whoso finds this (the penance of freeing a slave) beyond his means, he must fast for two consecutive months in order to seek repentance from Allâh. And Allâh is Ever All¬Knowing, All¬Wise. (92) And whoever kills a believer intentionally, his recompense is Hell to abide therein, and the Wrath and the Curse of Allâh are upon him, and a great punishment is prepared for him. (93) O you who believe! When you go (to fight) in the Cause of Allâh, verify (the truth), and say not to anyone who greets you (by embracing Islâm): "You are not a believer"; seeking the perishable goods of the worldly life. There are much more profits and booties with Allâh. Even as he is now, so were you yourselves before till Allâh conferred on you His Favours (i.e. guided you to Islâm), therefore, be cautious in discrimination. Allâh is Ever Well¬Aware of what you do. (94) Not equal are those of the believers who sit (at home), except those who are disabled (by injury or are blind or lame), and those who strive hard and fight in the Cause of Allâh with their wealth and their lives. Allâh has preferred in grades those who strive hard and fight with their wealth and their lives above those who sit (at home). Unto each, Allâh has promised good (Paradise), but Allâh has preferred those who strive hard and fight, above those who sit (at home) by a huge reward; (95) Degrees of (higher) grades from Him, and Forgiveness and Mercy. And Allâh is Ever Oft¬Forgiving, Most Merciful. (96) Verily! As for those whom the angels take (in death) while they are wronging themselves (as they stayed among the disbelievers even though emigration was obligatory for them), they (angels) say (to them): "In what (condition) were you?" They reply: "We were weak and oppressed on earth." They (angels) say: "Was not the earth of Allâh spacious enough for you to emigrate therein?" Such men will find their abode in Hell - What an evil destination! (97) Except the weak ones among men, women and children who cannot devise a plan, nor are they able to direct their way. (98)

4:101

And when you (Muslims) travel in the land, there is no sin on you if you shorten As-Salât (the prayer) if you fear that the disbelievers may put you in trial (attack you etc.), verily, the disbelievers are ever unto you open enemies.

4:105-115

Surely, We have sent down to you the Book (this Qur'ân) in truth that you might judge between men by that which Allâh has shown you (i.e. has taught you through Divine Revelation), so be not a pleader for the treacherous. (105) And seek the Forgiveness of Allâh, certainly, Allâh is Ever Oft¬Forgiving, Most Merciful (106) And argue not on behalf of those who deceive themselves. Verily, Allâh does not like anyone who is a betrayer of his trust, and sinner. (107) They may hide (their crimes) from men, but they cannot hide (them) from Allâh, for He is with them (by His Knowledge), when they plot by night in words that He does not approve, And Allâh ever encompasses what they do. (108) Lo! You are those who have argued for them in the life of this world, but who will argue for them on the Day of Resurrection against Allâh, or who will then be their defender? (109) And whoever does evil or wrongs himself but afterwards seeks Allâh's Forgiveness, he will find Allâh Oft¬Forgiving, Most Merciful. (110) And whoever earns sin, he earns it only against himself. And Allâh is Ever All-Knowing, All-Wise. (111) And whoever earns a fault or a sin and then throws it on to someone innocent, he has indeed burdened himself with falsehood and a manifest sin. (112) Had not the Grace of Allâh and His Mercy been upon you, a party of them would certainly have made a decision to mislead you, but (in fact) they mislead none except their own selves, and no harm can they do to you in the least. Allâh has sent down to you the Book (The Qur'ân), and Al¬Hikmah (Islâmic laws, knowledge of legal and illegal things i.e. the Prophet's Sunnah - legal ways), and taught you that which you knew not. And Ever Great is the Grace of Allâh unto you (113) There is no good in most of their secret talks save (in) him who orders Sadaqah (charity in Allâh's Cause), or Ma'rûf (Islâmic Monotheism and all the good and righteous deeds which Allâh has ordained), or conciliation between mankind, and he who does this, seeking the good Pleasure of Allâh, We shall give him a great reward (114) And whoever contradicts and opposes the Messenger after the right path has been shown clearly to him, and follows other than the believers' way. We shall keep him in the path he has chosen, and burn him in Hell - what an evil destination.

4:118-119

Allâh cursed him. And he [Shaitân (Satan)] said: "I will take an appointed portion of your slaves; (118) Verily, I will mislead them, and surely, I will arouse in them false desires; and certainly, I will order them to slit the ears of cattle, and indeed I will order them to change the nature created by Allâh." And whoever takes Shaitân (Satan) as a Walî (protector or helper) instead of Allâh, has surely suffered a manifest loss.

Verily, those who believe, then disbelieve, then believe (again), and (again) disbelieve, and go on increasing in disbelief; Allâh will not forgive them, nor guide them on the (Right) Way (137) Give to the hypocrites the tidings that there is for them a painful torment. (138) Those who take disbelievers for Auliyâ' (protectors or helpers or friends) instead of believers, do they seek honour, power and glory with them? Verily, then to Allâh belongs all honour, power and glory. (139) And it has already been revealed to you in the Book (this Qur'ân) that when you hear the Verses of Allâh being denied and mocked at, then sit not with them, until they engage in a talk other than that; (but if you stayed with them) certainly in that case you would be like them. Surely, Allâh will collect the hypocrites and disbelievers all together in Hell, (140) Those (hyprocrites) who wait and watch about you; if you gain a victory from Allâh, they say: "Were we not with you?" But if the disbelievers gain a success, they say (to them): "Did we not gain mastery over you and did we not protect you from the believers?" Allâh will judge between you (all) on the Day of Resurrection. And never will Allâh grant to the disbelievers a way (to triumph) over the believers. (141) Verily, the hypocrites seek to deceive Allâh, but it is He Who deceives them. And when they stand up for As-Salât (the prayer), they stand with laziness and to be seen of men, and they do not remember Allâh but little. (142) (They are) swaying between this and that, belonging neither to these nor to those, and he whom Allâh sends astray, you will not find for him a way (to the truth - Islâm). (143) O you who believe! Take not for Auliyâ' (protectors or helpers or friends) disbelievers instead of believers. Do you wish to offer Allâh a manifest proof against yourselves? (144) Verily, the hyprocrites will be in the lowest depths (grade) of the Fire; no helper will you find for them. (145) Except those who repent (from hypocrisy), do righteous good deeds, hold fast to Allâh, and purify their religion for Allâh (by worshipping none but Allâh, and do good for Allâh's sake only, not to show off), then they will be with the believers. And Allâh will grant the believers a great reward.

4:168-169

Verily, those who disbelieve and did wrong Allâh will not forgive them, nor will He guide them to any way,. (168) Except the way of Hell, to dwell therein forever, and this is ever easy for Allâh.

5:8

O you who believe! Stand out firmly for Allâh as just witnesses and let not the enmity and hatred of others make you avoid justice. Be just: that is nearer to piety, and fear Allâh. Verily, Allâh is Well-Acquainted with what you do.

5:13-14

So because of their breach of their covenant, We cursed them, and made their hearts grow hard. They change the words from their (right) places and have abandoned a good part of the Message that was sent to them. And you will not cease to discover deceit in them, except a few of them. But forgive them, and overlook (their misdeeds). Verily, Allâh loves Al¬Muhsinûn (good¬doers) And from those who call themselves Christians, We took their covenant, but they have abandoned a good part of the Message that was sent to them. So We planted amongst them enmity and hatred till the Day of Resurrection, and Allâh will inform them of what they used to do.

5:49-64

And so judge among them by what Allâh has revealed and follow not their vain desires, but beware of them lest they turn you far away from some of that which Allâh has sent down to you. And if they turn away, then know that Allâh's Will is to punish them for some sins of theirs. And truly, most of men are Fâsiqûn (rebellious and disobedient to

*Allâh). (49) Do they then seek the judgement of (the days of) Ignorance?
And who is better in judgement than Allâh for a people who have firm
Faith. (50) O you who believe! Take not the Jews and the Christians as
Auliyâ' (friends, protectors, helpers), they are but Auliyâ' of each other.
And if any amongst you takes them (as Auliyâ'), then surely he is one of
them. Verily, Allâh guides not those people who are the Zâlimûn
(polytheists and wrong-doers and unjust). (51) And you see those in
whose hearts there is a disease (of hypocrisy), they hurry to their
friendship, saying: "We fear lest some misfortune of a disaster may befall
us." Perhaps Allâh may bring a victory or a decision according to His
Will. Then they will become regretful for what they have been keeping as
a secret in themselves. (52) And those who believe will say: "Are these
the men (hypocrites) who swore their strongest oaths by Allâh that they
were with you (Muslims)?" All that they did has been in vain (because
of their hypocrisy), and they have become the losers. (53) O you who
believe! Whoever from among you turns back from his religion (Islâm),
Allâh will bring a people whom He will love and they will love Him;
humble towards the believers, stern towards the disbelievers, fighting in
the Way of Allâh, and never fear of the blame of the blamers. That is the
Grace of Allâh which He bestows on whom He wills. And Allâh is All-
Sufficient for His creatures' needs, All-Knower. (54) Verily, your Walî
(Protector or Helper) is none other than Allâh, His Messenger, and the
believers, - those who perform As-Salât (Iqâmat-as-Salât), and give
Zakât, and they are Rakiun (those who bow down or submit themselves
with obedience to Allâh in prayer). (55) And whosoever takes Allâh, His
Messenger, and those who have believed, as Protectors, then the party of
Allâh will be the victorious. (56) O you who believe! Take not as Auliyâ'
(protectors, friends, helpers) those who take your religion as a mockery
and fun from among those who received the Scripture before you, nor
from among the disbelievers; and fear Allâh if you indeed are true
believers. (57) And when you proclaim the call for As-Salât [call for the
prayer (Adhân)], they take it (but) as a mockery and fun; that is because
they are a people who understand not. (58) Say: "O people of the*

Scripture! Do you criticize us for no other reason than that we believe in Allâh, and in (the revelation) which has been sent down to us and in that which has been sent down before (us), and that most of you are Fâsiqûn [rebellious and disobedient (to Allâh)]?" (59) Say: "Shall I inform you of something worse than that, regarding the recompense from Allâh: those (Jews) who incurred the Curse of Allâh and His Wrath, those of whom (some) He transformed into monkeys and swines, those who worshipped Tâghût; such are worse in rank (on the Day of Resurrection in the Hell¬fire), and far more astray from the Right Path (in the life of this world)." (60) When they come to you, they say: "We believe." But in fact they enter with (an intention of) disbelief and they go out with the same. And Allâh knows all what they were hiding (61) And you see many of them (Jews) hurrying towards sin and transgression, and eating illegal things [as bribes and Ribâ (usury), etc.]. Evil indeed is that which they have been doing (62) Why do not the rabbis and the religious learned men forbid them from uttering sinful words and from eating illegal things. Evil indeed is that which they have been performing. (63) The Jews say: "Allâh's Hand is tied up (i.e. He does not give and spend of His Bounty)." Be their hands tied up and be they accursed for what they uttered. Nay, both His Hands are widely outstretched. He spends (of His Bounty) as He wills. Verily, the Revelation that has come to you from your Lord (Allâh) increases in most of them (their) obstinate rebellion and disbelief. We have put enmity and hatred amongst them till the Day of Resurrection. Every time they kindled the fire of war, Allâh extinguished it; and they (ever) strive to make mischief on earth. And Allâh does not like the Mufsidûn (mischief-makers).

5:67

O Messenger (Muhammad)! Proclaim (the Message) which has been sent down to you from your Lord. And if you do not, then you have not conveyed His Message. Allâh will protect you from mankind. Verily, Allâh guides not the people who disbelieve.

5:78-81

Those among the Children of Israel who disbelieved were cursed by the tongue of Dawûd (David) and 'Īsā (Jesus), son of Maryam (Mary). That was because they disobeyed (Allâh and the Messengers) and were ever transgressing beyond bounds. (78) They used not to forbid one another from Al-Munkar (wrong, evil-doing, sins, polytheism, disbelief) which they committed. Vile indeed was what they used to do. (79) You see many of them taking the disbelievers as their Auliyâ' (protectors, friends, helpers). Evil indeed is that which their ownselves have sent forward before them, for that (reason) Allâh's Wrath fell upon them and in torment they will abide. (80) And had they believed in Allâh, and in the Prophet (Muhammad) and in what has been revealed to him, never would they have taken them (the disbelievers) as Auliyâ' (protectors friends helpers), but many of them are the Fâsiqûn (rebellious, disobedient to Allâh). (81)

5:87

O you who believe! Make not unlawful the Tayyibât (all that is good as regards foods, things, deeds, beliefs, persons) which Allâh has made lawful to you, and transgress not. Verily, Allâh does not like the transgressors.

6:25

And of them there are some who listen to you; but We have set veils on their hearts, so they understand it not, and deafness in their ears; and even if they see every one of the Ayât (proofs, evidences, verses, lessons, signs, revelations, etc.) they will not believe therein; to the point that when they come to you to argue with you, the disbelievers say: "These are nothing but tales of the men of old."

6:39

Those who reject Our Ayât (proofs, evidences, verses, signs, revelations, etc.) are deaf and dumb in darkness. Allâh sends astray whom He wills and He guides on the Straight Path whom He wills.

6:50

Say: "I don't tell you that with me are the treasures of Allâh, nor (that) I know the unseen; nor I tell you that I am an angel. I but follow what is revealed to me." Say: "Are the blind and the one who sees equal? will you not then take thought?"

6:93

And who can be more unjust than he who invents a lie against Allâh, or says: "A revelation has come to me," whereas as no revelation has come to him in anything; and who says, "I will reveal the like of what Allâh has revealed." And if you could but see when the Zâlimûn (polytheists and wrong-doers) are in the agonies of death, while the angels are stretching forth their hands (saying): "Deliver your souls! This day you shall be recompensed with the torment of degradation because of what you used to utter against Allâh other than the truth. And you used to reject His Ayât (proofs, evidences, verses, lessons, signs, revelations etc.) with disrespect!

6:107-113

Had Allâh willed, they would not have taken others besides Him in worship. And We have not made you a watcher over them nor are you a Wakil (disposer of affairs, guardian or trustee) over them. (107) And insult not those whom they (disbelievers) worship besides Allâh, lest they insult Allâh wrongfully without knowledge. Thus We have made fair⁻seeming to each people its own doings; then to their Lord is their return and He shall then inform them of all that they used to do. (108) And they swear their strongest oaths by Allâh, that if there came to them a sign, they would surely believe therein. Say: "Signs are but with Allâh and what will make you (Muslims) perceive that (even) if it (the sign) came, they will not believe?" (109) And We shall turn their hearts and their eyes away (from guidance), as they refused to believe therein for the first time, and We shall leave them in their trespass to wander blindly. (110) And even if We had sent down unto them angels, and the dead had spoken unto them, and We had gathered together all things before their very eyes, they would not have believed, unless Allâh willed, but most of them behave ignorantly. (111) And so We have appointed for every Prophet enemies - Shayâtin (devils) among mankind and jinn, inspiring one another with adorned speech as a delusion (or by way of deception). If your Lord had so willed, they would not have done it, so leave them alone with their fabrications. (112) (And this is in order) that the hearts of those who disbelieve in the Hereafter may incline to such (deceit), and that they may remain pleased with it, and that they may commit what they are committing (all kinds of sins and evil deeds).

6:122-125

Is he who was dead (without Faith by ignorance and disbelief) and We gave him life (by knowledge and Faith) and set for him a light (of Belief) whereby he can walk amongst men — like him who is in the darkness (of disbelief, polytheism and hypocrisy) from which he can never come out? Thus it is made fair¬seeming to the disbelievers that which they used to do. (122) And thus We have set up in every town great ones of its wicked people to plot therein. But they plot not except against their ownselves, and they perceive (it) not. (123) And when there comes to them a sign (from Allâh) they say: "We shall not believe until we receive the like of that which the Messengers of Allâh had received." Allâh knows best with whom to place His Message. Humiliation and disgrace from Allâh and a severe torment will overtake the criminals (polytheists, sinners) for that which they used to plot. (124) And whomsoever Allâh wills to guide, He opens his breast to Islâm, and whomsoever He wills to send astray, He makes his breast closed and *constricted, as if he is climbing up to the sky. Thus Allâh puts the wrath on those who believe not.*

6:132

For all there will be degrees (or ranks) according to what they did. And your Lord is not unaware of what they do.

6:140-142

Indeed lost are they who have killed their children, foolishly, without knowledge, and have forbidden that which Allâh has provided for them, inventing a lie against Allâh. They have indeed gone astray and were not guided. (140) And it is He Who produces gardens trellised and untrellised, and date¬palms, and crops of different shape and taste (their fruits and their seeds) and olives, and pomegranates, similar (in kind) and different (in taste). Eat of their fruit when they ripen, but pay the due thereof (its Zakât, according to Allâh's Orders 1/10th or 1/20th) on the day of its harvest, and waste not by extravagance. Verily, He likes not Al-Musrifûn (those who waste by extravagance), (141) And of the cattle (are some) for burden (like camels) and (some are) small (unable to carry burden like sheep, goats for food, meat, milk, wool). Eat of what Allâh has provided for you, and follow not the footsteps of Shaitân (Satan). Surely he is to you an open enemy.

6:144

And of the camels two (male and female), and of oxen two (male and female). Say: "Has He forbidden the two males or the two females or (the young) which the wombs of the two females enclose? Or were you present when Allâh ordered you such a thing? Then who does more wrong than one who invents a lie against Allâh, to lead mankind astray without knowledge. Certainly Allâh guides not the people who are Zâlimûn (polytheists and wrong-doers)."

6:147-149

If they belie you say: "Your Lord is the Owner of Vast Mercy, and never will His Wrath be turned back from the people who are Mujrimûn (criminals, polytheists, or sinners)." (147) Those who took partners (in worship) with Allâh will say: "If Allâh had willed, we would not have taken partners (in worship) with Him, nor would our fathers, and we would not have forbidden anything (against His Will)." Likewise belied those who were before them, (they argued falsely with Allâh's Messengers), till they tasted Our Wrath. Say: "Have you any knowledge (proof) that you can produce before us? Verily, you follow nothing but guess and you do nothing but lie." (148) Say: "With Allâh is the perfect proof and argument, (i.e. the Oneness of Allâh, the sending of His Messengers and His Books to mankind), had He so willed, He would indeed have guided you all."

6:165

And it is He Who has made you generations coming after generations, replacing each other on the earth. And He has raised you in ranks, some above others that He may try you in that which He has bestowed on you. Surely your Lord is Swift in retribution, and certainly He is Oft-Forgiving, Most Merciful.

7:13-19

(Allâh) said: "(O Iblîs) get down from this (Paradise), it is not for you to be arrogant here. Get out, for you are of those humiliated and disgraced." (13) (Iblîs) said: "Allow me respite till the Day they are raised up (i.e. the Day of Resurrection)." (14) (Allâh) said: "You are of those respited." (15) (Iblîs) said: "Because You have sent me astray, surely I will sit in wait against them (human beings) on Your Straight Path (16) Then I will come to them from before them and behind them, from their right and from their left, and You will not find most of them as thankful ones (i.e. they will not be dutiful to You)." (17) (Allâh) said

(to Iblîs) "Get out from this (Paradise) disgraced and expelled. Whoever of them (mankind) will follow you, then surely I will fill Hell with you all." (18) "And O Adam! Dwell you and your wife in Paradise, and eat thereof as you both wish, but approach not this tree otherwise you both will be of the Zâlimûn (unjust and wrong-doers)."

7:23-24

They said: "Our Lord! We have wronged ourselves. If You forgive us not, and bestow not upon us Your Mercy, we shall certainly be of the losers." (23) (Allâh) said: "Get down, one of you is an enemy to the other [i.e. Adam, Hawwa (Eve), and Shaitân (Satan),]. On earth will be a dwelling-place for you and an enjoyment, - for a time."

7:30-31

A group He has guided, and a group deserved to be in error; (because) surely they took the Shayâtin (devils) as Auliyâ' (protectors and helpers) instead of Allâh, and think that they are guided. (30) O Children of Adam! Take your adornment (by wearing your clean clothes), while praying and going round (the Tawâf of) the Ka'bah, and eat and drink but waste not by extravagance, certainly He (Allâh) likes not Al-Musrifûn (those who waste by extravagance).

7:37-41

Who is more unjust than one who invents a lie against Allâh or rejects His Ayât (proofs, evidences, verses, lessons, signs, revelations)? For such their appointed portion (good things of this worldly life and their period of stay therein) will reach them from the Book (of Decrees) until, when Our Messengers (the angel of death and his assistants) come to them to take their souls, they (the angels) will say: "Where are those whom you used to invoke and worship besides Allâh," they will reply, "They have vanished and deserted us." And they will bear witness against themselves, that they were disbelievers. (37) (Allâh) will say:

"Enter you in the company of nations who passed away before you, of men and jinn, into the Fire." Every time a new nation enters, it curses its sister nation (that went before), until they will be gathered all together in the Fire. The last of them will say to the first of them: "Our Lord! These misled us, so give them a double torment of the Fire." He will say: "For each one there is double (torment), but you know not." (38) The first of them will say to the last of them: "You were not better than us, so taste the torment for what you used to earn." (39) Verily, those who belie Our Ayât (proofs, evidences, verses, lessons, signs, revelations) and treat them with arrogance, for them the gates of heaven will not be opened, and they will not enter Paradise until the camel goes through the eye of the needle (which is impossible). Thus do We recompense the Mujrimûn (criminals, polytheists, and sinners). (40) Theirs will be a bed of Hell (Fire), and over them coverings (of Hell-fire). Thus do We recompense the Zâlimûn (polytheists and wrong-doers).

7:44-45

And the dwellers of Paradise will call out to the dwellers of the Fire (saying): "We have indeed found true what our Lord had promised us; have you also found true, what your Lord promised (warnings)?" They shall say: "Yes." Then a crier will proclaim between them: "The Curse of Allâh is on the Zâlimûn (polytheists and wrong-doers)," (44) Those who hindered (men) from the Path of Allâh, and would seek to make it crooked, and they were disbelievers in the Hereafter.

7:55

Invoke your Lord with humility and in secret. He likes not the transgressors.

7:88-89

The chiefs of those who were arrogant among his people said: "We shall certainly drive you out, O Shu'aib, and those who have *believed with you from our town, or else you (all) shall return to our religion." He said: "Even though we hate it?" "We should have invented a lie against Allâh if we returned to your religion, after Allâh has rescued us from it. And it is not for us to return to it unless Allâh, our Lord, should will. Our Lord comprehends all things in His Knowledge. In Allâh (Alone) we put our trust. Our Lord! Judge between us and our people in truth, for You are the Best of those who give judgment."*

7:99-101

Did they then feel secure against the Plan of Allâh? None feels secure from the Plan of Allâh except the people who are the losers. (99) Is it not clear to those who inherit the earth in succession from its (previous) possessors, that had We willed, We would have punished them for their sins. And We seal up their hearts so that they hear not? (100) Those were the towns whose story We relate unto you (O Muhammad). And there came indeed to them their Messengers with clear proofs, but they were not such as to believe in that which they had rejected before. Thus Allâh does seal up the hearts of the disbelievers (from every kind of religious guidance)

7:146-147

I shall turn away from My Ayât (verses of the Qur'ân) those who behave arrogantly on the earth, without a right, and (even) if they see all the Ayât (proofs, evidences, verses, lessons, signs, revelations, etc.), they will not believe in them. And if they see the way of righteousness (monotheism, piety, and good deeds), they will not adopt it as the Way, but if they see the way of error (polytheism, crimes and evil deeds), they will adopt that way, that is because they have rejected Our Ayât (proofs, evidences, verses, lessons, signs, revelations, etc.) and were heedless (to learn a lesson) from them (146) Those who deny Our Ayât (proofs, evidences, verses, lessons, signs, revelations, etc.) and the

Meeting in the Hereafter (Day of Resurrection,), vain are their deeds. Are they requited with anything except what they used to do?

7:149

And when they regretted and saw that they had gone astray, they (repented and) said: "If our Lord have not mercy upon us and forgive us, we shall certainly be of the losers."

7:152

Certainly, those who took the calf (for worship), wrath from their Lord and humiliation will come upon them in the life of this world. Thus do We recompense those who invent lies.

7:155

And Mûsa (Moses) chose out of his people seventy (of the best) men for Our appointed time and place of meeting, and when they were seized with a violent earthquake, he said: "O my Lord, if it had been Your Will, You could have destroyed them and me before; would You destroy us for the deeds of the foolish ones among us? It is only Your Trial by which You lead astray whom You will, and keep guided whom You will. You are our Walî (Protector), so forgive us and have Mercy on us, for You are the Best of those who forgive.

7:175-179

And recite to them the story of him to whom We gave Our Ayât (proofs, evidences, verses, lessons, signs, revelations, etc.), but he threw them away, so Shaitân (Satan) followed him up, and he became of those who went astray. (175) And had We willed, We would surely have elevated him therewith but he clung to the earth and followed his own vain desire. So his parable is the parable of a dog: if you drive him away, he lolls his tongue out, or if you leave him alone, he (still) lolls his tongue out. Such is the parable of the people who reject Our Ayât (proofs, evidences, verses, lessons, signs, revelations, etc.). So relate the stories, perhaps they may reflect (176) Evil is the parable of the people who reject Our Ayât (proofs, evidences, verses and signs, etc.), and used to wrong their ownselves (177) Whomsoever Allâh guides, he is the guided one, and whomsoever He sends astray, then those! they are the losers (178) And surely, We have created many of the jinn and mankind for Hell. They have hearts wherewith they understand not, and they have eyes wherewith they see not, and they have ears wherewith they hear not (the truth). They are like cattle, nay even more astray; those! They are the heedless ones.

7:182

Those who reject Our Ayât (proofs, evidences, verses, lessons, signs, revelations, etc.), We shall gradually seize them with punishment in ways they perceive not.

7:186

Whomsoever Allâh sends astray, none can guide him; and He lets them wander blindly in their transgressions.

8:12-16

(Remember) when your Lord revealed to the angels, "Verily, I am with you, so keep firm those who have believed. I will cast terror into the hearts of those who have disbelieved, so strike them over the necks, and smite over all their fingers and toes." (12) This is because they defied and disobeyed Allâh and His Messenger. And whoever defies and disobeys Allâh and His Messenger, then verily, Allâh is Severe in punishment (13) This is (the torment), so taste it, and surely for the disbelievers is the torment of the Fire. (14) O you who believe! When you meet those who disbelieve, in a battle-field, never turn your backs to them. (15) And whoever turns his back to them on such a day - unless it be a stratagem of war, or to retreat to a troop (of his own), - he indeed has drawn upon himself wrath from Allâh. And his abode is Hell, and worst indeed is that destination!

8:20-23

O you who believe! Obey Allâh and His Messenger, and turn not away from him (i.e. Messenger Muhammad) while you are hearing. (20) And be not like those who say: "We have heard," but they hear not. (21) Verily! The worst of (moving) living creatures with Allâh are the deaf and the dumb, who understand not (i.e. the disbelievers) (22) Had Allâh known of any good in them, He would indeed have made them listen; and even if He had made them listen, they would but have turned away with aversion (to the truth). (23)

8:55

Verily, The worst of moving (living) creatures before Allâh are those who disbelieve, - so they shall not believe. (55)

8:58

If you (O Muhammad) fear treachery from any people throw back (their covenant) to them (so as to be) on equal terms). Certainly Allâh likes not the treacherous. (58)

9:19

Do you consider the providing of drinking water to the pilgrims and the maintenance of Al-Masjid-al-Harâm (at Makkah) as equal to the worth of those who believe in Allâh and the Last Day, and strive hard and fight in the Cause of Allâh? They are not equal before Allâh. And Allâh guides not those people who are the Zâlimûn (polytheists and wrong-doers).

9:23-24

O you who believe! Take not for Auliyâ' (supporters and helpers) your fathers and your brothers if they prefer disbelief to Belief. And whoever of you does so, then he is one of the Zâlimûn (wrong-doers). (23) Say: If your fathers, your sons, your brothers, your wives, your kindred, the wealth that you have gained, the commerce in which you fear a decline, and the dwellings in which you delight are dearer to you than Allâh and His Messenger, and striving hard and fighting in His Cause, then wait until Allâh brings about His Decision (torment). And Allâh guides not the people who are Al-Fâsiqûn (the rebellious, disobedient to Allâh)

9:30

And the Jews say: Uzair is the son of Allâh, and the Christians say: Messiah is the son of Allâh. That is their saying with their mouths, resembling the saying of the those who disbelieved aforetime. Allâh's Curse be on them, how they are deluded away from the truth!

9:32-33

They (the disbelievers, the Jews and the Christians) want to extinguish Allâh's Light (with which Muhammad has been sent - Islâmic Monotheism) with their mouths, but Allâh will not allow except that His Light should be perfected even though the Kâfirûn (disbelievers) hate (it). It is He Who has sent His Messenger (Muhammad) with guidance and the religion of truth (Islâm), to make it superior over all religions even though the Mushrikûn (polytheists, pagans, idolaters, disbelievers in the Oneness of Allâh) hate (it).

9:67-69

The hypocrites, men and women, are one from another, they enjoin (on the people) Al-Munkar (i.e. disbelief and polytheism of all kinds and all that Islâm has forbidden), and forbid (people) from Al-Ma'rûf (i.e. Islâmic Monotheism and all that Islâm orders one to do), and

~ 36 ~

they close their hands [from giving (spending in Allâh's Cause) alms].
They have forgotten Allâh, so He has forgotten them. Verily, the
hypocrites are the Fâsiqûn (rebellious, disobedient to Allâh). Allâh has
promised the hypocrites — men and women — and the disbelievers, the
Fire of Hell, therein shall they abide. It will suffice them. Allâh has
cursed them and for them is the lasting torment. (68) Like those before
you: they were mightier than you in power, and more abundant in
wealth and children. They had enjoyed their portion (awhile), so enjoy
your portion (awhile) as those before you enjoyed their portion (awhile);
and you indulged in play and pastime (and in telling lies against Allâh
and His Messenger Muhammad) as they indulged in play and pastime.
Such are they whose deeds are in vain in this world and in the Hereafter.
Such are they who are the losers.

9:73

O Prophet! Strive hard against the disbelievers and the
hypocrites, and be harsh against them, their abode is Hell, - and worst
indeed is that destination.

9:96

They (the hypocrites) swear to you (Muslims) that you may be
pleased with them, but if you are pleased with them, certainly Allâh is
not pleased with the people who are Al-Fâsiqûn (disobedient to Allâh)

9:107-109

And as for those who put up a mosque by way of harm and
disbelief, and to disunite the believers, and as an outpost for those who
warred against Allâh and His Messenger (Muhammad) aforetime, they
will indeed swear that their intention is nothing but good. Allâh bears
witness that they are certainly liars. (107) Never stand you therein.
Verily, the mosque whose foundation was laid from the first day on piety
is more worthy that you stand therein (to pray). In it are men who love

to clean and to purify themselves. And Allâh loves those who make themselves clean and pure (i.e. who clean their private parts with dust [which has the cleansing properties of soap) and water from urine and stools, after answering the call of nature]. (108) Is it then he who laid the foundation of his building on piety to Allâh and His Good Pleasure better, or he who laid the foundation of his building on the brink of an undetermined precipice ready to crumble down, so that it crumbled to pieces with him into the Fire of Hell. And Allâh guides not the people who are the Zâlimûn (cruel, violent, proud, polytheist and wrong-doer).

9:113-115

It is not (proper) for the Prophet and those who believe to ask Allâh's Forgiveness for the Mushrikûn (polytheists, idolaters, pagans, disbelievers in the Oneness of Allâh) even though they be of kin, after it has become clear to them that they are the dwellers of the Fire.(113) And Ibrâhîm's (Abraham) invoking (of Allâh) for his father's forgiveness was only because of a promise he [Ibrâhîm (Abraham)] had made to him (his father). But when it became clear to him [Ibrâhîm (Abraham)] that he (his father) is an enemy of Allâh, he dissociated himself from him. Verily Ibrâhîm (Abraham) was Awwah (one who invokes Allâh with humility, glorifies Him and remembers Him much) and was forbearing. And Allâh will never lead a people astray after He has guided them until He makes clear to them as to what they should avoid. Verily, Allâh is the All-Knower of everything

9:120

It was not becoming of the people of Al-Madinah and the bedouins of the neighbourhood to remain behind Allâh's Messenger (Muhammad when fighting in Allâh's Cause) and (it was not becoming of them) to prefer their own lives to his life. That is because they suffer neither thirst nor fatigue, nor hunger in the Cause of Allâh, nor they take any step to raise the anger of disbelievers nor inflict any injury upon an enemy but is written to their credit as a deed of righteousness. Surely, Allâh wastes not the reward of the Muhsinûn.

9:123

O you who believe! Fight those of the disbelievers who are close to you, and let them find harshness in you, and know that Allâh is with those who are the Al-Muttaqûn (the pious)

10:17

So who does more wrong than he who forges a lie against Allâh or denies His Ayât (proofs, evidences, verses, lessons, signs, revelations, etc.)? Surely, the Mujrimûn (criminals, sinners, disbelievers and polytheists) will never be successful!

10:99-100

And had your Lord willed, those on earth would have believed, all of them together. So, will you (O Muhammad) then compel mankind, until they become believers. (99) It is not for any person to believe, except by the Leave of Allâh, and He will put the wrath on those who are heedless.

11:18-21

And who does more wrong than he who invents a lie against Allâh. Such will be brought before their Lord, and the witnesses will say, "These are the ones who lied against their Lord!" No doubt! the curse of Allâh is on the Zâlimûn (polytheists, wrong-doers, oppressors) (18) Those who hinder (others) from the Path of Allâh (Islâmic Monotheism), and seek a crookedness therein, while they are disbelievers in the Hereafter. (19) By no means will they escape (from Allâh's Torment) on earth, nor have they protectors besides Allâh! Their torment will be doubled! They could not bear to hear (the preachers of the truth) and they used not to see (the truth because of their severe aversoin, inspite of the *fact that they had the sense of hearing and sight). (20) They are those who have lost their own selves, and their invented false deities will vanish from them.*

11:24

The likeness of the two parties is as the blind and the deaf and the seer and the hearer. Are they equal when compared? Will you not then take heed?

11:34

"And my advice will not profit you, even if I wish to give you good counsel, if Allâh's Will is to keep you astray. He is your Lord! and to Him you shall return."

11:38-39

And as he was constructing the ship, whenever the chiefs of his people passed by him, they mocked at him. He said: "If you mock at us, so do we mock at you likewise for your mocking "And you will know who it is on whom will come a torment that will cover him with disgrace and on whom will fall a lasting torment."

11:99

They were pursued by a curse in this (deceiving life of this world) and (so they will be pursued by a curse) on the Day of Resurrection. Evil indeed is the gift gifted [i.e., the curse (in this world) pursued by another curse (in the Hereafter)].

11:118-119

And if your Lord had so willed, He could surely have made mankind one Ummah [nation or community (following one religion only i.e. Islâm)], but they will not cease to disagree, – (118) Except him on whom your Lord has bestowed His Mercy (the follower of truth - Islâmic Monotheism) and for that did He create them. And the Word of your Lord has been fulfilled (i.e. His Saying): "Surely, I shall fill Hell with jinn and men all together."

12:5

He said: "O my son! Relate not your vision to your brothers, lest they arrange a plot against you. Verily! Shaitân (Satan) is to man an open enemy!

13:25

And those who break the Covenant of Allâh, after its ratification, and sever that which Allâh has commanded to be joined (i.e. they sever the bond of kinship and are not good to their relatives), and work mischief in the land, on them is the curse (i.e. they will be far away from Allâh's Mercy); and for them is the unhappy (evil) home (i.e. Hell)

13:27

And those who disbelieve say: "Why is not a sign sent down to him from his Lord?" Say: "Verily, Allâh sends astray whom He wills and guides unto Himself those who turn to Him in repentance."

13:31

And if there had been a Qur'ân with which mountains could be moved (from their places), or the earth could be cloven asunder, or the dead could be made to speak (it would not have been other than this Qur'ân). But the decision of all things is certainly with Allâh. Have not then those who believed yet known that had Allâh willed, He could have guided all mankind? And a disaster will not cease to strike those who disbelieve because of their (evil) deeds or it (i.e. the disaster) settle close to their homes, until the Promise of Allâh comes to pass. Certainly, Allâh does not fail in His Promise.

13:33-34

Is then He (Allâh) Who takes charge (guards, maintains, provides) of every person and knows all that he has earned (like any other deities who know nothing)? Yet they ascribe partners to Allâh. Say: "Name them! Is it that you will inform Him of something He knows not in the earth or is it (just) a show of false words." Nay! To those who disbelieved, their plotting is made fairseeming, and they have been hindered from the Right Path, and whom Allâh sends astray, for him, there is no guide. (33) For them is a torment in the life of this world, and certainly, harder is the torment of the Hereafter. And they have no Waq (defender or protector) against Allâh

14:2-4

Allâh to Whom belongs all that is in the heavens and all that is in the earth! And woe unto the disbelievers from a severe torment. (2) Those who prefer the life of this world to of the Hereafter, and hinder (men) from the Path of Allâh (i.e.Islâm) and seek crookedness therein - they are far astray. (3) And We sent not a Messenger except with the language of his people, in order that he might make (the Message) clear for them. Then Allâh misleads whom He wills and guides whom He wills. And He is the All-Mighty, the All-Wise

14:18

The parable of those who disbelieve in their Lord is that their works are as ashes, on which the wind blows furiously on a stormy day, they shall not be able to get aught of what they have earned. That is the straying, far away (from the Right Path).

14:21-22

And they all shall appear before Allâh (on the Day of Resurrection) then the weak will say to those who were arrogant (chiefs):

"Verily, we were following you; can you avail us anything against Allâh's Torment?" They will say: "Had Allâh guided us, we would have guided you. It makes no difference to us (now) whether we rage, or bear (these torments) with patience, there is no place of refuge for us." (21) And Shaitân (Satan) will say when the matter has been decided: "Verily, Allâh promised you a promise of truth. And I too promised you, but I betrayed you. I had no authority over you except that I called you, so you responded to me. So blame me not, but blame yourselves. I cannot help you, nor can you help me. I deny your former act in associating me (Satan) as a partner with Allâh (by obeying me in the life of the world). Verily, there is a painful torment for the Zâlimûn (polytheists and wrong-doers)."

14:27

Allâh will keep firm those who believe, with the word that stands firm in this world (i.e. they will keep on worshipping Allâh Alone and none else), and in the Hereafter. And Allâh will cause to go astray those who are Zâlimûn (polytheists and wrong-doers, etc.), and Allâh does what He wills.

15:33-35

[Iblîs (Satan)] said: "I am not the one to prostrate myself to a human being, whom You created from dried (sounding) clay of altered mud." (Allâh) said: "Then, get out from here, for verily, you are Rajîm (an outcast or a cursed one)." "And verily, the curse shall be upon you till the Day of Recompense (i.e. the Day of Resurrection)."

16:23

Certainly, Allâh knows what they conceal and what they reveal. Truly, He likes not the proud.

16:35-37

And those who joined others in worship with Allâh say: "If Allâh had so willed, neither we nor our fathers would have worshipped aught but Him, nor would we have forbidden anything without (Command from) Him." So did those before them. Then! Are the Messengers charged with anything but to convey clearly the Message? (35) And verily, We have sent among every Ummah (community, nation) a Messenger (proclaiming): "Worship Allâh (Alone), and avoid (or keep away from) Tâghût (all false deities, etc.)." Then of them were some whom Allâh guided and of them were some upon whom the straying was justified. So travel through the land and see what was the end of those who denied (the truth). (36) If you covet for their guidance, then verily Allâh guides not those whom He makes to go astray (or none can guide him whom Allâh sends astray). And they will have no helpers.

16:93

And had Allâh willed, He could have made you (all) one nation, but He sends astray whom He wills and guides whom He wills. But you shall certainly be called to account for what you used to do.

16:106-109

Whoever disbelieved in Allâh after his belief, except him who is forced thereto and whose heart is at rest with Faith, but such as open their breasts to disbelief, on them is wrath from Allâh, and theirs will be a great torment. (106) That is because they loved and preferred the life of this world over that of the Hereafter. And Allâh guides not the people who disbelieve. (107) They are those upon whose hearts, hearing (ears) and sight (eyes) Allâh has set a seal. And they are the heedless! (108) No doubt, in the Hereafter, they will be the losers.

18:17

And you might have seen the sun, when it rose, declining to the right from their Cave, and when it set, turning away from them to the left, while they lay in the midst of the Cave. That is (one) of the Ayât (proofs, evidences, signs) of Allâh. He whom Allâh guides, is rightly guided; but he whom He sends astray, for him you will find no Walî (guiding friend) to lead him (to the right Path).

18:50-51

And (remember) when We said to the angels; "Prostrate yourselves unto Adam." So they prostrated themselves except Iblîs (Satan). He was one of the jinn; he disobeyed the Command of his Lord. Will you then take him (Iblîs) and his offspring as protectors and helpers rather than Me while they are enemies to you? What an evil is the exchange for the Zâlimûn (polytheists, and wrong-doers). (50) I (Allâh) made them (Iblîs and his offspring) not to witness (nor took their help in) the creation of the heavens and the earth and not (even) their own creation, nor was I (Allâh) to take the misleaders as helpers

18:57

And who does more wrong than he who is reminded of the Ayât (proofs, evidences, verses, lessons, signs, revelations, etc.) of his Lord, but turns away from them forgetting what (deeds) his hands have sent forth. Truly, We have set veils over their hearts lest they should understand this (the Qur'ân), and in their ears, deafness. And if you call them to guidance, even then they will never be guided.

18:103-106

Say: "Shall We tell you the greatest losers in respect of (their) deeds? (103) "Those whose efforts have been wasted in this life while they thought that they were acquiring good by their deeds!(104) "They are those who deny the Ayât (proofs, evidences, verses, lessons, signs, revelations, etc.) of their Lord and the Meeting with Him (in the Hereafter). So their works are in vain, and on the Day of Resurrection, We shall assign not weight for them. (105) "That shall be their recompense, Hell; because they disbelieved and took My Ayât (proofs, evidences, verses, lessons, signs, revelations, etc.) and My Messengers by way of jest and mockery.

19:37-39

Then the sects differed, so woe unto the disbelievers from the Meeting of a great Day. (37) How clearly will they (polytheists and disbelievers in the Oneness of Allâh) see and hear, the Day when they will appear before Us! But the Zalimûn (polytheists and wrong-doers) today are in plain error (38) And warn them of the Day of grief and regrets, when the case has been decided, while (now) they are in a state of carelessness, and they believe not

19:83

See you not that We have sent the Shayâtin (devils) against the disbelievers to push them to do evil.

20:61

Mûsa (Moses) said to them: "Woe unto you! Invent not a lie against Allâh, lest He should destroy you completely by a torment. And surely, he who invents a lie (against Allâh) will fail miserably."

20:117

Then We said: "O Adam! Verily, this is an enemy to you and to your wife. So let him not get you both out of Paradise, so that you will be distressed.

20:123-127

He (Allâh) said: "Get you down (from the Paradise to the earth), both of you, together, some of you are an enemy to some others. Then if there comes to you guidance from Me, then whoever follows My

Guidance he shall neither go astray, nor shall be distressed. (123) "But whosoever turns away from My Reminder (i.e. neither believes in this Qur'ân nor acts on its teachings) verily, for him is a life of hardship, and We shall raise him up blind on the Day of Resurrection." (124) He will say:"O my Lord! Why have you raised me up blind, while I had sight (before)." (125) (Allâh) will say: "Like this, Our Ayât (proofs, evidences, verses, lessons, signs, revelations, etc.) came unto you, but you disregarded them (i.e. you left them, did not think deeply in them, and you turned away from them), and so this Day, you will be neglected (in the Hell-fire, away from Allâh's Mercy)." (126) And thus do We requite him who transgresses beyond bounds [i.e. commits the great sins and disobeys his Lord (Allâh) and believes not in His Messengers, and His revealed Books, like this Qur'ân, etc.], and believes not in the Ayât (proofs, evidences, verses, lessons, signs, revelations) of his Lord, and the torment of the Hereafter is far more severe and more lasting.

22:38

Truly, Allâh defends those who believe. Verily! Allâh likes not any treacherous ingrate to Allâh [those who disobey Allâh but obey Shaitân (Satan)].

22:72

And when Our Clear Verses are recited to them, you will notice a denial on the faces of the disbelievers! They are nearly ready to attack with violence those who recite Our Verses to them. Say: "Shall I tell you of something worse than that? The Fire which Allâh has promised to those who disbelieved, and worst indeed is that destination!"

24:4

And those who accuse chaste women, and produce not four witnesses, flog them with eighty stripes, and reject their testimony forever, They indeed are the Fâsiqûn (liars, disobedient to Allâh).

24:6-9

And for those who accuse their wives, but have no witnesses except themselves, let the testimony of one of them be four testimonies (i.e. testifies four times) by Allâh that he is one of those who speak the truth. (6) And the fifth (testimony should be) the invoking of the Curse of Allâh on him if he be of those who tell a lie (against her). (7) But it shall avert the punishment (of stoning to death) from her, if she bears witness four times by Allâh, that he (her husband) is telling a lie. (8) And the fifth (testimony) should be that the Wrath of Allâh be upon her if he (her husband) speaks the truth.

24:19

Verily, those who like that illegal sexual intercourse should be propagated among those who believe, they will have a painful torment in this world and in the Hereafter. And Allâh knows and you know not.

24:23

Verily, those who accuse chaste women, who never even think of anything touching their chastity and are good believers, — are cursed in this life and in the Hereafter, and for them will be a great torment

24:39-40

As for those who disbelieve, their deeds are like a mirage in a desert. The thirsty one thinks it to be water, until he comes up to it, he finds it to be nothing, but he finds Allâh with him, Who will pay him his due (Hell). And Allâh is Swift in taking account. (39) Or [the state of a disbeliever] is like the darkness in a vast deep sea, overwhelmed with waves topped by waves, topped by dark clouds, (layers of) darkness upon darkness: if a man stretches out his hand, he can hardly see it! And he for whom Allâh has not appointed light, for him there is no light.

25:41-44

And when they see you, they treat you only in mockery (saying):"Is this the one whom Allâh has sent as a Messenger? (41) "He would have nearly misled us from our âlihah (gods), had it not been that we were patient and constant in their worship!" And they will know when they see the torment, who it is that is most astray from the (Right) Path! (42) Have you seen him who has taken as his ilâh (god) his own vain desire? Would you then be a Wakîl (a disposer of his affairs or a watcher) over him? (43) Or do you think that most of them hear or understand? They are only like cattle; nay, – they are even farther astray from the Path. (i.e. even worse than cattle).

26:69-77

And recite to them the story of Ibrâhim (Abraham). (69) When he said to his father and his people: "What do you worship?" (70) They said: "We worship idols, and to them we are ever devoted." (71) He said: "Do they hear you, when you call on (them)? (72) "Or do they benefit you or do they harm (you)?" (73) They said: "(Nay), but we found our fathers doing so." He said: "Do you observe that which you have been worshipping, – (75) "You and your ancient fathers? (76) "Verily! they are enemies to me, save the Lord of the 'Alamîn (mankind, jinn and all that exists);

26:165-168

"Go you in unto the males of the 'Alamîn (mankind), (165) "And leave those whom Allâh has created for you to be your wives? Nay, you are a trespassing people!" (166) They said: "If you cease not. O Lut (Lot)! Verily, you will be one of those who are driven out!" (167) He said: "I am, indeed, of those who disapprove with severe anger and fury your (this evil) action (of sodomy).

27:4-5

Verily, those who believe not in the Hereafter, We have made their deeds fair-seeming to them, so that they wander about blindly (4) They are those for whom there will be an evil torment (in this world). And in the Hereafter they will be the greatest losers.

28:39-42

And he and his hosts were arrogant in the land, without right, and they thought that they would never return to Us. (39) So We seized him and his hosts, and We threw them all into the sea (and drowned them). So behold what was the end of the Zâlimûn [wrong-doers, polytheists and those who disbelieved in the Oneness of their Lord (Allâh), or rejected the advice of His Messenger Mûsa (Moses)] (40) And We made them leaders inviting to the Fire, and on the Day of Resurrection, they will not be helped. (41) And We made a curse to follow them in this world, and on the Day of Resurrection, they will be among Al-Maqbuhûn (those who are prevented to receive Allâh's Mercy or any good, despised or destroyed).

28:50

But if they answer you not (i.e. do not bring the book nor believe in your doctrine of Islâmic Monotheism), then know that they only follow their own lusts. And who is more astray than one who follows his own lusts, without guidance from Allâh? Verily! Allâh guides not the people who are Zâlimûn (disobedient to Allâh, and polytheists)

28:76-77

Verily, Qârûn (Korah) was of Mûsâ's (Moses) people, but he behaved arrogantly towards them. And We gave him of the treasures, that of which the keys would have been a burden to a body of strong men. Remember when his people said to him: "Do not exult (with riches, being ungrateful to Allâh). Verily Allâh likes not those who exult (with riches, being ungrateful to Allâh). But seek, with that which Allâh has bestowed on you, the home of the Hereafter, and forget not your portion of lawful enjoyment in this world, and do good as Allâh has been good to you, and seek not mischief in the land. Verily, Allâh likes not the Mufsidûn (those who commit crimes/sins, oppressors, mischief-makers, corrupters).

28:86

And you were not expecting that the Book (this Qur'ân) would be sent down to you, but it is a mercy from your Lord. So never be a supporter of the disbelievers.

29:41

The likeness of those who take (false deities as) Auliyâ' (protectors helpers) other than Allâh is the likeness of a spider, who builds (for itself) a house, but verily, the frailest (weakest) of houses is the spider's house; if they but knew.

29:52-53

Say: "Sufficient is Allâh for a witness between me and you. He knows what is in the heavens and on earth." And those who believe in Bâtil (all false deities other than Allâh), and disbelieve in Allâh and (in His Oneness), it is they who are the losers. (52) And they ask you to hasten on the torment (for them), and had it not been for a term appointed, the torment would certainly have come to them. And surely, it will come upon them suddenly while they perceive not!

29:68

And who does more wrong than he who invents a lie against Allâh or denies the truth (Muhammad and his doctrine of Islâmic Monotheism and this Qur'ân), when it comes to him? Is there not a dwelling in Hell for disbelievers?

30:29

Nay, but those who do wrong follow their own lusts without knowledge, Then who will guide him whom Allâh has sent astray? And for such there will be no helpers.

30:37

Do they not see that Allâh enlarges the provision for whom He wills and straitens (it for whom He wills). Verily, in that are indeed signs for a people who believe.

30:45

That He may reward those who believe (in the Oneness of Allâh Islâmic Monotheism), and do righteous good deeds, out of His Bounty. Verily, He likes not the disbelievers.

31:18

And turn not your face away from men with pride, nor walk in insolence through the earth. Verily, Allâh likes not any arrogant boaster

32:13

And if We had willed, surely! We would have given every person his guidance, but the Word from Me took effect (about evil¬doers), that I will fill Hell with jinn and mankind together

32:18

Is then he who is a believer like him who is Fâsiq (disbeliever and disobedient to Allâh)? Not equal are they

32:22

And who does more wrong than he who is reminded of the Ayât (proofs, evidences, verses, lessons, signs, revelations, etc.) of his Lord, then turns aside therefrom? Verily, We shall exact retribution from the Mujrimûn (criminals, disbelievers, polytheists, sinners, etc.)

33:19

Being miserly towards you (as regards help and aid in Allâh's Cause). Then when fear comes, you will see them looking to you, their eyes revolving like (those of) one over whom hovers death, but when the fear departs, they will smite you with sharp tongues, miserly towards (spending anything in any) good (and only covetous of booty and wealth). Such have not believed. Therefore Allâh makes their deeds fruitless, and that is ever easy for Allâh.

33:57-58

Verily, those who annoy Allâh and His Messenger Allâh has cursed them in this world, and in the Hereafter, and has prepared for them a humiliating torment. (57) And those who annoy believing men and women undeservedly, they bear (on themselves) the crime of slander and plain sin.

33:60-62

If the hypocrites, and those in whose hearts is a disease, and those who spread false news among the people in Al¬Madinah, stop not, We shall certainly let you overpower them; then they will not be able to stay in it as your neighbours but a little while. (60) Accursed, they shall be seized wherever found and killed with a (terrible) slaughter. (61) That was the Way of Allâh in the case of those who passed away of old, and you will not find any change in the Way of Allâh.

33:64

Verily, Allâh has cursed the disbelievers, and has prepared for them a flaming Fire.

34:16-17

But they turned away (from the obedience of Allâh), so We sent against them Sail Al¬'Arim (flood released from the dam), and We converted their two gardens into gardens producing bitter bad fruit, and tamarisks, and some few lote¬trees. (16) Like this We requited them because they were ungrateful disbelievers. And never do We requite in such a way except those who are ungrateful, (disbelievers).

35:6-8

Surely, Shaitân (Satan) is an enemy to you, so take (treat) him as an enemy. He only invites his Hizb (followers) that they may become the dwellers of the blazing Fire. Those who disbelieve, theirs will be a severe torment; and those who believe (in the Oneness of Allâh Islâmic Monotheism) and do righteous good deeds, theirs will be forgiveness and a great reward (i.e. Paradise). (7) Is he, then, to whom the evil of his deeds made fair¬seeming, so that he considers it as good (equal to one who is rightly guided)? Verily, Allâh sends astray whom He wills, and guides whom He wills. So destroy not yourself in sorrow for them. Truly, Allâh is the All¬Knower of what they do!

35:39

He it is Who has made you successors generations after generations in the earth, so whosoever disbelieves (in Islâmic Monotheism) on him will be his disbelief. And the disbelief of the disbelievers adds nothing but hatred of their Lord. And the disbelief of the disbelievers adds nothing but loss.

36:8-10

Verily! We have put on their necks iron collars reaching to the chins, so that their heads are raised up. (8) And We have put a barrier before them, and a barrier behind them, and We have covered them up, so that they cannot see. (9) It is the same to them whether you warn them or you warn them not, they will not believe.

36:60

Did I not command for you, O Children of Adam, that you should not worship Shaitân (Satan). Verily, he is a plain enemy to you.

37:151-152

Verily, it is of their falsehood that they say: (151) "Allâh has begotten?" And, verily, they are liars!

38:27-28

And We created not the heaven and the earth and all that is between them without purpose! That is the consideration of those who disbelieve! Then woe to those who disbelieve (in Islâmic Monotheism) from the Fire! (27) Shall We treat those who believe (in the Oneness of Allâh — Islâmic Monotheism) and do righteous good deeds, as Mufsidûn (those who associate partners in worship with Allâh and commit crimes) on earth? Or shall We treat the Muttaqûn (pious), as the Fujjâr (criminals, disbelievers, the wicked)?

38:78

And verily!, My Curse is on you till the Day of Recompense.

39:3

Surely, the religion (i.e. the worship and the obedience) is for Allâh only. And those who take Auliyâ' (protectors, friends, helpers, lords, gods) besides Him (say): "We worship them only that they may bring us near to Allâh." Verily, Allâh will judge between them concerning that wherein they differ. Truly, Allâh guides not him who is a liar, and a disbeliever.

39:9

Is one who is obedient to Allâh, prostrating himself or standing (in prayer) during the hours of the night, fearing the Hereafter and hoping for the Mercy of his Lord (like one who disbelieves)? Say: "Are those who know equal to those who know not?" It is only men of understanding who will remember (i.e. get a lesson from Allâh's Signs).

39:15

So worship what you like besides Him. Say: "The losers are those who will lose themselves and their families on the Day of Resurrection. Verily, that will be a manifest loss!"

39:19

Is, then one against whom the Word of punishment is justified (equal to one who avoids evil)? Will you rescue him who is in the Fire?

39:22

Is he whose breast Allâh has opened to Islâm, so that he is in light from His Lord (as the non-Muslim)? So, woe to those whose hearts are hardened against remembrance of Allâh! They are in plain error!

39:24-26

Is he then, who will confront with his face the awful torment on the Day of Resurrection (as he who enters peacefully in Paradise)? And it will be said to the Zâlimûn (polytheists and wrong-doers): "Taste what you used to earn!" (24) Those before them belied, and so the torment came on them from directions they perceived not. (25) So Allâh made them to taste the disgrace in the present life, but greater is the torment of the Hereafter if they only knew!

39:29

Allâh puts forth a similitude: a (slave) man belonging to many partners (like those who worship others along with Allâh) disputing with one another, and a (slave) man belonging entirely to one master, (like those who worship Allâh Alone). Are those two equal in comparison? All the praises and thanks are to Allâh! But most of them know not.

39:32

Then, who does more wrong than one who utters a lie against Allâh, and denies the truth, when it comes to him! Is there not in Hell an abode for the disbelievers?

39:65

And indeed it has been revealed to you, as it was to those before you: "If you join others in worship with Allâh, (then) surely (all) your deeds will be in vain, and you will certainly be among the losers

40:10

Those who disbelieve will be addressed: "Allâh's aversion was greater towards you (in the worldly life when you used to reject the Faith) than your aversion towards one another (now in the Fire of Hell, as you are now enemies to one another), when you were called to the Faith but you used to refuse."

40:28

And a believing man of Fir'aun's (Pharaoh) family, who hid his faith said: "Would you kill a man because he says: My Lord is Allâh, and he has come to you with clear signs (proofs) from your Lord? And if he is a liar, upon him will be (the sin of) his lie; but if he is telling the truth, then some of that (calamity) wherewith he threatens you will befall on you." Verily, Allâh guides not one who is a Musrif (a polytheist, or a murderer who shed blood without a right, or those who commit great sins, oppressor, transgressor), a liar!

40:34-35

*And indeed Yûsuf (Joseph) did come to you, in times gone by,
with clear signs, but you ceased not to doubt in that which he did bring
to you, till when he died you said: "No Messenger will Allâh send after
him." Thus Allâh leaves astray him who is a Musrif (a polytheist, an
oppressor, a criminal, sinner who commit great sins) and a Murtâb (one
who doubts Allâh's Warning and His Oneness). (34) Those who dispute
about the Ayât (proofs, evidences, verses, lessons, signs, revelations, etc.)
of Allâh, without any authority that has come to them, it is greatly
hateful and disgusting to Allâh and to those who believe. Thus does
Allâh seal up the heart of every arrogant, tyrant. (So they cannot guide
themselves to the Right Path)*

40:52

*The Day when their excuses will be of no profit to Zâlimûn
(polytheists, wrong-doers and disbelievers in the Oneness of Allâh).
Theirs will be the curse, and theirs will be the evil abode (i.e. painful
torment in Hell-fire).*

40:58

*And not equal are the blind and those who see, nor are (equal)
those who believe (in the Oneness of Allâh − Islâmic Monotheism), and
do righteous good deeds, and those who do evil. Little do you remember!*

41:6-7

*Say: "I am only a human being like you. It is revealed to me that
your Ilâh (God) is One Ilâh (God - Allâh), therefore take Straight Path to
Him (with true Faith − Islâmic Monotheism) and obedience to Him,
and seek forgiveness of Him. And woe to Al-Mushrikûn (the polytheists,
disbelievers in the Oneness of Allâh). (6) Those who give not the Zakât
and they are disbelievers in the Hereafter.*

41:25

And We have assigned them (devils) intimate companions (in this world), who have made fair-seeming to them, what was before them (evil deeds which they were doing in the present worldly life and disbelief in the Reckoning and the Resurrection) and what was behind them (denial of the matters in the coming life of the Hereafter as regards punishment or reward). And the Word (i.e. the torment) is justified against them as it was justified against those who were among the previous generations of jinn and men that had passed away before them. Indeed they (all) were the losers.

41:34

The good deed and the evil deed cannot be equal. Repel (the evil) with one which is better (i.e. Allâh orders the faithful believers to be patient at the time of anger, and to excuse those who treat them badly), then verily! he, between whom and you there was enmity, (will become) as though he was a close friend.

42:8

And if Allâh had willed, He could have made them one nation, but He admits whom He wills to His Mercy. And the Zâlimûn (polytheists and wrong-doers) will have neither a Walî (protector, or guardian) nor a helper.

42:16

And those who dispute concerning Allâh (His religion of Islâmic Monotheism, with which Muhammad has been sent), after it has been accepted (by the people), of no use is their dispute before their Lord, and on them is wrath, and for them will be a severe torment

42:44-46

And whomsoever Allâh sends astray, for him there is no Walî (protector, helper, guardian) after Him. And you will see the Zâlimûn (polytheists, wrong-doers, oppressors) when they behold the torment, they will say: "Is there any way of return (to the world)?" (44) And you will see them brought forward to it (Hell) made humble by disgrace , (and) looking with stealthy glance. And those who believe will say: "Verily, the losers are they who lose themselves and their families on the Day of Resurrection. Verily, the Zâlimûn [i.e. Al-Kâfirûn (disbelievers in Allâh, in His Oneness and in His Messenge, polytheists, wrong-doers)] will be in a lasting torment. (45) And they will have no Auliyâ' (protectors, helper, guardian, lords) to help them other than Allâh. And he whom Allâh sends astray, for him there is no way.

43:36-37

And whosoever turns away blindly from the remembrance of the Most Gracious (Allâh) (i.e. this Qur'ân and worship of Allâh), We appoint for him Shaitân (Satan devil) to be a Qarîn (a intimate companion) to him. (36) And verily, they (Satans / devils) hinder them from the Path (of Allâh), but they think that they are guided aright!

43:62

And let not Shaitân (Satan) hinder you (from the right religion, i.e. Islâmic Monotheism), Verily, he (Satan) to you is a plain enemy.

43:65

But the sects from among themselves differed. So woe to those who do wrong from the torment of a painful Day!

43:67

Friends on that Day will be foes one to another except the righteous

45:7-9

Woe to every sinful liar, Who hears the Verses of Allâh (being) recited to him, yet persists with pride as if he heard them not. So announce to him a painful torment! And when he learns something of Our Verses (this Qur'ân), he makes them a jest. For such there will be a humiliating torment.

45:21

Or do those who earn evil deeds think that We shall hold them equal with those who believe and do righteous good deeds, in their present life and after their death? Worst is the judgement that they make.

45:23

Have you seen him who takes his own lust (vain desires) as his ilâh (god)? and Allâh knowing (him as such), left him astray, and sealed his hearing and his heart, and put a cover on his sight. Who then will guide him after Allâh? Will you not then remember?

46:17-19

But he who says to his parents: "Fie upon you both! Do you hold out the promise to me that I shall be raised up (again) when generations before me have passed away (without rising)?" While they (father and mother) invoke Allâh for help (and rebuke their son): "Woe to you! Believe! Verily, the Promise of Allâh is true." But he says: "This is nothing but the tales of the ancient." (17) They are those against whom the Word (of torment) is justified among the previous generations of jinn and mankind that have passed away. Verily, they are ever the losers (18) And for all, there will be degrees according to that which they did, that He (Allâh) may recompense them in full for their deeds. And they will not be wronged.

46:32

And whosoever does not respond to Allâh's Caller, he cannot escape on earth, and there will be no Auliyâ' (lord, helpers, supporters, protectors) for him besides Allâh (from Allâh's Punishment). Those are in manifest error.

47:1

Those who disbelieve [in the Oneness of Allâh, and in the Message of Prophet Muhammad], and hinder (men) from the Path of Allâh (Islâmic Monotheism), He will render their deeds vain

47:7-9

O you who believe! If you help (in the cause of) Allâh, He will help you, and make your foothold firm. (7) But those who disbelieve (in the Oneness of Allâh Islâmic Monotheism), for them is destruction, and (Allâh) will make their deeds vain. (8) That is because they hate that which Allâh has sent down (this Qur'ân and Islâmic laws etc.), so He has made their deeds fruitless.

47:14-16

Is he who is on a clear proof from his Lord, like those for whom their evil deeds that they do are beautified for them, while they follow their own lusts (evil desires)? The description of Paradise which the Muttaqûn (pious) have been promised (is that) in it are rivers of water the taste and smell of which are not changed, rivers of milk of which the taste never changes, rivers of wine delicious to those who drink; and rivers of clarified honey (clear and pure) therein for them is every kind of fruit; and forgiveness from their Lord. (Are these) like those who shall dwell for ever in the Fire, and be given, to drink, boiling water, so that it cuts up their bowels? (15) And among them are some who listen to you (O Muhammad) till, when they go out from you, they say to those who have received knowledge: "What has he said just now? Such are men whose hearts Allâh has sealed, and they follow their lusts (evil desires).

47:22-23

Would you then, if you were given the authority, do mischief in the land, and sever your ties of kinship? (22) Such are they whom Allâh has cursed, so that He has made them deaf and blinded their sight.

47:25-34

Verily, those who have turned back (have apostatise) as disbelievers after the guidance has been manifested to them — Shaitân (Satan) has beautified for them (their false hopes), and (Allâh) prolonged their term (age). (25) This is because they said to those who hate what Allâh has sent down: "We will obey you in part of the matter," but Allâh knows their secrets. (26) Then how (will it be) when the angels will take their souls at death, smiting their faces and their backs? (27) That is because they followed that which angered Allâh, and hated that which pleased Him. So He made their deeds fruitless. (28) Or do those in whose hearts is a disease (of hypocrisy), think that Allâh will not bring to light all their hidden ill-wills? (29) Had We willed, We could have shown them to you, and you should have known them by their marks; but surely, you will know them by the tone of their speech! And Allâh knows (all) your deeds. (30) And surely, We shall try you till We test those who strive hard (for the Cause of Allâh) and As-Sabirun (the patient ones), and We shall test your facts (i.e. the one who is a liar, and the one who is truthful). (31) Verily, those who disbelieve, and hinder (men) from the Path of Allâh (i.e. Islâm), and oppose the Messenger, after the guidance has been clearly shown to them, they will not hurt Allâh in the least, but He will make their deeds fruitless, O you who believe! Obey Allâh, and obey the Messenger and render not vain your deeds. (33) Verily, those who disbelieve, and hinder (men) from the Path of Allâh (i.e. Islâm); then die while they are disbelievers, - Allâh will not forgive them.

48:6

And that He may punish the Munâfiqûn (hypocrites), men and women, and also the Mushrikûn men and women, who think evil thoughts about Allâh, for them is a disgraceful torment, And the Anger of Allâh is upon them, and He has cursed them and prepared Hell for them — and worst indeed is that destination.

48:28-29

He it is Who has sent His Messenger with guidance and the religion of truth (Islâm), that He may make it (Islâm) superior over all religions. And All-Sufficient is Allâh as a Witness. (28) Muhammad is the Messenger of Allâh, And those who are with him are severe against disbelievers, and merciful among themselves. You see them bowing and falling down prostrate (in prayer), seeking Bounty from Allâh and (His) Good Pleasure. The mark of them (i.e. of their Faith) is on their faces (foreheads) from the traces of prostration (during prayers). This is their description in the Taurât. But their description in the Injeel is like a (sown) seed which sends forth its shoot, then makes it strong, and becomes thick, and it stands straight on its stem, delighting the sowers that He may enrage the disbelievers with them. Allâh has promised those among them who believe and do righteous good deeds, forgiveness and a mighty reward (i.e. Paradise).

51:10

Cursed be the liars

51:60

Then, woe to those who disbelieve from their Day which they have been promised (for their punishment).

52:42

Or do they intend a plot? But those who disbelieve are themselves plotted against!

52:47

And verily, for those who do wrong, there is another punishment before this, but most of them know not.

57:22-23

No calamity befalls on the earth or in yourselves but is inscribed in the Book of Decrees (Al-Lauh Al-Mahfûz), before We bring it into existence. Verily, that is easy for Allâh. (22) In order that you may not grieve at the things that you fail to get, nor rejoice over that which has been given to you. And Allâh likes not prideful boasters.

58:5

Verily, those who oppose Allâh and His Messenger (Muhammad) will be disgraced, as those before them (among the past nation), were disgraced. And We have sent down clear Ayât (proofs, evidences, verses, lessons, signs, revelations, etc.). And for the disbelievers is a disgracing torment.

58:14-22

Have you not seen those (hypocrites) who take as friends a people upon whom is the Wrath of Allâh (i.e. Jews and Christians)? They are neither of you (Muslims) nor of them (Jews and Christians), and they swear to a lie while they know. (14) Allâh has prepared for them a severe torment. Evil indeed is that which they used to do. (15) They have made their oaths a screen (for their evil actions). Thus they hinder (men) from the Path of Allâh, so they shall have a humiliating torment. (16) Their children and their wealth will avail them nothing against Allâh. They will be the dwellers of the Fire, to dwell therein forever. (17) On the Day when Allâh will resurrect them all together (for their account), then they will swear to Him as they swear to you (O Muslims). And they think that they have something (to stand upon). Verily, they are liars! (18)

Shaitân (Satan) has overpowered them. So he has made them forget the remembrance of Allâh. They are the party of Shaitân (Satan). Verily, it is the party of Shaitân (Satan) that will be the losers! (19) Those who oppose Allâh and His Messenger (Muhammad), they will be among the lowest (most humiliated). (20) Allâh has decreed: "Verily! It is I and My Messengers who shall be the victorious." Verily, Allâh is All-Powerful, All-Mighty. (21) You will not find any people who believe in Allâh and the Last Day, making friendship with those who oppose Allâh and His Messenger, even though they were their fathers or their sons or their brothers or their kindred (people). For such He has written Faith in their hearts, and strengthened them with Rûh (proofs, light and true guidance) from Himself. And He will admit them to Gardens (Paradise) under which rivers flow to dwell therein (forever). Allâh is pleased with them, and they with Him. They are the Party of Allâh. Verily, it is the Party of Allâh that will be the successful.

59:2-4

He it is Who drove out the disbelievers among the people of the Scripture (i.e. the Jews of the tribe of Banu An-Nadîr) from their homes at the first gathering. You did not think that they would get out. And they thought that their fortresses would defend them from Allâh! But Allâh's (Torment) reached them from a place whereof they expected it not, and He cast terror into their hearts, so that they destroyed their own dwellings with their own hands and the hands of the believers. Then take admonition, O you with eyes (to see). (2) And had it not been that Allâh had decreed exile for them, He would certainly have punished them in this world, and in the Hereafter theirs shall be the torment of the Fire. (3) That is because they opposed Allâh and His Messenger (Muhammad). And whosoever opposes Allâh, then verily, Allâh is Severe in punishment.

59:11

Have you not observed the hypocrites who say to their friends among the people of the Scripture who disbelieve: "(By Allâh) If you are expelled, we (too) indeed will go out with you, and we shall never obey any one against you, and if you are attacked (in fight), we shall indeed help you." But Allâh is Witness, that they verily, are liars.

59:20

Not equal are the dwellers of the Fire and the dwellers of the Paradise. It is the dwellers of Paradise that will be successful.

60:1-2

O you who believe! Take not My enemies and your enemies (i.e. disbelievers and polytheists) as friends, showing affection towards them, while they have disbelieved in what has come to you of the truth (i.e. Islâmic Monotheism, this Qur'ân, and Muhammad) and have driven out the Messenger and yourselves because you believe in Allâh your Lord! If you have come forth to strive in My Cause and to seek My Good Pleasure, (then take not these disbelievers and polytheists, as your friends). You show friendship to them in secret, while I am All-Aware of what you conceal and what you reveal. And whosoever of you (Muslims) does that, then indeed he has gone (far) astray, from the Straight Path. (1) Should they gain the upper hand over you, they would behave to you as enemies, and stretch forth their hands and their tongues against you with evil, and they desire that you should disbelieve.

60:4-10

Indeed there has been an excellent example for you in Ibrâhîm and those with him, when they said to their people: "Verily, we are free from you and whatever you worship besides Allâh, we have rejected you, and there has started between us and you, hostility and hatred for ever, until you believe in Allâh Alone," except the saying of Ibrâhîm (Abraham) to his father: "Verily, I will ask forgiveness (from Allâh) for

you, but I have no power to do anything for you before Allâh ." Our
Lord! In You (Alone) we put our trust, and to You (Alone) we turn in
repentance, and to You (Alone) is (our) final Return, (4) "Our Lord!
Make us not a trial for the disbelievers, and forgive us, Our Lord! Verily,
You, only You are the All-Mighty, the All-Wise." (5) Certainly, there
has been in them an excellent example for you to follow — for those who
look forward to (the Meeting with) Allâh and the Last Day. And
whosoever turns away, then verily, Allâh is Rich (Free of all needs),
Worthy of all Praise. (6) Perhaps Allâh will make friendship between you
and those whom you hold as enemies. And Allâh has power (over all
things), and Allâh is Oft-Forgiving, Most Merciful. (7) Allâh does not
forbid you to deal justly and kindly with those who fought not against
you on account of religion nor drove you out of your homes. Verily,
Allâh loves those who deal with equity. (8) It is only as regards those
who fought against you on account of religion, and have driven you out
of your homes, and helped to drive you out, that Allâh forbids you to
befriend them. And whosoever will befriend them, then such are the
Zâlimûn (wrong-doers those who disobey Allâh). (9) O you who believe!
When believing women come to you as emigrants, examine them, Allâh
knows best as to their Faith, then if you ascertain that they are true
believers, send them not back to the disbelievers, They are not lawful
(wives) for the disbelievers nor are the disbelievers lawful (husbands) for
them. But give (the disbelievers) that (amount of money) which they have
spent [as their Mahr] to them. And there will be no sin on you to marry
them if you have paid their Mahr to them. Likewise hold not the
disbelieving women as wives, and ask for (the return of) that which you
have spent (as Mahr) and let them (the disbelievers) ask back for that
which they have spent. That is the Judgement of Allâh. He judges
between you. And Allâh is All-Knowing, All-Wise.

60:13

O you who believe! Take not as friends the people who incurred
the Wrath of Allâh. Surely, they have despaired of (receiving any good

in) the Hereafter, just as the disbelievers have despaired of those (buried) in graves (that they will not be resurrected on the Day of Resurrection).

61:3

Most hateful it is with Allâh that you say that which you do not do.

61:7

And who does more wrong than the one who invents a lie against Allâh, while he is being invited to Islâm? And Allâh guides not the people who are Zâlimûn (wrong-doers and disbelievers) folk.

62:5

The likeness of those who were entrusted with the (obligation of the) Taurât (Torah) (i.e. to obey its commandments), but who subsequently failed in those (obligations), is as the likeness of a donkey which carries huge burdens of books (but understands nothing from them). How bad is the example of people who deny the Ayât (proofs, evidences, verses, signs, revelations) of Allâh. And Allâh guides not the people who are Zâlimûn (wrong-doers, disbelievers).

63:1-4

When the hypocrites come to you (O Muhammad), they say: "We bear witness that you are indeed the Messenger of Allâh." Allâh knows that you are indeed His Messenger and Allâh bears witness that the hypocrites are liars indeed. (1) They have made their oaths a screen (for their hypocrisy). Thus they hinder (men) from the Path of Allâh. Verily, evil is what they used to do. (2) That is because they believed, then disbelieved, therefore their hearts are sealed, so they understand not. (3) And when you look at them, their bodies please you; and when they speak, you listen to their words. They are as blocks of wood propped up. They think that every cry is against them. They are the enemies, so beware of them. May Allâh curse them! How are they denying (or deviating from) the Right Path?

63:9

O you who believe! Let not your properties or your children divert you from the remembrance of Allâh. And whosoever does that, then they are the losers.

64:14

O you who believe! Verily, among your wives and your children are your enemies (who may stop you from the obedience of Allâh), therefore beware of them! But if you pardon (them) and overlook, and forgive (their faults), then verily, Allâh is Oft-Forgiving, Most Merciful.

66:9-11

O Prophet! Strive hard against the disbelievers and the hypocrites, and be severe against them;, their abode will be Hell, and worst indeed is that destination. (9) Allâh sets forth an example for those who disbelieve, the wife of Nûh (Noah) and the wife of Lut (Lot). They were under two of our righteous slaves, but they both betrayed them (their husbands by rejecting their doctrine) So they availed them (their respective wives) not, against Allâh, and it was said: "Enter the Fire along with those who enter!" (10) And Allâh has set forth an example for those who believe; the wife of Fir'aun (Pharaoh), when she said: "My Lord! Build for me a home with You in Paradise, and save me from Fir'aun and his work, and save me from the people who are Zâlimûn (polytheists, wrong-doers and disbelievers in Allâh).

67:20

Who is he besides the Most Gracious that can be an army to you to help you? The disbelievers are in nothing but delusion

68:35-44

Shall We then treat the Muslims like the Mujrimûn (criminals, polytheists and disbelievers)? (35) What is the matter with you? How judge you? (36) Or have you a Book where in you learn, (37) That you shall therein have all that you choose? (38) Or have you oaths from Us, reaching to the Day of Resurrection that yours will be what you judge? (39) Ask them, which of them will stand surety for that! (40) Or have they "partners"? Then let them bring their "partners" if they are truthful! (41) (Remember) the Day when the Shin shall be laid bare (i.e. the Day of Resurrection) and they shall be called to prostrate themselves (to Allâh), but they (hypocrites) shall not be able to do so. (42) Their eyes will be cast down and ignominy will cover them; they used to be called to prostrate themselves (offer prayers), while they were healthy and good (in the life of the world, but they did not). (43) Then leave Me Alone with such as belie this Qur'ân. We shall punish them gradually from directions they perceive not.

71:26-28

And Nûh (Noah) said: "My Lord! Leave not one of the disbelievers on the earth! (26) "If You leave them, they will mislead Your slaves, and they will beget none but wicked disbelievers." (27) "My Lord! Forgive me, and my parents, and him who enters my home as a believer, and all the believing men and women. And to the Zâlimûn (wrong-doers, and disbelievers) grant You no increase but destruction!"

74:19-20

So let him be cursed! how he plotted! (19) And once more let him be cursed, how he plotted!

75:31-35

So he (the disbeliever) neither believed (in this Qur'ân, and in the Message of Muhammad) nor prayed! (31) But on the contrary, he belied (this Qur'ân and the Message of Muhammad) and turned away! (32) Then he walked in conceit to his family admiring himself! (33) Woe to you! And then (again) woe to you! (34) Again, woe to you! And then (again) woe to you!

77:15

Woe that Day to the deniers (of the Day of Resurrection)!

77:19

Woe that Day to the deniers (of the Day of Resurrection)!

77:24

Woe that Day to the deniers (of the Day of Resurrection)!

77:28

Woe that Day to the deniers (of the Day of Resurrection)!

77:34

Woe that Day to the deniers (of the Day of Resurrection)!

77:37

Woe that Day to the deniers (of the Day of Resurrection)!

77:40

Woe that Day to the deniers (of the Day of Resurrection)!

77:45-49

Woe that Day to the deniers (of the Day of Resurrection)! (45) (O you disbelievers)! Eat and enjoy yourselves (in this worldly life) for a little while. Verily, you are the Mujrimûn (polytheists, disbelievers, sinners, criminals). (46) Woe that Day to the deniers (of the Day of Resurrection)! (47) And when it is said to them: "Bow down yourself (in prayer)!" They bow not down (offer not their prayers). (48) Woe that Day to the deniers (of the Day of Resurrection)!

80:17

Be cursed man! How ungrateful he is!

83:1-3

Woe to Al-Mutaffifun (those who give less in measure and weight). (1) Those who, when they have to receive by measure from men, demand full measure, (2) And when they have to give by measure or weight to (other) men, give less than due.

85:4

Cursed were the people of the Ditch

91:10

And indeed he fails who corrupts his ownself

95:4-6

Verily, We created man in the best stature (mould), (4) Then We reduced him to the lowest of the low, (5) Save those who believe (in Islâmic Monotheism) and do righteous deeds, Then they shall have a reward without end (Paradise).

98:6

Verily, those who disbelieve from among the people of the Scripture (Jews and Christians) and Al-Mushrikûn will abide in the Fire of Hell. They are the worst of creatures.

103:2-3

Verily, man is in loss, (2) Except those who believe (in Islâmic Monotheism) and do righteous good deeds, and recommend one another to the truth, and recommend one another to patience

104:1

Woe to every slanderer and backbiter.

107:4-7

So woe to those who pray (4) [But] who are heedless of their prayer –(5) Those who do good deeds only to be seen (6) and refuse to give 'even the simplest' aid. (7)

108:3

For he who hates you (O Muhammad), he will be cut off (from every posterity good thing in this world and in the Hereafter).

111:1-5

Perish the two hands of Abû Lahab, and perish he! His wealth and his children will not benefit him! He will be burnt in a Fire of blazing flames! And his wife [as well] - the carrier of firewood. Around her neck is a rope of [twisted] fiber.

Hadith Citations showing Anger For or Hatred Toward Certain Beings

Abu Hurairah reported:

The Prophet said, "When Allah loves a slave, calls out Jibril and says: 'I love so-and-so; so love him'. Then Jibril loves him. After that he (Jibril) announces to the inhabitants of heavens that Allah loves so- and-so; so love him; and the inhabitants of the heavens (the angels) also love him and then make people on earth love him".

[Al- Bukhari and Muslim].

Another narration of Muslim is: *Messenger of Allah, said: "When Allah loves a slave, He calls Jibril (Gabriel) and says: 'I love so-and-so; so love him.' And then Jibril loves him. Then he (Jibril) announces in the heavens saying: Allah loves so-and-so; so love him; then the inhabitants of the heavens (the angels) also love him; and then people on earth love him. And when Allah hates a slave, He calls Jibril and says: 'I hate so- and-so, so hate him.' Then Jibril also hates him. He (Jibril) then announces amongst the inhabitants of heavens: 'Verily, Allah hates so- and-so, so you also hate him.' Thus they also start to hate him. Then he becomes the object of hatred on the earth also".*

[Al- Bukhari and Muslim].

Narrated AbuUmamah:

The Prophet said: If anyone loves for Allah's sake, hates for Allah's sake, gives for Allah's sake and withholds for Allah's sake, he will have perfect faith.

Sunan Abi Dawud 4681 Grade: Sahih

It was narrated that Abu Hurairah said:

"The Messenger of Allah said: 'Whoever loves Hasan and Husain, loves me; and whoever hates them, hates me.'"

Sunan Ibn Majah Grade: Hasan

Ahmad (18524) narrated from al-Baraa' ibn 'Aazib, that the Messenger of Allah said:

"Indeed the strongest bond of faith is to love for the sake of Allah and hate for the sake of Allah."

Classed as hasan by the commentators on al-Musnad; also classed as hasan by al-Albaani in Saheeh at-Targheeb (3030).

Narrated Al-Bara:

I heard the Prophet saying, "None loves the Ansar but a believer, and none hates them but a hypocrite. So Allah will love him who loves them, and He will hate him who hates them."

Sahih al-Bukhari 3783

Muhammad bin Sirin narrated from Abu Hurairah - and I think he (narrated it from the Prophet) who said:

"Love your beloved moderately, perhaps he becomes hated to you someday. And hate whom you hate moderately, perhaps he becomes your beloved someday."

Jami` at-Tirmidhi 1997 Grade: Hasan

Narrated `Aisha:

The Prophet said, "The most hated person in the sight of Allah is the most quarrelsome person."

Sahih al-Bukhari 2457

Narrated Abu Dharr:

The Prophet said: The best of the actions is to love for the sake of Allah and to hate for the sake of Allah.

Sunan Abi Dawud 4599 Grade: Daif (Al-Albani)

Abu ad-Darda narrated that the Messenger of Allah said:

"Allah hates the profligate and the obscene."

Related by At-Tirmidhi who graded it to be Sahih.

Narrated Abdullah ibn Amr ibn al-'As:

The Messenger of Allah said: Allah , the Exalted, hates the eloquent one among men who moves his tongue round (among his teeth), as cattle do.

Sunan Abi Dawud 5005 Grade: Sahih

Abu Hurairah said:

The Prophet said, "The most disgraceful man near Allah is a man who calls himself Malikul-Amlak (i.e., king of kings)."

[Al-Bukhari and Muslim].

Umar bin Al-Khattab narrated that the Prophet said:

"Shall I not inform you of the best of your leaders and the worst of them: The best of them are those whom you love and they love you, you supplicate for them, and they supplicate for you. And the evilest of your *leaders are those who hate you, and you hate them, and they curse you and you curse them."*

Jami` at-Tirmidhi 2264 Grade: Sahih

Narrated Anas bin Malik:

that the Messenger of Allah said: "There are three things for which whomever has them, then he has tasted the sweetness of faith: The one for whom Allah and His Messenger are more beloved than anything else; whoever loves someone and he does not love him except for the sake of Allah, and whoever hates to return to disbelief after Allah has saved him from it, just as he hates to be thrown into fire."

Jami` at-Tirmidhi 2624 Grade: Sahih

Narrated 'Abdullah bin Mughaffal:

that the Messenger of Allah said: "(Fear) Allah! (Fear) Allah regarding my Companions! Do not make them objects of insults after me. Whoever loves them, it is out of love of me that he loves them. And whoever hates them, it is out of hatred for me that he hates them. And whoever harms them, he has harmed me, and whoever harms me, he has offended Allah, and whoever offends Allah, [then] he shall soon be punished."

Jami at-Tirmidhi Grade: Daif (Darussalam)

It has been narrated on the authority of 'Auf bin Malik that the Messenger of Allah said:

The best of your rulers are those whom you love and who love you, who invoke God's blessings upon you and you invoke His blessings upon them. And the worst of your rulers are those whom you hate and who hate you and whom you curse and who curse you. It was asked (by those present): Shouldn't we overthrow them with the help of the sword?

He said: *No, as long as they establish prayer among you. If you then find anything detestable in them. You should hate their administration, but do not withdraw yourselves from their obedience.*

Sahih Muslim 1855

Abu Huraira reported Allah's Messenger as saying:

A believing man should not hate a believing woman; if he dislikes one of her characteristics, he will be pleased with another.

Sahih Muslim 1468

Sahl bin Mu'adh[bin Anas] Al-Juhni narrated from his father that the Prophet said:

"Whoever gives for the sake of Allah, withholds for the sake of Allah, loves for the sake of Allah, hates for the sake of Allah, and marries for the sake of Allah, he has indeed perfected his faith."

Jami at-Tirmidhi Grade: Hasan

Abu Sa'eed narrated that the Messenger of Allah said:

"Indeed, the most beloved of people to Allah on the Day of Judgement, and the nearest to Him in the status is the just Imam. And the most hated of people to Allah and the furthest from Him in status is the oppressive Imam."

Jami at-Tirmidhi 1329 Grade: Daif (Darussalam)

It was narrated from Abu Hurairah that the Messenger of Allah said:

"There are four whom Allah, the Mighty and Sublime, hates: The vendor who sells his wares by means of false oaths, the poor man

who shows off, the old man who commits Zina and the Imam who is unjust."

Sunan an-Nasa'i 2576 Grade: Sahih

Aslam said, " '*Umar ibn al-Khattab said, 'Do not let your love be a total infatuation. Do not let your anger be destruction.' I asked, 'How is that?' He replied, 'When you love, you are infatuated like a child. When you hate, you desire destruction for your companion.'* "

Al-Adab Al-Mufrad 1322 Grade: Sahih

It has been narrated on the authority of Umm Salama (wife of the Prophet) that he said:

Amirs will be appointed over you, and you will find them doing good as well as bad deeds. One who hates their bad deeds is absolved from blame. One who disapproves of their bad deeds is safe (so far as Divine wrath is concerned). But one who approves of their bad deeds and imitates them (is doomed). People asked: Messenger of Allah, shouldn't we fight against them? He replied: No, as long as they say their prayer. (" Hating + disapproving" refers to liking and disliking from the heart.)

Sahih Muslim 1854

Narrated Ibn `Abbas:

The Prophet said, "The most hated persons to Allah are three: (1) A person who deviates from the right conduct, i.e., an evil doer, in the Haram (sanctuaries of Mecca and Medina); (2) a person who seeks that the traditions of the Pre-Islamic Period of Ignorance, should remain in Islam (3) and a person who seeks to shed somebody's blood without any right."

Sahih al-Bukhari 6882

Anas ibn Malik reported *that the Messenger of Allah, said,
"Do not hate one another nor envy one another nor shun one another.
Slaves of Allah, be brothers! It is not lawful for a Muslim to refuse to
speak to his brother (Muslim) for more than three nights."*

Al-Adab Al-Mufrad 398 Grade: Sahih

Abu Hurayra reported *that the Prophet, said, "Allah loves
sneezing and hates yawning. When one of you sneezes and praises Allah
Almighty, it is a duty for every Muslim who hears him to say to him,
'May Allah have mercy on you.' Yawning comes from Shaytan. When
one of you yawns, he should control it as much as possible. When a man
says, 'Aawh!,' Shaytan laughs at him."*

Al Adab al Murfad Grade: Sahih

On the authority of Abu Hurayrah who said:

*The Messenger of Allah said, "Do not envy one another, and do
not inflate prices for one another, and do not hate one another, and do
not turn away from one another, and do not undercut one another in
trade, but [rather] be slaves of Allah and brothers [amongst yourselves].
A Muslim is the brother of a Muslim: he does not oppress him, nor does
he fail him, nor does he lie to him, nor does he hold him in contempt.
Taqwa (piety) is right here [and he pointed to his chest three times]. It is
evil enough for a man to hold his brother Muslim in contempt. The whole
of a Muslim is inviolable for another Muslim: his blood, his property,
and his honour."*

40 Hadith of Nawwawi #35 Grade: Sahih

It was narrated that Ibrahim said:

*"Abdullah used to say: 'May Allah curse the women who have
tattoos done and Al-Mutanammisat(those who pluck eyebrows), and*

have the women who have their teeth separated. Should I not curse those whom the Messenger of Allah cursed?'"

Sunan an-Nasa'i 5255 Grade: Sahih

Narrated Ibn `Abbas:

I heard `Umar saying, "May Allah Curse so-and-so! Doesn't he know that the Prophet said, 'May Allah curse the Jews for, though they were forbidden (to eat) fat, they liquefied it and sold it. "

Sahih al-Bukhari 3460

Abu Hurairah narrated that the Messenger of Allah said:

"Lo! Indeed the world is cursed. What is in it is cursed, except for remembrance of Allah, what is conducive to that, the knowledgeable person and the learning person."

Jami` at-Tirmidhi 2322 Grade: Hasan

Abu Bakr As-Siddiq narrated that the Messenger of Allah said:

"Cursed are those who harm a believer, or plot to do so."

Jami` at-Tirmidhi 1941 Grade: Daif (Darussalam)

Abdullah bin 'Amr narrated:

"The Messenger of Allah cursed the one who bribes and the one who takes a bribe."

Jami` at-Tirmidhi 1337 Grade: Hasan

Narrated Ibn 'Abbas:

"*The Messenger of Allah cursed the women who imitate men and the men who imitate women.*"

Jami at-Tirmidhi Grade: Sahih

It was narrated from Ibn 'Umar that:

The Messenger of Allah cursed the woman who affixes hair extensions.

Sunan an-Nasa'i 5249 Grade: Sahih

It was narrated from 'Umar bin Khattab that the Messenger of Allah said:

"*The importer is blessed with provision and the hoarder is cursed.*"

Sunan Ibn Majah Grade: Daif (Darussalam)

Abu Tufail reported:

We said to 'Ali bin Abi Talib: Inform us about something which Allah's Messenger told you in secret, whereupon he said: He told me nothing in secret which he hid from people, but I heard him say: Allah cursed him who sacrificed for anyone besides Allah; and cursed him who accommodated an innovator; and Allah cursed him who cursed his parents and Allah cursed him who changed the boundary lines (of the land possessed by him).

Sahih Muslim 1978 b

Narrated Abu Juhaifa:

The Prophet cursed the lady who practices tattooing and the one who gets herself tattooed, and one who eats (takes) Riba' (usury) and the one who gives it. And he prohibited taking the price of a dog, and the money earned by prostitution, and cursed the makers of pictures.

Sahih al-Bukhari 5347

Abu Hurairah narrated that the Prophet said:

"Whoever points a piece of iron at his brother, the angels curse him."

Jami` at-Tirmidhi 2162 Grade: Sahih

It was narrated that Ibn 'Umar said; "I heard the Messenger of Allah say:

'May Allah curse the one who disfigures an animal.

Sunan an-Nasa'i 4442 Grade: Sahih

Narrated Abdullah ibn Mas'ud:

The Messenger of Allah cursed the one who accepted usury, the one who paid it, the witness to it, and the one who recorded it.

Sunan Abi Dawud 3333 Grade: Sahih

It was narrated that Abu Musa said:

"The Messenger of Allah cursed the one who separates a mother and her child, or a brother from his brother."

Sunan Ibn Majah Grade: Daif (Darussalam)

Abu Huraira reported:

The Messenger of Allah said: Let there be curse of Allah upon the Jews and the Christians for they have taken the graves of their apostles as places of worship.

Sahih Muslim 530 b

Narrated Abu Huraira:

Allah's Messenger said, "If a husband calls his wife to his bed (i.e. to have sexual relation) and she refuses and causes him to sleep in anger, the angels will curse her till morning."

Sahih al-Bukhari 3237

Narrated Abu Huraira:

Allah 's Apostle said, "Allah curses the thief who steals an egg (or a helmet) for which his hand is to be cut off, or steals a rope, for which his hand is to be cut off."

Sahih al-Bukhari 6799

Ibn 'Abbas reported:

that the Messenger of Allah, may Allah bless him and grant him peace, said, "Allah curses anyone who misguides a blind person and leads him away from the path."

Al-Adab Al-Mufrad 892 Grade: Hasan Sahih

Aishah narrated that the Messenger of Allah said:

" Six are cursed, being cursed by Allah and by every Prophet that came: The one who adds to Allah's Book, the one who denies Allah's Qadar, the one who rules with tyranny by which he honors whom Allah has debased, and he dishonors whom Allah has honored, and the one who legalizes what Allah forbade, and the one from my family who legalizes what Allah forbade, and the abandoner of my Sunnah."

Jami at-Tirmidhi Grade: Hasan

It was narrated from Anas:

"The Messenger of Allah said the Qunut for a month."- (One of the narrators) Shu'bah said: "He cursed some men." Hisham said: "He *supplicated against some of the tribes of Arabs."-"Then he stopped doing that after bowing." This is what Hisham said. Shu'bah said, narrating from Qatadah, from Anas that the Prophet said the Qunut for a month, cursing Ri'l, Dhawkan and Lihyan.*

Sunan an-Nasa'i 1077 Grade: Sahih

Narrated `Ali:

We have nothing except the Book of Allah and this written paper from the Prophet (wherein is written:) Medina is a sanctuary from the 'Air Mountain to such and such a place, and whoever innovates in it a heresy or commits a sin, or gives shelter to such an innovator in it will incur the curse of Allah, the angels, and all the people, none of his compulsory or optional good deeds of worship will be accepted. And the asylum (of protection) granted by any Muslim is to be secured (respected) by all the other Muslims; and whoever betrays a Muslim in this respect incurs the curse of Allah, the angels, and all the people, and none of his compulsory or optional good deeds of worship will be accepted, and whoever (freed slave) befriends (take as masters) other than his manumitters without their permission incurs the curse of Allah, the angels, and all the people, and none of his compulsory or optional good deeds of worship will be accepted.

Sahih al-Bukhari 1870

Abu Darda' reported:

Allah's Messenger stood up (to pray) and we heard him say:" I seek refuge in Allah from thee." Then said:" curse thee with Allah's curse" three times, then he stretched out his hand as though he was taking hold of something. When he finished the prayer, we said: Messenger of Allah, we heard you say something during the prayer which we have not heard you say before, and we saw you stretch out your hand. He replied: Allah's enemy Iblis came with a flame of fire to put it in my face, so I said three times:" I Seek refuge in Allah from thee." Then I said three times:" I curse thee with Allah's full curse." But he did not retreat (on any one of these) three occasions. Thereafter I meant to seize him. I swear by Allah that had it not been for the supplication of my brother Sulaiman he would have been bound, and made an object of sport for the children of Medina.

Sahih Muslim 542

Jabir reported that there happened to pass before Allah's Apostle an ass the face of which had been cauterized, whereupon he said:

Allah has cursed one who has cauterized it (on the face).

Sahih Muslim 2117

Narrated Mu'awiyah ibn Jaydah al-Qushayri:

The Messenger of Allah said: Woe to him who tells things, speaking falsely, to make people laugh thereby. Woe to him! Woe to him!.

Sunan Abi Dawud 4990 Grade: Hasan

Narrated Jabir:

`Umar came cursing the disbelievers (of Quraish) on the day of Al-Khandaq (the battle of Trench) and said, "I could not offer the `Asr prayer till the sun had set. Then we went to Buthan and he offered the (`Asr) prayer after sunset and then he offered the Maghrib prayer.

Sahih al-Bukhari 598

Narrated Anas:

The Prophet said, "Medina is a sanctuary from that place to that. Its trees should not be cut and no heresy should be innovated nor any sin should be committed in it, and whoever innovates in it a heresy or commits sins (bad deeds), then he will incur the curse of Allah, the angels, and all the people."

Sahih al-Bukhari 1867

Narrated Abu Salama:

Abu Hurairah said, "No doubt, my Salat is similar to that of the Prophet." Abu Hurairah used to recite Qunut after saying Sami' Allahu liman hamida in the last Rak'a of the Zuhr, Isha and Fajr Prayers. He would ask Allah's Forgiveness for the true believers and curse the disbelievers.

Sahih al-Bukhari 797

Anas bin Malik narrated:

"Allah's Messenger cursed three people: A man who leads people (in Salat) while they dislike him, a woman who spends a night while her husband is angry with her, and a man who hears: 'Hayya Alal Falah (come to success)' then does not respond."

Jami` at-Tirmidhi 358 Grade: Daif (Darussalam)

Narrated Ali ibn Abu Talib:

(The narrator Isma'il said: I think ash-Sha'bi attributed this tradition to the Prophet)

The Prophet said: Curse be upon the one who marries a divorced woman with the intention of making her lawful for her former husband and upon the one for whom she is made lawful.

Sunan Abi Dawud 2076 Grade: Sahih

Narrated Abdullah ibn Umar:

The Prophet said: Allah has cursed wine, its drinker, its server, its seller, its buyer, its presser, the one for whom it is pressed, the one who conveys it, and the one to whom it is conveyed.

Sunan Abi Dawud 3674 Grade: Sahih

Narrated Abdullah ibn Abbas:

The Prophet said: If anyone is killed blindly or, when people are throwing stones, by a stone or a whip, his blood-wit is the blood-wit for an accidental murder. But if anyone is killed intentionally, retaliation is due. If anyone tries to prevent it, the curse of Allah, of angels, and of all the people will rest on him.

Sunan Abi Dawud 4591 Grade: Sahih

Abu Hurairah reported the Prophet as saying :

if a man becomes the client of any people without the permission of his patrons (i.e. those who have freed him), on him will be the curse of Allah, of angels and of all people; no obligatory or supererogatory worship will be accepted from him.

Sunan Abi Dawud 5114 Grade: Sahih

Anas bin Malik reported the Messenger of Allah as saying:

If anyone pretends to be the son of a man other than his father, or attributes his freedom to people other than those who set him free, on him will be the curse of Allah that will continue till the day of resurrection.

Sunan Abi Dawud 5115 Grade: Sahih

It was narrated that 'Aishah said:

"The Prophet was stung by a scorpion while he was performing prayer, and he said: 'May Allah curse the scorpion, for it does not spare anyone, whether he is praying or not. Kill them whether you are in Ihram or not.'" In Al-Hill (outside the sacred precincts of Makkah) or Al-Haram (the sacred precincts or Makkah).

Sunan Ibn Majah Grade: Hasan

Sa'id b. Jubair reported that Ibn 'Umar happened to pass by some young men of the Quraish who had tied a bird (and th, is made it a target) at which they had been shooting arrows Every arrow that they missed came into the possession of the owner of the bird. So no sooner did they see Ibn 'Umar they went away. Thereupon Ibn 'Umar said:

Who has done this? Allah has cursed him who does this. Verily Allah's Messenger invoked curse upon one who made a live thing the target (of one's marksmanship).

Sahih Muslim 1958 b

Narrated Ibn `Abbas:

When Allah's Messenger came to Mecca, he refused to enter the Ka`ba with idols in it. He ordered (idols to be taken out). So they were taken out. The people took out the pictures of Abraham and Ishmael holding Azlams in their hands. Allah's Messenger said, "May Allah curse these people. By Allah, both Abraham and Ishmael never did the game of chance with Azlams." Then he entered the Ka`ba and said Takbir at its corners but did not offer the prayer in it.

Sahih al-Bukhari 1601

Abu Huraira reported that Allah's Messenger said:

Verily Allah created the universe and when He had finished that, ties of relationship came forward and said This is the place for him who seeks refuge from severing (of blood-relationship). He said: Yes. Are you not satisfied that I should keep relationship with one who joins your ties of relationship and sever it with one who severs your (ties of relationship)? They (the ties of blood) said: Certainly so. Thereupon He said: Well, that is how things are for you. Allah's Messenger then said: Recite if you like:" But if you turn away you are sure to make mischief in the land and cut off the ties of kinship. Those it is whom Allah has cursed, so He has made them deaf and blinded their eyes. Do they not reflect on the Qur'an? Or, are there locks on their hearts?".

Sahih Muslim 2554

Al-Bara' reported:

When Allah's Messenger went forth from Mecca to Medina, Suraqa bin Malik bin Ju'shum pursued him. Allah's Messenger invoked curse upon him, and his horse sank (in the desert). He (Suraqa) said: (Allah's Messenger), invoke blessings for me and I will do no harm to you. He (the Prophet) then supplicated Allah. (At that time) he (the Prophet) felt thirsty, and they happened to pass by a shepherd. Abu Bakr Siddiq said: I took hold of a bowl and milked some milk into it for Allah's Messenger and gave it to him. He drank it and I was pleased.

Sahih Muslim 2009 b

Narrated `Abdullah:

While the Prophet was prostrating, surrounded by some of Quraish, `Uqba bin Abi Mu'ait brought the intestines (i.e. Abdominal contents) of a camel and put them over the back of the Prophet. The Prophet did not raise his head, (till) Fatima, came and took it off his back and cursed the one who had done the harm. The Prophet said, "O Allah! Destroy the chiefs of Quraish, Abu Jahl bin Hisham, `Utba bin Rabi`al,

Shaba bin Rabi`a, Umaiya bin Khalaf or Ubai bin Khalaf." (The sub-narrator Shu`ba, is not sure of the last name.) I saw these people killed on the day of Badr battle and thrown in the well except Umaiya or Ubai whose body parts were mutilated but he was not thrown in the well.

Sahih al-Bukhari 3854

It was narrated that 'Aishah said:

"While the Messenger of Allah was sitting in the mosque, a woman from Muzainah (tribe) entered, trailing her garment in the mosque. The Prophet said: 'O people, tell your women not to wear their adornments and show pride in the mosque, for the Children of Israel were not cursed until their women wore adornments and walked proudly in their places of worship.'"

Sunan Ibn Majah 4001 Grade: Daif (Darussalam)

Narrated Abu Huraira:

The Prophet said, "A group of Israelites were lost. Nobody knows what they did. But I do not see them except that they were cursed and changed into rats, for if you put the milk of a she-camel in front of a rat, it will not drink it, but if the milk of a sheep is put in front of it, it will drink it." I told this to Ka`b who asked me, "Did you hear it from the Prophet?" I said, "Yes." Ka`b asked me the same question several times.; I said to Ka`b. "Do I read the Torah? (I tell you this from the Prophet.)"

Sahih al-Bukhari 3305

Narrated `Abdullah bin Mulaika:

`Aisha said that the Jews came to the Prophet and said, "As-Samu 'Alaikum" (death be on you). `Aisha said (to them), "(Death) be on you, and may Allah curse you and shower His wrath upon you!" The Prophet said, "Be calm, O `Aisha ! You should be kind and lenient, and

beware of harshness and Fuhsh (i.e. bad words)." She said (to the Prophet), "Haven't you heard what they (Jews) have said?" He said, "Haven't you heard what I have said (to them)? I said the same to them, and my invocation against them will be accepted while theirs against me will be rejected (by Allah). "

Sahih al-Bukhari 6030

Narrated Abu Huraira:

When Khaibar was conquered, a roasted poisoned sheep was presented to the Prophet as a gift (by the Jews). The Prophet ordered, "Let all the Jews who have been here, be assembled before me." The Jews were collected and the Prophet said (to them), "I am going to ask you a question. Will you tell the truth?" They said, "Yes." The Prophet asked, "Who is your father?" They replied, "So-and-so." He said, "You have told a lie; your father is so-and-so." They said, "You are right." He said, "Will you now tell me the truth, if I ask you about something?" They replied, "Yes, O Abu Al-Qasim; and if we should tell a lie, you can realize our lie as you have done regarding our father." On that he asked, "Who are the people of the (Hell) Fire?" They said, "We shall remain in the (Hell) Fire for a short period, and after that you will replace us." The Prophet said, "You may be cursed and humiliated in it! By Allah, we shall never replace you in it." Then he asked, "Will you now tell me the truth if I ask you a question?" They said, "Yes, O Abu Al-Qasim." He asked, "Have you poisoned this sheep?" They said, "Yes." He asked, "What made you do so?" They said, "We wanted to know if you were a liar in which case we would get rid of you, and if you are a prophet then the poison would not harm you."

Sahih al-Bukhari 3169

Abdullah ibn al-'As reported that the Prophet , said,

"Show mercy and you will be shown mercy. Forgive and Allah will forgive you. Woe to the vessels that catch words (i.e. the ears). Woe to those who persist and consciously continue in what they are doing."

Al-Adab Al-Mufrad 380 Grade: Sahih

It was narrated from Ibn 'Umar that the Messenger of Allah said:

"Woe to you! Do not turn back into disbelievers after I am gone, striking one another's necks.

Sunan Ibn Majah 3943 Grade: Sahih

Narrated Abu Sa`id Al-Khudri:

The Prophet said, "When a funeral is ready and the men carry the deceased on their necks (shoulders), if it was pious then it will say, 'Present me quickly', and if it was not pious, then it will say, 'Woe to it (me), where are they taking it (me)?' And its voice is heard by everything except mankind and if he heard it he would fall unconscious."

Sahih al-Bukhari 1316

It was narrated from Abu Sa'eed Al-Khudri that the Messenger of Allah said:

"Woe to the most wealthy except those who do such and such with the money, and such and such" – four things, (pointing) to his right, to his left, in front of him and behind him.

Sunan Ibn Majah Book 37, Hadith 4268 Grade: Hasan

It was narrated from Sahl bin Sa'd that:

The Messenger of Allah said: "This goodness contains many treasures, and for those there are keys. So glad tidings to the one whom

~ 96 ~

Allah makes a key to good and a lock for evil, and woe to the one whom Allah makes a key to evil and a lock to good."

Sunan ibn Majah Grade: Daif

Ibn 'Umar saw a shepherd with some sheep in a bad place and saw a place which was better than it.

He told him, "Woe to you, shepherd! Move them! I heard the Messenger of Allah, may Allah bless him and grant him peace, say, 'Every shepherd is responsible for his flock.'"

Al-Adab Al-Mufrad 416 Grade: Sahih

Ibn 'Abbas reported that the polytheists also pronounced (Talbiya) as:

Here I am at Thy service, there is no associate with Thee. The Messenger of Allah said: Woe be upon them, as they also said: But one associate with Thee, you possess mastery over him, but he does not possess mastery (over you). They used to say this and circumambulate the Ka'ba.

Sahih Muslim 1185

Narrated Abu Bakra:

A man praised another man in front of the Prophet. The Prophet said thrice, "Wailaka (Woe on you) ! You have cut the neck of your brother!" The Prophet added, "If it is indispensable for anyone of you to praise a person, then he should say, "I think that such-and-such person (is so-and-so), and Allah is the one who will take his accounts (as he knows his reality) and none can sanctify anybody before Allah (and that only if he knows well about that person.)".

Sahih al-Bukhari 6162

Narrated 'Amr bin Shu'aib:

from his father, from his grandfather that the Messenger of Allah said: "The Muslim is not killed for disbeliever." And with this chain, it has been narrated that the Prophet said: "The blood-money paid for disbeliever is half of the blood-money paid for a believer."

Jami` at-Tirmidhi 1413 Grade: Hasan

Narrated Usama bin Zaid:

the Prophet said, "A Muslim cannot be the heir of a disbeliever, nor can a disbeliever be the heir of a Muslim."

Sahih al-Bukhari 6764

Abu Huraira reported Allah's Messenger as saying:

Do not greet the Jews and the Christians before they greet you and when you meet any one of them on the roads force him to go to the narrowest part of it.

Sahih Muslim 2167 a

It has been narrated by 'Umar bin al-Khattab that he heard the Messenger of Allah say:

I will expel the Jews and Christians from the Arabian Peninsula and will not leave any but Muslim.

Sahih Muslim 1767 a

It is narrated on the authority of Abu Huraira that the Messenger of Allah observed:

By Him in Whose hand is the life of Muhammad, he who amongst the community of Jews or Christians hears about me, but does not affirm his belief in that with which I have been sent and dies in this state (of disbelief), he shall be but one of the denizens of Hell-Fire.

Sahih Muslim 153

Abu Musa' reported that Allah's Messenger said:

When it will be the Day of Resurrection Allah would deliver to every Muslim a Jew or a Christian and say: That is your rescue from Hell-Fire.

Sahih Muslim 2767 a

It was narrated from Ibn 'Umar that the Messenger of Allah passed by some women of 'Abdul-Ashhal who were weeping for their slain on the Day of Uhud. The Messenger of Allah said:

"But there is no one to weep for Hamzah." So the women of Ansar started to weep for Hamzah. The messenger of Allah woke up and said, 'Woe to them, have they not gone home yet? Tell them to go home and not to weep for anyone who dies after this day.'"

Sunan ibn Majah Book 6, Hadith 1659 Grade: Hasan

It was narrated from Abu Zubair that Jabir bin 'Abdullah said:

"The Messenger of Allah was in Ji'ranah and he was distributing gold nuggets and spoils of war which were in Bilal's lap. A man said: 'Do justice, O Muhammed!' He said: 'Woe to you! Who will do justice after me if I do not do justice?' 'Umar said: 'O Messenger of Allah! Let me strike the neck of this hypocrite!' The Messenger of Allah said: 'This man has some companions who recite the Qur'an but it does not go any deeper than their collarbones. They will pass through Islam like an arrow passing through its target.'"

Sunan Ibn Majah Book 1, Hadith 177 Grade: Sahih

Sahl (b. Sa'd) reported:

I heard Allah's Apostle as saying: I shall go to the Cistern before you and he who comes would drink and he who drinks would never feel thirsty, and there would come to me people whom I would know and who would know me. Then there would be intervention between me and them. Abu Hazim said that Nu'man b. Abu 'Ayyash heard it and I narrated to them this hadith, and said: Is it this that you heard Sahl saying? He said: Yes, and I bear witness to the fact that I heard it from Abu Sa'id Khudri also, but he made this addition that he (the Holy Prophet) would say: They are my followers, and it would be said to him: You do not know what they did after you and I will say to them: Woe to him who changes (his religion) after me.

Sahih Muslim 2290, 2291 a

It was narrated from 'Awf bin Malik that the Messenger of Allah said:

"The Jews split into seventy-one sects, one of which will be in Paradise and seventy in Hell. The Christians split into seventy-two sects, seventy-one of which will be in Hell and one in Paradise. I swear by the One Whose Hand is the soul of Muhammad, my nation will split into seventy-three sects, one of which will be in Paradise and seventy-two in Hell." It was said: "O Messenger of Allah, who are they?" He said: "The main body."(Al-Jamah)

Sunan Ibn Majah 3992 Grade: Hasan

Abdullah bin Mughfal narrated that the Messenger of Allaah said:

"Allaah, Allaah My Companions! Do not make them targets (of slander etc.) after me! Whoever loves them, loves them by loving me.

~ 100 ~

Whoever hates them, hates them by hating me. And whoever does (something to) hurt them, hurts me. And whoever does (something to) hurt me, (tries to) hurt Allaah. And whoever does (try to) hurt Allaah, (he) will be seized (by Allaah)."

Sunan Tirmidhi, 3862 Grade: Hasan

Ibn 'Abbaas and Anas bin Malik reported that the Messenger of Allaah said:

"Whoever abuses my Companions, upon them is the curse of Allaah, the Angels and the whole of mankind."

At-Tabarani, 3/174 Grade: Hasan

Abdullah bin Amr narrated that:

the Prophet said: "The Lord's pleasure is in the parent's pleasure, and the Lord's anger is in the parent's anger."

Jami` at-Tirmidhi 1899 Grade: Hasan

Abu Ad-Dardh narrated that the Messenger of Allah said:

"Nothing is heavier on the believer's Scale on the Day of Judgment than good character. For indeed Allah, Most High, is angered by the shameless obscene person."

Jami` at-Tirmidhi 2002 Grade: Sahih

It was narrated from Abu Hurairah that the Messenger of Allah said:

"A man may speak a word that angers Allah and not see anything wrong with it, but it will cause him to sink down in Hell the depth of seventy autumns."

Sunan Ibn Majah 3970 Grade: Sahih

Ibn 'Umar reported that the Prophet, said,

"If anyone behaves insolently or walks with an arrogant, he will meet Allah Almighty covered with His anger."

Al-Adab Al-Mufrad 549 Grade: Sahih

Isma'll bin Umayyah said:

I asked about a man who intertwines his fingers while he is engaged in prayer. He said that Ibn 'Umar had said: This is the prayer of those who earn the anger of Allah.

Sunan Abi Dawud 993 Grade: Sahih

Muhammed bin 'Amr narrated from his father, from his grandfather who said:

"I heard Bilal bin Al-Harith Al Muzani, the Companion of the Messenger of Allah saying: 'I heard the Messenger of Allah saying: "Indeed one of you says a statement pleasing to Allah, not realizing that you have achieved what you have achieved. Then for it, Allah writes for him His pleasure until the Day of Meeting Him. And one of you says a statement angering Allah, not realizing that you have achieved what you have achieved. Then for it, Allah writes for him His anger until the Day of Meeting with Him."

Jami' at-Tirmidhi 2319 Grade: Hasan

Narrated Ibn `Abbas:

Allah's Wrath gets severe on a person killed by a prophet, and Allah's Wrath became severe on him who had caused the face of Allah's Messenger to bleed.

Sahih al-Bukhari 4076

It was narrated from Ibn 'Umar that the Messenger of Allah said:

"Whoever takes the wrongdoer's side in a dispute or supports wrongdoing, he will remain subject to the wrath of Allah until he gives it up."

Sunan Ibn Majah 2320 Grade: Hasan

It was narrated from Anas bin Malik that the Messenger of Allah said:

"The greatest reward comes with the greatest trial. When Allah loves a people He tests them. Whoever accepts that wins His pleasure but whoever is discontent with that earns His wrath."

Sunan Ibn Majah 4031 Grade: Hasan

Narrated 'Adiyy bin Hatim:

that the Prophet said: "The Jews are those who Allah is wrath with, and the Christians have strayed."

Jami ath-Tirmidhi Grade: Hasan

Mu'adh ibn Anas reported:

The Messenger of Allah, peace and blessings be upon him, said, "The best of faith is to love for the sake of Allah, to hate for the sake of Allah, and to work your tongue in the remembrance of Allah." Mu'adh said, "How is it, O Messenger of Allah?" The Prophet said, "That you love for people what you love for yourself, and you hate for them what you hate for yourself, and you speak goodness or remain silent."

Musnad Aḥmad 21627 Grade: Sahih

Ibn Abbas said:

"One night, when he exited his Salat, I heard the Messenger of Allah saying: 'O Allah, I ask You of Your mercy, that You guide by it my heart, and gather by it my affair, and bring together that which has

been scattered of my affairs, and correct with it that which is hidden from me, and raise by it that which is apparent from me, and purify by it my actions, and inspire me by it with that which contains my guidance, and protect me by it from that which I seek protection, and protect me by it from every evil. O Allah give me faith and certainty after which there is no disbelief, and mercy, by which I may attain the high level of Your generosity in the world and the Hereafter. O Allah, I ask You for success [in that which You grant, and relief] in the Judgment, and the positions of the martyrs, and the provision of the successful, and aid against the enemies. O Allah, I leave to You my need, and my actions are weak, I am in need of Your mercy, so I ask You, O Decider of the affairs, and O Healer of the chests, as You separate me from the punishment of the blazing flame, and from seeking destruction, and from the trial of the graves. O Allah, whatever my opinion has fallen short of, and my intention has not reached it, and my request has not encompassed it, of good that You have promised to anyone from Your creation, or any good You are going to give to any of Your slaves, then indeed, I seek it from You and I ask You for it, by Your mercy, O Lord of the Worlds. O Allah, Possessor of the strong rope, and the guided affair, I ask You for security on the Day of the Threat, and Paradise on the Day of Immortality along with the witnesses, brought-close, who bow and prostrate, who fulfill the covenants, You are Merciful, Loving, and indeed, You do what You wish. **_O Allah, make us guided guiders and not misguided misguiders, an ally to Your friends, an enemy to Your enemies. We love due to Your love, those who love You, and hate, due to Your enmity those who oppose You._** O Allah, this is the supplication (that we are capable of), and it is upon You to respond, and this is the effort (that we are capable of), and upon You is the reliance. O Allah, appoint a light in my heart for me, and a light in my grave, and light in front of me, and light behind me, and light on my right, and light on my left, and light above me, and light below me, and light in my hearing, and light in my vision, and light in my hair, and light in my skin, and light in my flesh, and light in my blood, and light in my bones. O Allah, magnify for *me light, and appoint for me a light. Glory is to the One who wears Glory and grants by it. Glory is to the One for Whom glorification is not fitting except for Him, the Possessor of Honor and Bounties, Glory is to the Possessor of Glory and Generosity, Glory is to the Possessor of Majesty and Honor'*

Jami` at-Tirmidhi 3419 Grade: Daif

Yahya related to me from Malik from Da'ud ibn al-Husayn that he heard al-Araj say,

"I never saw the people in Ramadan, but that they were cursing the disbelievers." He added, "The reciter of Qur'an used to recite surat al-Baqara in eight rakas and if he did it in twelve rakas the people would think that he had made it easy."

Muwatta Imam Malik

Abu Musa Ashari reported that the Prophet said:

"He who begs in Allah's name is accursed. He who is asked for something in Allah's name but he refuses to give is also accursed unless an indecent or unlawful thing is sought."

Reported by Tabarani

It is reported that Sufyān Al-Thawrī said:

"If you loved a man for Allāh and then he innovates in Islām and you don't hate him for it, you never [truly] loved him for Allāh."

Abū Nu'aym, Hilyatu Al-Awliyā` 7:34.

Al-Miswar ibn Rifa'a al-Quruzi said,

"I heard a man ask Ibn 'Abbas, 'Should I do wudu' after I have eaten bread and meat?' He replied, 'Woe to you! Would you do wudu' on account of good things?'"

Al-Adab Al-Mufrad 773 Grade: Sahih

It is reported that 'Umar bin Al-Khattāb said:

"We were once in a time when we did not think anyone learned the Quran seeking anything but Allāh the Exalted, but now I fear there are men who learn it and intend the people and what they can get from them. So seek Allāh with your recitation and deeds. For verily, we used to know you when Allāh's Messenger was amongst us, when revelation would descend and Allāh would tell us about you. As for today, Allāh's Messenger has passed on, and the revelation has stopped; and I only know you as I say: whoever shows what is good, we love him for it and think good of him, and whoever shows what is evil, we hate him for it and suspect him. Your secret and private matters are between you and your Lord the Mighty and Majestic."

Al-Ājurrī, Akhlāq Ḥamalat Al-Qurʾān article 26.

It is reported that Bishr bin Al-Ḥārith said:

"I heard Al-Fuḍayl bin ʿAyyāḍ say, "It has reached me that Allāh has barred repentance from every adherent of bid'ah (religious innovation), and the worst of the people of bid'ah are those who hate the Companions of Allāh's Messenger." He then turned to me and said, "Make the firmest of your deeds with Allāh your love for the Companions of His Prophet, for [then], were you to come to the standing of judgment (on the Day of Resurrection) with the likes of the Earth in sins, Allāh would forgive you; but if you come [on that Day] with even the smallest amount of hatred for them, no deed will benefit you.""

Abū Bakr Al-Daynūrī, Al-Mujālasah wa Jawāhir Al-'Ilm 5: 412.

It is reported that Al-Ḥasan bin Al-Ḥasan bin 'Alī bin Abī Ṭālib said to a person from the Rāfiḍah:

"Love us, but if we disobey Allāh, then hate us; for if Allāh was going to benefit anyone because of his relation to the Messenger of Allāh, without obedience [to Allāh], He would have benefitted the mother and father [of the Prophet]."

Al-Dhahabī, Siyar A'lām Al-Nubalāʾ 4:486.

It is reported that ʿAbdullāh bin ʿAbbās said,

"Love for Allāh and hate for Allāh, make your enmity because of Allāh and your allegiance because of Allāh; for indeed, the love and support of Allāh is not achieved save through this. And a man will never taste true faith (īmān) – though he may pray and fast much – except when he is like that. Today, the people's brotherhood is based upon worldly considerations (dunyā), but this will not do anything for them on the Day of Resurrection."

Ibn Al-Mubārak, Al-Zuhd wa Al-Raqā`iq article 353.

Abu Mahdhura said,

"I was sitting with 'Umar when Safwan ibn Umayya brought him a bowl which some people were carrying in a robe. They set it down in front of 'Umar. 'Umar then invited some poor people and some slaves belonging to the people around him and they ate with him. Then he said, 'Allah will do a people - or else he said, 'Allah will curse a people' - who dislike having their slaves eat with them.' Safwan said, 'By Allah, we do not dislike them, but we prefer ourselves to them, and by Allah, we do not find good food which we can eat and feed it to them as well.'"

Al-Adab Al-Mufrad 201 Grade: Sahih

Narrated Ibn 'Umar:

Zaid bin 'Amr bin Nufail went to Sham, inquiring about a true religion to follow. He met a Jewish religious scholar and asked him about their religion. He said, "I intend to embrace your religion, so tell me something about it." The Jew said, "You will not embrace our religion unless you receive your share of Allah's Anger." Zaid said, "'I do not run except from Allah's Anger, and I will never bear a bit of it if I have the power to avoid it. Can you tell me of some other religion?" He said, "I do not know any other religion except the Hanif." Zaid enquired, "What is Hanif?" He said, "Hanif is the religion of (the prophet) Abraham who was neither a Jew nor a Christian, and he used to worship

None but Allah (Alone)" Then Zaid went out and met a Christian religious scholar and told him the same as before. The Christian said, "You will not embrace our religion unless you get a share of Allah's Curse." Zaid replied, "I do not run except from Allah's Curse, and I will never bear any of Allah's Curse and His Anger if I have the power to avoid them. Will you tell me of some other religion?" He replied, "I do not know any other religion except Hanif." Zaid enquired, "What is Hanif?" He replied, Hanif is the religion of (the prophet) Abraham who was neither a Jew nor a Christian and he used to worship None but Allah (Alone)" When Zaid heard their Statement about (the religion of) Abraham, he left that place, and when he came out, he raised both his hands and said, "O Allah! I make You my Witness that I am on the religion of Abraham."

Sahih al-Bukhari 3827

Ibn Taymiyyah said:

"Love for the sake of Allah and hate for the sake of Allah are an obligation and it is one of the strongest bonds of faith."

'Minhaaj As-Sunnah'

Exposition on the Sunnah of Sacred Hatred

Firstly the preceding chapters do not include every ayat or hadith that supports the position that Allah has anger/hatred to/for certain beings, nevertheless I hope such a small compilation of the available evidence will be sufficient to prove the point. To proceed, modern Christians teach God loves everybody so much that he gave his only begotten son or himself as a sacrifice for the sins of all. Classical Christians and non-Modernist Christians taught/teach hatred for Jews and non-Christians. Among religious people the "Hate the Sin but not the sinner" and the "Love everybody no matter how bad they are" doctrines come from a combination of that modern Christian love-sacrifice theology and what is called the "Abrahamic faiths" notion. The disgusting myth is that since Abraham pbuh was the biological common ancestor of Islamic, Jewish and Christian prophets, then all 3 religions of Judaism, Christianity and Islam are equal and they all count. So everyone should just love each other and get along, admitting we all worship the same God and will go to paradise together despite practicing different "Abrahamic faiths". This doctrine was invented by Yoakim Moubarac in the 1950s CE. Yoakim Moubarac was a Lebanese Maronite priest who had been ordained June 29, 1947 CE, about 1 month after the state of Israel was created. His mentor was a French Catholic orientalist named Louis Massignon who was influential during the Second Vatican Council changing certain Church doctrines and a friend of the famous British T.E. Lawrence. A graduate of "Jesus College" in Oxford, England, during WWI T.E. Lawrence was the guy who tricked the Arab Muslims to fight against the Ottomon Empire in support of the British. This then led to the British conquering

Palestine and the allied powers taking much of the middle eastern Muslim lands. T.E. Lawrence's friend Louis Massignon made it his life mission to enforce French control and influence over Muslim lands and ensure Palestinians and Arabs accepted the Israeli occupation. Louis Massignon said Catholicism and Islam were both Abrahamic faiths in order to make the Muslims in French colonies stop revolting and waging Jihad. Massignon's student Yoakim Moubarac continued the Israeli platform of his mentor's mission adding Judaism and broadened the club to include Judaism, Christianity and Islam as Abrahamic faiths. Why? This was because Israel was waging a religious war against Islam and Christianity in the name of Judaism. Whereas Israel could not win such a war unless the Muslims and Christians didn't fight back. Thus the Abrahamic faith mythology of Judaism, Christianity and Islam all stemming from Abraham pbuh was formulated and has been preached ever since in the name of tolerance and peace. So this Abrahamic faiths notion is pure Zionist propaganda so the state of Israel can fight a religious war in the holy land without having the other religious groups fight back. If any claims otherwise then ask for proof of this doctrine being preached by Jews, Christians or Muslims prior to the state of Israel being created in 1947. The Anti-Semitic Europeans never heard this doctrine before WWII. This Abrahamic faiths doctrine is false and constitutes disbelief in Judaism, and in Christianity and in Islam. Yet this is the premise of "inter-faith". Abraham pbuh did not teach, preach or practice 3 different religions. To show the stupidity of this "inter-faith" corruption you can just say, "*Well most every religion agrees that mankind all comes from one original pair of humans. Therefore all the religions go back to Adam pbuh because we are all his descendants. Thus all religions are Adamic faiths which stem from his teachings. Since God made us all and we have religions then they must all count and all must lead to heaven. So that means everyone's religion is correct hooray! Let's all love each other while we wait to go to paradise, every human goes to heaven. It's impossible to be wrong! If you are a human then your religion is automatically correct. Now we could say only aliens go to hell, but then might have to change that belief if we meet aliens. We could say hell isn't real and God loves everybody but few will fall for that because we know it's not true. Thus our doctrine shall be God loves everybody except for those who say God hates people for what they believe. So only those intolerant extremists who hate people for believing something different than they believe will go to hell. Of course this doesn't mean we think we will go to hell, because we don't hate the haters we love them, even though they are crazy intolerant extremists. God loves everyone who loves everyone and God hates anyone who hates anyone."* Obviously such a doctrine is sheer satanic stupidity, similar to the Santa Claus methodology of X being true only if you believe it is and X being false if you don't believe X is true, but it's exactly the same as the "Abrahamic faiths" movement. This disease is based on promoting tolerance and love in order to achieve peace. Not one prophet in the world taught this and this is well known. Yet were all the prophets extremists who killed everyone who disagreed with them? No. Were they intolerant of every other religion? Yes. Were they peaceful? Yes. Did they love everyone? No. Did they hate other people because of what they believed? Yes. So the fundamental issue with "inter-faith" is that it's not prophetic and is an entirely different religion that's based on a hatred for intolerance. Which is ironic because such people claim to be all about tolerance and combating extremism but in reality they are extremists who are intolerant towards the very intolerance the prophets taught and preached and practiced. Intolerance doesn't mean violence! Just consider if Abraham pbuh himself walked into one of these collusions of "Abrahamic faiths". Do you think Abraham pbuh would look at the Jews, Christians and Muslims and say, "*All your religions are true, you Jews keep on being Jews, you Christians keep on being Chrsitians, you Muslims keep on being Muslims. Nobody should change, but if anyone does it doesn't matter because all of you are going to heaven despite having 3 different religions and I only taught 1.*" Likewise do you think Jesus pbuh would attend such a meeting and tell Jews to remain as Jews, Christians to stay Christians and Muslims to remain Muslims. No, Jesus pbuh would tell at least 2 groups to change their faith, as would all the prophets. In fact in John 8:37-46 biblical Jesus pbuh himself says explicitly that Jews are not related to the faith of Abraham pbuh but are related to the devil and are nothing but liars. In context the biblical Jews were pulling the same ruse people preach today saying Jews, Christians and Muslims are all "children of Abraham" pbuh. The bible itself says Jesus pbuh said NO and he even told Jews he knows their lineages to link to Abraham pbuh but he still said their father was the devil and their religion was the devil's. If you say Jews, Christians and Muslims are all "children of Abraham" then you might as well say everyone is because Abraham pbuh was reportedly the first human to start wearing underwear under their pants, so technically anyone who wears underwear is following the religion of Abraham pbuh. But who would dare say because you wear underwear that makes you a follower of Abraham pbuh on the road to heaven and God loves you? A heaven-bound global Abrahamic underwear club makes more sense than the Abrahamic faiths doctrine. By wearing underwear you have more in common with Abraham pbuh than those preaching there are 3 Abrahamic faiths, the funny part is those who preach the "Abrahamic faiths" mythology don't even know Abraham pbuh is reportedly the first to wear underwear. That's how little they know about Abraham pbuh. The names they use show how ridiculous and illegitimate the concept is. They'll use the term inter-faith and Abrahamic faiths together. Which label is it? They'll claim to be both types but in reality are neither. Perhaps the most important refutation from the Muslim side is that Muhammad pbuh himself fought Jews during the battle of Khaibar for religious reasons and he fought the Christians during the battle of Tabuk for religious reasons because he considered both Jews and Christians disbelievers with those specific ones being worthy of fighting and killing in battle. So clearly Muhammad pbuh would not have fought Jews and Christians if he thought their religions were valid or true, and he wouldn't have taught that Jews and Christians go to hell either if he thought differently. On top of that every time Muslims pray we ask God to not make us like the Jews or Christians while also asking Allah to exalt and bless the followers of Abraham pbuh. Who do Muslims consider to be the followers of Abraham pbuh? The Quran is crystal clear when Allah says the Jews and Christians have nothing to do with Abraham pbuh and that those who follow Muhammad pbuh are following Abraham pbuh as well. Thus everytime a Muslim prays and says the fatihah and the durood Ibrahim we are explicitly saying that Jews and Christians are not following the religion of Abraham pbuh and he has nothing to do with their religions. So how is it people today fall for this "inter-faith Abrahamic faiths" stuff? They are simply idiots who don't know at least 3 religions. All those who know religion know this and all who promote inter-faith are extremists upon different faiths than the very faiths they are trying to bring together. The real word for "Abrahamic faiths" is pluralism. Pluralism is the religion that says more than one religion is true and that people can believe in different religions and still all end up in paradise. Abraham pbuh was not a pluralist, those preaching Abrahamic faiths in his name as well as most types of "Inter-faith" types are. Those who promote the Abrahamic faiths movement have the least to do with the religion of Abraham pbuh out of all 3 groups claiming to be connected to Abraham pbuh. The thing is we can all be tolerant of persons with different religious opinions but we cannot be tolerant of different religions. There is a difference between peaceful intolerance and violent intolerance and extremist intolerance and violent extremist intolerance. The first 2 are prophetic, the second 2 are satanic. There is no such thing in the prophetic religion as peaceful tolerance. Moses, Jesus and Muhammad pbut taught both peaceful intolerance as well as violent intolerance when certain situations arose. Yet I personally know some Muslims who don't understand what prophetic peaceful intolerance is. It is more accurate to say Publicly Peaceful Aggressive Intolerance which is sometimes polite depending on the specific person or people one is communicating with. One thing many fail to understand is that while prophets were frequently peaceful, during those peaceful moments they were not always polite. The majority of the time prophets interacted with disbelievers they were confrontational. Sometimes the prophets were rudely confrontational but they were politely confrontational more. Rarely were prophets peacefully politely non-confrontational with disbelievers when it came to discussing religion. They would act like that only with people who were genuinely deeply interested in learning about what they believed and preached. Usually the prophets were boldly confrontational because confrontation causes motivation for the one confronted to quickly and correctly resolve the confrontation. Unfortunately many Muslims, particularly in the West, are not confrontational when discussing religion with disbelievers when they should be. While those who are, might sometimes be only confrontational, too confrontational, or not as polite as they should be because they lack knowledge and manners. Yet overall the world in general, due to secularism, freedom, equality, tolerance, etc, has forgotten that confrontationalism is central to religion. This causes most today to incorrectly mistake confrontational people as extreme just because they are confrontational. The true prophetic religion is only spread by theological confrontation.

As an example of Hating both the sin and the sinner consider the "sinner" known to history as Adolf Hitler. Do Muslims love Adolf Hitler but hate his sins? No we hate him and his sins. The same applies to the Shia Iranian Ayatollah Khomeini. Likewise for the Khariji Osama bin Laden. The same rule goes for Ghandi, the Popes and Martin Luther King Jr. Muslims even hate Abu Talib, who was the uncle of Muhammad pbuh and his guardian since the age of 8 who raised him and protected him from his enemies until he died when Muhammad pbuh was 50 years old. I must admit that Abu Talib was very kind to Muslims and helped them very much, but he never embraced Islam because he feared his idolatrous family members would make fun of him. Thus Abu Talib died as a disbeliever despite Muhammad's deepest desires that he embrace Islam. As a result, even though Muhammad pbuh really cared about Abu Talib and was greatly assisted by him throughout his life he made it publicly known that Abu Talib will be in the hellfire forever and he didn't attend his own uncle's funeral. Muhammad pbuh wished Abu Talib had become a Muslim but he didn't, so Muhammad pbuh hated him even though he always treated him kindly as his closest relative. Likewise despite Abu Talib never harming Muslims and even aiding Muslims and Islam, all Muslims hated/hate Abu Talib because he never accepted Islam and died a polytheist. He was a very moral man and he even believed Muhammad pbuh was a prophet of God but his sin of disbelief requires him to be hated. So because Allah hates him then all Muslims hate him too. Nobody would dare to say "I love Abu Talib but hate his sins", this would be blasphemous for a Muslim to think, unless they were a complete fool and didn't know better. There is not a single verse in the Quran, not 1 authentic hadith and no statements from any companions of Muhammad pbuh which teach this doctrine of "Hate the sin, but not the sinner." Whereas there are many verses in the Quran, many hadith and every single Sahabah taught Muslims to hate people based on them being disbelievers alone, as individuals. Sins also justify hating someone, but different sins are given different values and good deeds counterbalance the sins as well. Although it is a tilted scale where belief or disbelief determines the final outcome. This is how it is with God too. God hates all sinners because of their sins, like disbelief. Whereas God loves all believers because of their good deeds, like belief. Yet the weight of our scales constantly fluctuate as long as we are alive and circumstances can change the weight of our deeds/sins. For example repentance can forgive one's sins while to disbelieve eliminates any and all credit for one's good deeds. While major sins and minor sins can erase some good deeds and some good deeds can erase minor sins, with repentance being needed for major sins and belief being needed to forgive the sin of disbelief. Yet major sins can become disbelief and minor sins can become major sins so it's a very complex relationship each individual has with God and it fluctuates until we die. Regardless though God loves those on the side of belief and hates those on the side of disbelief, and aside from these two criterion God hates sinners for their sins. Although as it concerns believers God's love for them outweighs the hate God has for them because of their sins. God might still punish them for those sins but there is still love there, but the disbeliever has no love from God until they believe. This is inspite of any "good deeds" they have. In reality disbelievers can never do 1 good deed because the condition for a good deed is to do it sincerely for the sake of Allah and according to the Sunnah of their prophet, whereas since no disbeliever believes in Allah accurately they cannot qualify for their deed to be accepted since they cannot do something sincerely for God's sake. However humans are not God, but the revelations and prophets God sent us tell us to love what God loves and hate what God hates. Thus God wants us to hate the sins and to hate the sinners, even if they are believers, but with believers our love for their belief outweighs our hate for them because of their sin, so we love believers more than we hate them. Yet the true slaves of God hate all sinners, even themselves. Of course, prophets are an exception because since God forgives all their sins it means God does not hate prophets thus believers cannot hate prophets even an iota nor any other specific person God expressed his love for, such as all the companions of Muhammad pbuh via Quranic text and authentic hadith. Although God's love has not been made known for anyone on earth today. Therefore technically we should all hate everybody a tiny bit, because they sin but if they believe then our love for them is greater than the hate, while if they disbelieve then our hate will overpower any emotional affection they or Satan may inspire us to have towards them. However there is another caveat to this intricate but very important facet of Muslims hating Muslims due to their sins. First of all since many Muslims are ignorant they sometimes don't know Islam teaches Muslims to hate sinners even if they're Muslims, so since they don't know their Aqeedah then they sometimes make up their own and call it Islam. One solid proof to establish that Islam teaches Muslims to hate sinful Muslims is the ruling regarding bida(religious innovations). Most Muslims know that bida is a sin and that innovators are to be hated and even treated differently due to the gravity of the bida in the hopes that they stop.

However there are different types of bida, some types make one a disbeliever but it is possible in some instances for one to still be Muslim while doing a bida or preaching a bida, despite being extremely sinful. An example would be one who uses prayer beads, it's bad to do but such a person is still a Muslim in most cases. Thus a preacher or practitioner of bida could still be a Muslim, and as such other Muslims would love them because they are Muslims while hating their bida and them as individuals because of their bida, with the level of hate varying based on the severity of the bida. The interactions would also vary between Muslims and sinful Muslims depending on how the sinful Muslim would react and based on their knowledge level. Sometimes sinful Muslims get shunned by Muslims so they stop sinning, other times they don't because shunning them would make them become bigger sinners or even possibly leave Islam. Extensive knowledge is required by all involved regarding such complexities of social interaction. Many Muslims today unfortunately are not knowledgeable enough to know how to interact with each other. For example if someone's bida took them to the level of disbelief in Islam then the Muslim would have nothing at all to do with them and abandon them completely, even though the person may claim to be Muslim and believe/do lots of correct things. The people of bida whom Muslims avoid and dissociate from completely, whom we oppose openly, are those who differ with us over very fundamental aspects of Iman(faith) or Aqeedah(Creed); it does not include simple differences of opinion amongst the scholars, over finer points of jurisprudence. Although I said before that everyone sins, thus every Muslim alive today must be sinful. Does that mean Muslims have to hate all Muslims even those who don't practice bida? No. The reason why is because we only judge what is apparent, we don't delve into the hearts or private deeds. Only

God can judge the hidden but we can and must judge the apparent. Since we are restricted to the apparent judgement only, if publicly there is no Islamic reason to hate then no hate would exist even if there were private reasons to hate, we would never hate Muslims for things we don't know of. While if Muslims commit public sins then we would hate their sins and them as individuals according to their level of sinfulness, while our love for them as Muslims would outweigh the hatred we have for them as sinners. However that hatred would still exist temporarily until we see them stop publicly sinning and/or repent. We might not even know if they repented or whether they truly gave up the sins in their life or if God forgave them, but we go based on what is apparent. Apparently they'd be Muslims who repented and stopped sinning in public and who we'd assume God forgave. Not knowing of any sins that would cause us to hate them, we'd have nothing but love for them, even though in private they could be evil sinners worthy of immense hatred. Now this benefit of the doubt regarding hatred only applies to Muslims, this does not apply to non-Muslims. This is because since Muslims hate the sinful individual Muslim due to their known levels of sinfulness, it's impossible not to hate one guilty of the sin of disbelief. The sin of disbelief is worse than any sin a believer could be committing. Therefore the best disbeliever is always hated more than the worst believer. Whereas for disbelievers there is never any love for them only hatred, as individuals, with the amount of hatred varying based on their level of sinfulness. To make it easier to comprehend the love/hate relationship Muslims have I've included a chart which I think explains this very intricate and crucial doctrine of Islamic faith known as "Walaa Wabaraa", though Walaa Wabaraa covers more than just love and hate.

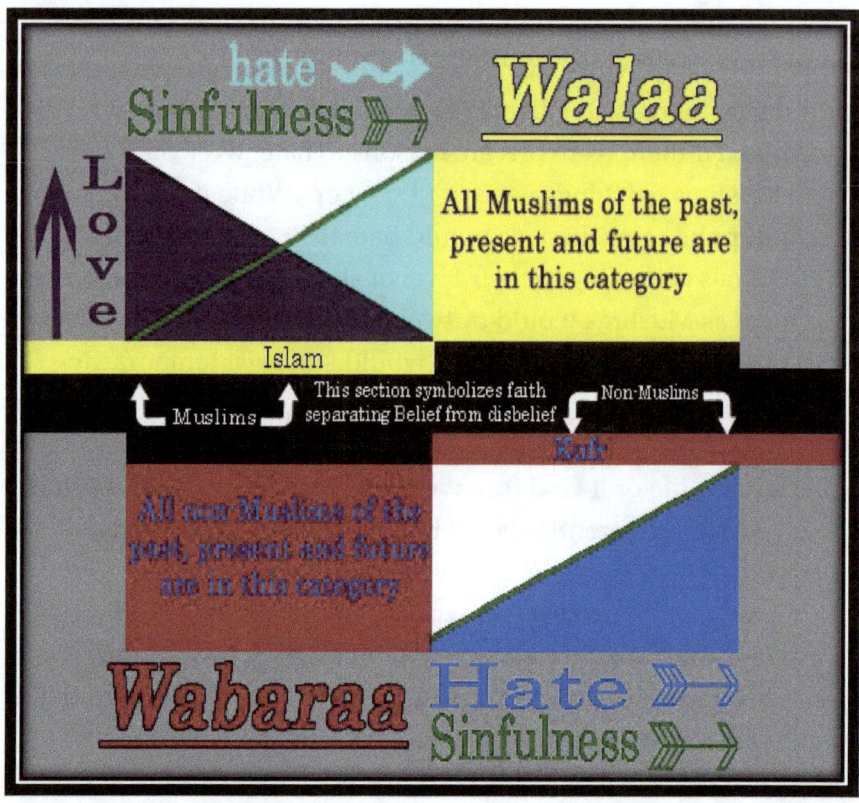

Keep in mind this chart's sinfulness is the one constant present in both charts from left to right in an uptrend. The hate for the Muslim is different than the hate for kafirs because there is love involved which outweighs the hate and turns it into a hate of a different shade/flavor. Whereas although the chart for the non-Muslim is below the Muslim chart, that is only because the Muslim chart has love involved making the y axis(longitudinal) act as the point where love crosses over into zero and the x axis (latitudinal) be the line separating belief from disbelief. At zero love the kafir starts by default automatically hated to a higher degree because their sin of disbelief outweighs all the Muslims sins combined. Thus don't be fooled by the dark blue hate on the bottom seeming small at first, it's a darker and deeper hatred than the turqouis hate Muslims have for sinful Muslims. The bottom hate chart's lowest point is higher than the highest hate point on the upper chart, the reason it is depicted below is because Islam is above kufr and not to be below or equal. Also the love is above hate as well so the kafir chart cannot be alongside nor above the love chart because their chart has no love because there is no islam. The prophet Muhammad pbuh even repeatedly said in famous well-known authentic hadiths recorded in both Sahih Bukhari and Sahih Muslim what means, "*Everyone will be with those whom he loves.*" in regards to the afterlife. This teaching was clarified by Muhammad pbuh to mean that if you love God and his prophets then you would be with them in paradise. But what does that mean? Who doesn't claim to love God and the prophets? Al-Hassan thoroughly explained this by saying: "*Don't be mislead into thinking that all is well when a person is to be with whom he loves, if the people he loves are still following the old ways (of pre-Islamic ignorance). You will never be allowed to join the best of humanity, until you follow in their footsteps; follow their example and adopt their way of life; morning, evening and night you must live like them, strive to be one of them, to follow the road they have trod. For even though you may fall short in deeds, the heart of the matter is that you tried to do what was right. As for the Jews and the Christians and others like them, they loved their prophets but they would not support them; for they differed with them both in word and in deed, and chose for themselves some other path and so their destiny is the fire.*" However there is another lesson from the statement of Muhammad pbuh that, "*Everyone will be with those whom he loves.*" which directly pertains to love/hate. This is because the only way such a statement could be true is if there were categories of people whom people did not love. Since if you love everybody then the statement would necessitate everybody being together, but we

~ 121 ~

know that some go to paradise and some go to hell thus it's impossible for someone to "love everybody". The Jewish and Christian example explained by Hassan shows how despite their claim the Jews and Christians don't really love the prophets, but those who lied about the prophets whom they really follow, like Paul. However what if a Muslim claims to love both Muslims and non-Muslims? Well then there is a problem because if Muslims are going to paradise and all the non-Muslims go to hell such a person can't end up in both places forever "with those whom they love". Thus this also proves that Muslims cannot love those outside of Islam because to do so would be to end up with them in the hellfire, since Muhammad pbuh taught how everyone will be with those they love. As a result this is more than enough proof to prove false the claim of modernist extremists that Muslims are supposed to love kafirs. Those who love disbelievers will end up with the disbelievers in the afterlife. Therefore all Muslims who go to paradise according to Muhammad pbuh do not love disbelievers but have only hate for them. Some may concede that there is a "natural love" but personally I think that is a poor choice of words because that "natural love" is not "love" as I've defined it throughout this book. Likewise some Muslims will argue the Quran mentions Allah telling Muhammad pbuh he can't guide whom he loves or use as an argument that Muslim men can sometimes marry practicing chaste Christian or Jewish women(which I don't think exist today since nobody follows the bible) thus how can they marry a disbeliever and have hate for them without love when Allah says he puts love/affection between husband and wife? Rather the "natural love" is simply a biological affinity for a member of the same species that is impossible for a human not to have for another human. For example Moses pbuh did not love Pharaoh but there was still a biological affinity for him as a human being. Likewise Jesus pbuh will have a "natural love" for the anti-christ but nobody would dare to say that Jesus pbuh loves the anti-christ. It's a type of humanist love or racist love because we are all humans who belong to the same human race. So "natural love" can also be called "racist love". Yet nobody would say "racist love" was "love" as they do with "natural love". That's why I say there is no love in the heart of a Muslim towards a non-Muslim, despite the biological affinity for all humans in general that cannot be denied. Because the singular english word "love" doesn't convey the correct meaning to most people but can convey an incorrect forbidden meaning. The main problem that leads to disbelief or misunderstandings and rejection of Islamic doctrines regarding love and hate is the english language and people just use the word "love" and that's it. There are many emotions/attitudes that get called "love" in english but because of the variety of "loves" to just say "love" is dangerous without specifying which of the types of "love" it is. Typically when a non-Muslim hears the word love they only think of 2 types, "true love" that they see in hollywood movies and fairytales and the exaggerated fake love type as in someone who "loves" the warm summer weather. Disbelievers don't really have a concept of "love" for a person not being "true 100% love", unless the person doesn't really mean it when they say it and are lying to you, but then they are a liar. Most people don't know of other types of "love". The Muslim scholar Ibn al-Qayyim commented on this, saying what means:

There are four kinds of "love", which we must differentiate between, and those who go astray do so because they do not make this distinction. The first of them is love of Allaah, but this alone is not sufficient to save a person from the punishment of Allaah and to earn him His reward. The Mushrikeen, worshippers of the cross, Jews and others all love Allaah. The second is love of that which Allaah loves. This is what brings a person into Islam and out of Kufr. The most beloved *of people to Allaah is the one who is most correct and most devoted in this kind of love. **The third** kind is love for the sake of Allaah, which is one of the essentials of loving that which Allaah loves. A person's love of that which Allaah loves cannot be complete until he also loves for the sake of Allaah. **The fourth** is love for something alongside Allaah, and this love has to do with shirk. Everyone who loves things alongside Allaah but not for the sake of Allaah has taken that thing as a rival to Allaah.** This is the love of the Mushrikeen. **There remains a fifth kind of love which has nothing to do with our topic; this is the natural love which is a person's inclination towards that which suits his nature,** such as the love of a thirsty person for water or of a hungry person for food, or the love of sleep, or of one's wife and children. **There is nothing wrong with this unless it distracts a person from remembering Allaah and keeps him from loving Him.** Allaah says (what means):"O you who believe! Let not your properties or your children divert you from the remembrance of Allaah" [63:9]*

"Men whom neither trade nor sale (business) diverts from the remembrance of Allaah" [24:37] (Al-Jawaab al-Kaafi, 1/134)

Ibn Al-Qayyim also said:

The difference between loving for the sake of Allaah and loving something alongside Allaah is one of the most important distinctions. Everyone needs to make this distinction and is indeed obliged to do so. Loving for the sake of Allaah is a sign of the perfection of faith, but loving something alongside Allaah is the essence of shirk. *The difference between them is that a person's love for the sake of Allaah is connected to his love of Allaah; if this love becomes strong in his heart, this love dictates that he will love that which Allaah loves. If he loves that which his Lord loves and he loves those who are the friends of Allaah, this is love for the sake of Allaah. So he loves His Messengers, Prophets, angels and close friends because Allaah loves them, and he hates those who hate them because Allaah hates those people.* **The sign of the love and hatred for the sake of Allaah is**

that his hatred for the one whom Allaah hates will not turn into
love merely because that person treats him kindly, does him a service or
meets some need he has ; and his love for those whom Allaah loves will
not turn to hatred simply because that person does something that upsets
or hurts him, whether it is done by mistake or deliberately, in obedience
to Allaah or because the person feels that he has a duty to do it for some
reason, or because the person is a wrongdoer who may yet give up his
wrongdoing and repent. **The entire religion revolves around four**
principles: love and hatred, and stemming from them, **action and**
abstinence. The person whose love and hatred, action and abstinence,
are all for the sake of Allaah, has perfected his faith so that when he loves,
he loves for the sake of Allaah, when he hates, he hates for the sake of
Allaah, when he does something, he does it for the sake of Allaah, and
when he abstains from something, he abstains for the sake of Allaah. To
the extent that he is lacking in these four categories, he is lacking in faith
and commitment to religion. **This is in contrast to the love of things**
alongside Allaah, which is of two types. One is diametrically
opposed to the principle of Tawheed and is shirk; the other is opposed to
perfection of sincerity and love towards Allaah, but does not put a person
beyond the pale of Islam.

The first kind is like the love of the Mushrikeen for their idols and
gods. Allaah says (interpretation of the meaning):"And of mankind are
some who take (for worship) others besides Allaah as rivals (to Allaah).
They love them as they love Allaah" [2:165]

These Mushrikeen love their idols and gods alongside Allaah as they love
Allaah. This love and devotion is accompanied by fear, hope, worship and
supplication. This love is pure Shirk which Allaah does not forgive.

Faith cannot be perfected unless a person regards these idols as
enemies and hates them intensely, and hates the people who
worship them, and regards them as enemies and strives against
them. This is the message with which Allaah sent all His Messengers
and revealed all His Books. He created Hell for the people of shirk who
love these rivals, and He created Paradise for those who strive against

them and take them as enemies for His sake and to earn His Pleasure. Anybody who worships anything from the vicinity of the Throne to the lowest depths of the earth and takes a god and a supporter besides Allaah and associates another beings in worship with Him, will be disowned by the object of his worship when he is most in need of it [i.e., on the Day of Judgement]. **The second kind is love for the things which Allaah has made attractive to people,** *such as women, children, gold, silver, branded beautiful horses, cattle and well-tilled land. People love them with a kind of desire, like the love of the hungry person for food and the thirsty person for water.* **This love is of three kinds.** *If a person loves them for the sake of Allaah and as a means of obeying Allaah, he will be rewarded for that; it will be counted as a part of love for the sake of Allaah and a means of reaching Him, and he will still find enjoyment in them. This is how the best of creation [i.e. the Prophet] was, to whom women and perfume were made dear in this world, and his love for them helped him to love Allaah more and to convey His Message and fulfil His commands.* **If a person loves them** *because they suit his nature and his own desires, but he does not give them preference over that which Allaah loves and is pleased with, and he gets them* **because of his natural inclination,** *then they come under the heading of things which are permissible, and he will not be punished for that, but* **his love of Allaah and for the sake of Allaah will be lacking somewhat.** *If his sole purpose in life is to get these things, and he gives priority to that over that which Allaah loves and is pleased with, then he is wronging himself and following his own desires. The first is the love of al-Saabiqoon (those who are foremost in Islam, the friends of God); the second is the love of al-muqtasidoon (those who are average) and the third is the love of al-zaalimoon (wrongdoers). (Al-Rooh by Ibn al-Qayyim, 1/254.)*

Non-Muslims don't usually know about these distinctions of love, especially if they are westernized non-Muslims. They consider the permissible type of "natural love" to be "like" or "care". Most don't think love and enmity can exist together, they think "love" means the person likes you 100% and has 0% hatred for you no matter what they believe, say or do and they might disagree or dislike something but there will never be hate because of the love. So to a non-Muslim their vocabulary doesn't allow us to say "love" without giving a huge lecture on all the various types of love and how we don't really mean what everyone else does when they say "love". Then after you give that big lecture they will forget it 5 minutes after you finish explaining it to them because they want to believe what they hear and prefer, thus it's best to just say you "care" rather than call it "natural love". They can understand what you mean when you say "I care about you but I don't love you." But to just say "love" without even specifying it as a certain type of "natural love that Muslims have for all creatures" is not going to convey the correct meaning and will convey sinful unislamic messages to them and make them think disbelief is no big deal no matter what else you say, because no matter what you say about kufr/shirk/disbelief as long as they think you love them they don't care. If you let them know you don't love them because of kufr/shirk then they realize that kufr/shirk is a really bad thing that is coming between them and love. Thus they will see kufr/shirk as a bad thing rather than just a *"difference of opinion"*.

Today because of the religions of humanism and pluralism the "love for each other" is stressed in order to establish true racism of love for humans just because they are humans. This is done so that in case of Aliens vs. Humans all humans will side with humans, even if they are wrong, because of "love for species" overcoming justice and hate for evil/evildoers and hate for the sake of Allah. Traditionally it was love of white skin that led to the enslavement of blacks and genocide of native Americans, now they promote "love of humans" so that the genocide and enslavement of Aliens can be done easily without moral dilemmas or conflicted loyalties. They will say one must love their own species more than aliens, no matter what. You might think this whole "love everybody, hate nobody" nonsense is innocent but it's evil, in reality human Muslims love Muslim jinn more than we do any individual non-Muslim human even if they be our own family. Muslim humans love Muslim jinn more than they do kafir kin. If they ever fought the proper Muslims would side with the Muslim Jinn against the non-Muslim humans.

Once again I must stress that having hate does not mean being nasty or hurtful. It is a prophetic hatred that is peaceful in most instances, except during war. Every classical religion teaches this fundamental principle to some extent, the difference is that in Islam it's intricacies are actually explained so one knows what God expects from us. The other religions know they should hate those of other faiths if theirs is true, but their doctrines on hate are extremely vague because their religious doctrines never came from a genuine prophet of God or if they did it has been corrupted beyond repair. So they don't really know how much love and hate is too much or too little. If you "love everybody" then you are guaranteed to burn in hell no matter what religion is correct because to love an enemy of God is treason and a betrayal of the prophets and their religion. One can't be afraid to hate for the sake of God. Rationally if you are ever going to hate for any reason then for the sake of God is the only justifiable reason to hate anyone ever. If you hate for a reason other than the sake of God then you got no business hating anyone, because only something you worship can instill within you the emotion of hatred towards another human. Likewise only something you worship can instill within you the emotion of love towards another human. Remember when I say "love" I do not consider the biological affinity humans have for each other to be "love". I'm belaboring this point so it becomes well-known the politically popular "Hate the sin, but not the sinner"(or love the sinner) doctrine is not from God, his revelations, nor his prophets. It might sound clever, cute and tolerant but it's a satanic false doctrine. Regarding sinners, Muslims have a "tough love" for knowledgeable sinful Muslims, a "gentle loving criticism" for ignorant/weak Muslims, a "tender hate" for peaceful disbelievers who don't oppose Islam or Muslims and a "polite harsh hate" for evil enemies of Islam. However no Muslim loves a sinner but hates their actions, instead we hate the sin and the sinner while we love all believers and those sinners who repent. Repentance from a sin eliminates any hatred a Muslim has for someone due to that sin. Whereas depending on the sin such repentance may not even need be publicized by the Muslim sinner for the hatred to be eliminated from the Muslim's heart, sometimes one can assume another Muslim repented and sometimes one cannot. As a principle it is forbidden to love a sinner in Islam, we love Muslims, and sometimes Muslims sin thus we can have a level of love for them because they are Muslim while hating them for being a sinner at the same time until we get an indication they may have repented and been forgiven for their sin thereupon we have nothing but love for them unless they are unrepentant sinners. For instance good deeds eliminate bad deeds and apparently every Muslim does many good deeds such as the 5 daily prayers, fasting Ramadan, paying charity, giving the salams, Hajj, Umrah, Hijra, Jihad etc. So because so many good deeds are public knowledge, based on the apparent most Muslims appear sinless either due to lack of sins or an overabundance of good deeds that would make one assume their good deeds erased their apparently known evil deeds. In the case of unrepentant Muslim sinners Muslims love and hate them simultaneously, loving them more than they hate them as long as they are Muslims. While since a non-Muslim sinner is hated for their false faith and cannot perform a valid repentance to be forgiven by God then the hatred Muslims have for non-Muslims will always remain until they become a Muslim. We hate all the non-Muslims both for their sin of disbelief as well as their other sins. Since their good deeds don't qualify as acceptable to God they don't count and therefore don't erase their sins no matter what good they do, so the disbeliever has disbelief + sins + 0 valid good deeds. Thus they are hated accordingly to their level of sinfulness without their "good deeds" influencing any love towards them. They are hated based on sinfulness, the less sinful the less hatred but all disbelievers are by default of disbelief more sinful than the most sinful Muslim. Though disbelievers do get worldly reward for their good deeds from Allah out of his appreciation for the good even though it will have no weight in the afterlife, it doesn't convert into love from Allah or his allies/friends. To say "Hate the sin but love the sinner" is exactly like saying "Hate disbelief but love the disbeliever" or "Hate the evil Satan does but love Satan for who he is". Sadly many would agree with the first 2 of those 3 statements but then disagree with the third, however they are all the same. If you love disbelievers then you must love them all, including Satan. Hence this doctrine of "Hate the sinner but not the sin" or "Hate disbelief but not the disbeliever" is pure satanist doctrine. The Satanists know Satan is a bad creature, but they love him anyways despite his sins. Just as a believer would reject this loving of Satan the believer also rejects the notion of loving disbelievers. People err often but its hatred of others error that should lead you to correct them.

The main problem leading to disbelief or misunderstandings and rejection of Islamic doctrines regarding love and hate is the english language and people just use the word "love" and that's it. Most never clarify what they mean, so when a practicing Muslim says "It's forbidden to love non-Muslims and equals disbelief " it's common for the average Muslim to think we're talking about "natural love" when we're talking about spiritual love and the hate we are saying is obligatory does not negate the "natural love". With me, I define love as being "true love"/conditional/ for the sake of Allah. So when I say the english word "love" I'm using my definition but frequently others don't know my definition of love. So I explain and redefine "natural love" as " simply a biological affinity for a member of the same species that is impossible for a human not to have for another human." or "racist love for the human race" for short. Yet a problem occurs with non-Arabic speaking Muslims who then teach this to Arabic speaking Muslims and get labeled as extremists who don't know Arabic and thus don't understand Islam and how it teaches love for others. This happens a lot. Arabic speaking Muslims will try to say Islam really teaches love for non-Muslims and then they quote Arabic words. But the problem is when they translate those words into english those words that in Arabic mean love don't mean love in english. Yet because they also speak english they don't understand how the problem is not with the Arabic but it is with them misunderstanding the english language when translating Arabic words into english. In other cases this can even lead to strict practicing Muslims making takfir of other Muslims due to this linguistic confusion where the translations amount to disbelief in Islam in some people's vocabulary even though the Muslim themself doesn't believe in the unislamic translation's meanings. For example people can tell if I am saying arabic words and don't know the meaning, but Muslim reverts who only know 1 language can't always tell that other people don't know what they are saying when they say it because the way they say it is understood by the ear. Also mono-lingual people aren't used to having to decode meanings behind speech and we think people know what the words they are using mean. Typically we never define our words when we speak to people, we tend to think everyone's definition of words matches our own definition. So while a Muslim revert might not know more than 1 language, some of us tend to know our 1 and only language a lot more than those bi-linguists we speak to, but the Muslim reverts don't know that we know our one language better than those who know more than 1 language. Thus when an ignorant Muslim who knows Arabic tells a revert *"You are a new Muslim and don't know Arabic so you don't understand Islam."* then the Muslim revert should say: *"Well perhaps you don't know english as well as I do, so you don't know how to teach Islam or interpret what I say. Of course you know some english words just as I know some Arabic but knowing words and base meanings doesn't mean one knows how to communicate ideas of complexity or even simplicity."* Thus I think many cases involving takfir could simply be solved and avoided if people just discussed the linguistic barriers that is leading to their opposing statements and thereby learned that they actually fundamentally agree, but linguistically the words they are using are making them both think the other is an extremist or even a non-Muslim. Basically a Muslim can't just judge another Muslim to be unislamic or sinful based on what they say alone, you have to know what they mean and it can be tricky because they might not know how to express themselves correctly the Islamic way in a language all parties know. Therefore Muslims must be careful to communicate the ideas they mean effectively so there is the least possibility for confusion. Ambiguous and general statements can be dangerous for all. The knowledge of another person's definitions of words can make the difference between mislabeling someone as a Muslim, an extremist or a disbeliever. Sadly proper Muslims frequently get misunderstood when they speak, particularly by non-Muslims, especially if/when extremists use the same statements as them but mean very different things when they say them. Hence the confusion some have when they hear a proper Muslim say: *"It's obligatory in Islam to hate all non-Muslims and it's disbelief in Islam to love any of them."* Then when a less informed Muslim disputes this sometimes another Muslim overreacts and ignorantly makes takfir and as a result gets labeled as a takfiri and then people think proper Muslims are takfiris all because of linguistic confusion by them saying that it's forbidden/disbelief to express love for non-Muslims, even though that is what Islam teaches. We still insist on saying this despite the confusion it can cause because circumstances have made the utterance of "love" for non-Muslims forbidden in the english language. For example when boyfriends and girlfriends date even they don't say they love each other, even if they are having sex with each other they still don't say that. Instead they say "like" because to say "love" is a very big thing and means a lot which they don't feel for each other even if they are dating and fornicating, until they get nearer the engagement period. To say you love someone in the western and non-Muslim world or in the english language is a huge thing and means you are loyally allied and/or want to spend your life together with them. Most western non-Muslims don't love strangers, or co-workers, or members of the same religion even, they only love family and extremely close friends. Even gang members don't say they love each other, they are just loyal to each other. They'll die and kill for each other and go to prison for each other for the cause of Satan but still they will never say they love each other. In the West and in english the word "love" is the strongest type of positive feelings one can have for another person. To say you love someone is the nicest thing you can ever say to someone. In english there are no stronger words, except perhaps for saying "I worship you." After "I worship you" to say "I love you" is the most endearing phrase one can say. Thus it is a huge thing for non-Muslims to hear and in my opinion and experience the word "love" should not be used because the way I was raised "love" does not explain what Muslims are supposed to feel for non-Muslims. I'd say "care about" is. Or a biological affinity. At the end of the day we want to convey the truth. So if you say "love" in english people might get the wrong message. Thus if you don't say love then it is much safer because Satan will make people misunderstand the word love and they will not get the correct islamic message. So I stick to care or natural affinity while stressing hate for whoever doesn't believe in Allah, Islam and the prophethood of Muhammad pbuh yet being kind and just despite the hate and always treating people as the prophets taught us even though I may hate them. Also I stress that the hate is only due to religious beliefs or sins and once such hateful false religious beliefs change and one becomes a Muslim then I would love them and that is when I use the word love. I don't give the message "I'll never love you" but instead explain "I will only love them if God does and God only loves Muslims and hates all the non-Muslims". As a result people realize religion is important and that if I am willing to have strained social interactions due to their religious beliefs then maybe their beliefs really are quite bad afterall and they might reconsider and think of changing them as a result, if they are that bad as to prevent love and cause hatred. One cannot say you love them in the present as a non-Muslim and then say you'll love them as a Muslim, it won't seem like there is any difference between the two faiths. But if you never say you love them and maintain that you won't until they become Muslims then they will understand and see how important it is to be Muslim and that "love" is not a meaningless word to you. It also teaches that Muslims must really care for each other even more than regular people care for regular people, since regular people don't love each other. Seriously most non-Muslim best friends don't even use the word "love". So when a Muslim says they only love Muslims and love all Muslims the non-Muslim realizes the ties of Islam are stronger than their strongest unislamic friendship. Yet many never let the non-Muslims know this as the Sahabah did because they are afflicted with kafirphobia and care too much about what people think instead of what Allah thinks. In reality such folk don't truly love Allah.

One must follow the prophetic methods. No prophet I know of ever started a violent revolution, nor did they use indiscriminate violence in civilian areas, nor did they harm innocents or non-combatants who just happened to be living their lives in ignorance. Likewise no prophet declared war on every country in the world simultaneously. So just because Muslims may be oppressed in every country, one has to be practical in that the sword is not the answer to all forms of oppression. Diplomacy can work, if it's done correctly. Moses pbuh didn't start a revolution, Jesus pbuh didn't start a revolution, Muhammad pbuh didn't start a revolution. Yet at the same time keep in mind none of them voted in elections and none of them ran for political office or held "inter-faith" dialogues to unite the various religious faiths living in the same localities. I repeat Moses pbuh didn't vote, Jesus pbuh didn't vote and Muhammad pbuh didn't vote. The prophetic method is not the revolutionary method, it is not the democratic method, it is not the capitalist method, it is not the machiavellian method and it is not the "Inter-faith" method. It's the pure fundamental Islamic method, as taught to mankind in the Quran and Sunnah which was adhered to by the salaf through sincerity and knowledge. It is not the "moderate Islam" which the disbelievers want and promote. For example most Muslims in the

West have a delusion that as a persecuted minority in Mecca the Muslims didn't ruffle any feathers or press for Shariah. Such a notion is entirely false, they got persecuted because they were preaching an entirely different way of life that contradicted, denounced and rejected the status quo and values of the pagan majority who were in power. Umar bin Khattab is well known to have tortured Muslims in Mecca on a daily basis, before he embraced Islam. He explained the reason was because Muslims were insulting his faith and threatening the political, economic and social stability of his city disrupting the status quo turning families against each other. Umar said he considered them to be political criminals/rebels because of their teachings against the idols, tourism industry and government system. Yet on his first day after Umar became a Muslim he publicly declared his Islam and rejection of the idols and the disbelievers ways. On his first day as a Muslim, Umar went to his uncle Abu Jahl to tell him the news at the crack of dawn. Why did he do that? He said because he knew Abu Jahl was the worst enemy of Islam and he knew it would make him upset to learn Umar of all people became a Muslim, and it did. The conversation went as follows:

"*Who comes*", asked Abu Jahl.

"*It's Umar*", said Umar.

Abu Jahl opened the door and said, "*Welcome nephew*".

Umar: "*Uncle do you know, I have become a Muslim?*"

Abu Jahl: "*Do not talk like that. I know that a man of your views can never become a Muslim*".

Umar: "*No, uncle it is a fact that I have become a Muslim. I have come to tell you that I have embraced the religion of Allah and His Messenger, Muhammad.*"

Abu Jahl:"*If what you say is true then be damned. May God ruin you and what you have brought!*"

Then Abu Jahl slammed the door in the face of Umar. So Umar went and told all the leaders of his tribe and the city of Mecca the same thing and got similar responses. Then Umar went to the Kaba and told the biggest town gossiper the news, because he wanted everyone to know it, and as soon as the town gossiper heard he shouted out, "*O ye Quraish, know that Umar bin al Khattab has been converted to Islam, and apostatized from the faith of his forefathers!*" Nearly immediately Umar got beat up by a mob and they spent the entire day fighting him, with Umar fighting back all by himself. He was a good fighter and whenever he was getting too hurt he'd put his fingers in the eyes of an enemy and threaten that if they all don't stop hitting him then he would take out the eyes of his hostage. Then they would stop hitting him and he let the hostage go. Then they ganged up again on him until again Umar would grab somebody put his fingers over their eyes and threaten to take them out if they didn't stop hitting him and whoever the hostage was they always shouted to the mob to stop hitting Umar because they didn't want to lose their eyes. This was how Umar spent his first day as a Muslim, getting beat up except for brief interludes of rest. Umar's own uncle Abu Jahl was the biggest enemy of Islam during the time of Muhammad pbuh, yet even he gave Umar pity when he saw how he was being treated and offered protection because he was getting abused so much. Abu Jahl was even the first polytheist to kill a Muslim when he killed his slave girl Sumayyah bint Khabbab because she was Muslim. So that shows just how bad Umar was persecuted after embracing Islam for Abu Jahl to offer him protection on the very same day that he started out by damning Umar to his face asking God to ruin him. Yet when Abu Jahl, the man who hated Muslims the most and hurt them the most out of all, offered to protect his nephew from the mob that had been beating him up all day long, do you know what Umar said? He briskly replied: *"Uncle I don't need your protection. For me the protection of Allah is enough."* Which of course did not make his polytheistic uncle who hated Islam happy, it embarrassed and infuriated him since it was so uncharacteristic of Abu Jahl to offer protection to a Muslim when he was their top enemy. Abu Jahl was truly only offering protection to be nice out of fear his nephew would die and then the nephew rebukes him and maintains his religion is true and Abu Jahl's is false. A similar event happened with Bilal ibn Raba'ah who was a black slave. Many Muslims are familiar with the famous incident when Bilal was tortured in the desert by his polytheist owner who put rocks on him to try to get him to leave Islam. In reply Bilal would only say "The One", referring to there only being 1 God and all the idols not being gods at all. During which and later Bilal said that he only said the Arabic word for "The One" because he knew it was the most hateful thing he could say to make his disbelieving torturer upset and Bilal swore to God that if he knew anything that could've made his disbelieving torturer more angry he would've said it. Bilal even told his owner/torturer this several times while being tortured. So by definition even under torture Bilal was a "hate preacher" deliberately saying things against disbelief to make disbelievers upset and realize their faith was false. Although keep in mind he wasn't mean, he was just saying "The One" but the reason he said that was not just because it was true, there was hatred behind his truthful peaceful polite speech. The other thing about Bilal's famous incident Muslims tend not to know is what Bilal did that got him into the tortuous situation. Now Bilal had been tortured by his owner ever since he became a Muslim, just because he was a Muslim but there was a specific action Bilal did that triggered the torture in the desert that nearly killed him. It had to do with what Bilal did after he became a Muslim and his owner found out. Bilal's Owner, Umayyah ibn Khalaf, learned of his slave's Islamic faith after another polytheist informed him while he was with Abu Jahl. Also know that this took place about 6 years before Abu Jahl's nephew Umar had become Muslim and Abu Jahl offered Umar his protection which was adamantly rejected. The conversation went as follows:

Umayyah ibn Khalaf: *"Are you sure (that Bilal accepted Islam)?"*

Informer: *"Certainly."*

Umayyah ibn Khalaf: *"Did you see him going to Muhammad?"*

Informer: *"Many times."*

Umayyah ibn Khalaf: *"That thought never crossed my mind."*

Informer: *"But I saw something worse!"*

Umayyah ibn Khalaf: *"What did you see?"*

Informer: *"I cannot really tell you. It is so sacrilegious I cannot describe what I saw."*

Umayyah ibn Khalaf: *"What did you see? Tell me."*

Informer: *"I saw him spitting in the face of our great god Hubal!"*

The informer had followed Bilal unbeknownst to him to the Kaba where the idols of the city were prominently displayed and witnessed Bilal say to the major idol: "And you, the feeble god!

Where were you when you broke your arm? (The idol's arm had broken off years prior and been replaced with a golden arm.) *Couldn't you defend yourself? How, in your majestic pride could you permit yourself to be repaired by your servants, your worshippers? Truly you have no hand. What can you do if I smash you or spit in your face?"* After spitting on Hubal's face, Bilal proclaimed, *"You do not even deserve that. The day will come when your neck shall be broken and shall never be replaced!"* Also note this happened in public during the first year of Muhammad's prophethood in Mecca. Bilal was just the second man to become a Muslim after Abu Bakr did. Plus Bilal was a slave, so Muslims didn't have much political clout and were a clear minority living amongst disbelievers. Now I'm not saying Muslims should spit at statues today, but this is what Bilal did in Mecca when there were only a few Muslims. Today Muslims should just strongly condemn kufr & kafirs without spitting, since Bilal said *"you do not even deserve that"* it means that kufr and kafirs don't deserve spittle.

Ummayah ibn Khalaf, furious at what the informer told him his slave (Bilal) had done to his god said: *"Did he dare do that?"*

Informer: *"Yes, he did."*

Umayyah ibn Khalaf: *"What a most sacrilegious and unpardonable abomination!"* and he ran away from the meeting crying with tears streaming down his face.

Abu Jahl went after him and asked what was wrong.

Umayyah ibn Khalaf: *"My slave, Bilal!"*

Abu Jahl: *"What happened to him?"*

Umayyah ibn Khalaf: *"He has rejected our gods **and** entered the religion of Muhammad."*

Abu Jahl: *"And what do you intend to do? It is indeed a most intolerable situation."*

Umayyah ibn Khalaf: *"If it is true, Bilal will suffer the consequences."*

Abu Jahl: *"But woe to us, if we are going to leave Muhammad to spread his poisonous views and let him corrupt our slaves and the people of weaker minds and the disobedient, and allow him supporters. Go Umayyah, fetch your mean slave and punish him. Let him taste the painful chastisement so that he becomes a good example to those whose weak minds might induce them to abandon our heritage. Go Umayyah and torture him mercilessly. Those deviators deserve no sympathy. As for me, I shall do everything possible to strangle that new religion in its infancy, and shall never rest until the prestige and dignity of our gods are restored. And as for you, Muhammad, you are my declared enemy forever and my blood relation to you shall never diminish my hatred for you or generate any sympathy for you. My heart shall ever be hardened and I shall let you taste varieties of punishments and tortures as **you have planted the seeds of enmity** between a son and his father, between a brother and his brother and brought about shame never suffered before by a people at the hand of one of its members."*

Six years after making this statement Umar was getting beaten up so bad for becoming a Muslim Abu Jahl offered Umar protection and got rebuffed, so it really does show the firmness Umar had on just his first day as a Muslim to put up with such a beating that softened the heart of Abu Jahl towards him. Yet Bilal and Umar are famous examples so one may think they had extraordinary circumstances to act the way they did towards disbelief and that the hatred wasn't really a part of Muhammad's message at all pbuh. Yet that would be a mistake to make as proven by the story of Amr ibn Abasah and Al-Husain(the father of Imran bin Husain). The way Amr ibn Abasah became a Muslim is related in the authentic collection of hadith known as

~ 141 ~

Sahih Muslim. Amr related his interaction with Muhammad pbuh as follows: *"I heard about a man in Mecca, who was informing (people) about much (significant) news. I sat on my mount and went to him. At the time the Messenger of Allah's people were brazen and insolent in their dealings with him, and so I proceeded gently until I entered upon him in Mecca. I said, "Who are you?" He said, "I am a Prophet." I asked, "And what is a Prophet?" He said, "Allah(God) has sent me" I asked "with what (message) did he send you? He said, "He sent me with (the message of) joining ties of relation, breaking idols, and believing in the Oneness of Allah(God)(worshipping Him alone), without associating any (partner) with Him." I asked, "And who is with you upon this?" He said, "The free one and the slave." Among those who followed him at that time were Abu Bakr and Bilal. I said, Indeed I will follow you (here)."* Afterwards Amr was told by Muhammad pbuh that he essentially wouldn't be able to handle the persecution in Mecca so he told Amr to go live elsewhere until he heard Muhammad pbuh and the Muslims had overcome the persecution and then Amr should come back to be with him. Whereas if you notice according to Amr at the time there were only a few Muslims yet while under persecution Muhammad pbuh told a non-Muslim that God sent him to "break the idols" BEFORE he told him about worshipping God alone. Understand that at that time to say one was sent to break the idols was quite a statement to make when almost everyone worshipped idols, it was also a very big economic statement to make as well. Yet Muhammad pbuh made it his 2nd point after joining kinship ties prior to his message of monotheism. When Muhammad pbuh said he was sent to "break the idols" he would not fulfill this purpose until decades later after getting political authority to do so. Although as a sidenote Muhammad pbuh did break the idols on top of the Kaba with Ali one night, before emigrating; they just didn't get caught. In public Muhammad pbuh always made his message clear about what his beliefs and goals were even when he couldn't fulfill them and could get in serious harm for expressing his future plans. Al-Husain the father of Imran bin Husain also had a similar encounter with Muhammad pbuh in Mecca. The leaders of Mecca knew Al-Husain was intelligent so they told him to come get Muhammad pbuh to stop his hate preaching. The Quraish told Al-Husain, "*Speak to this man on our behalf, for indeed, he speaks(badly) of our gods and curses them.*" So Al-Husain went to Muhammad pbuh and told him, "*What is this that has reached us about you: You speak about our gods and curse them? Your father was indeed good and wise (for having adhered to the religion of his fathers).*" What do you think Muhammad pbuh said in reply? Really take a minute and think how do you think the merciful and kind Muhammad pbuh replied, the same Muhammad pbuh who when he was chased out of Taaif was pelted with stones that led his shoes to fill with blood yet refused to curse those people but asked God to guide their children to Islam. Most Western Muslims use this example of Muhammad pbuh at Taaif to say how Muslims must always be extra nice to disbelievers and such. Yet this incident happened years before Taaif and the supplication for Taaif was in private where the disbelievers never knew about it. So that supplication cannot be used as a template for public interactions with disbelievers. Also the calamity of Taaif happened after Muhammad pbuh preached there for 10 days, those people fully knew what Muhammad pbuh meant and the leaders of Taaif told Muhammad pbuh that if they accepted Islam then they would lose their positions since a prophet of God would have to be in charge. Thus because the people of Taaif didn't want to make political changes that would be necessary if as a people they accepted Islam then they rejected Islam and pelted Muhammad pbuh with stones. Most people ignore this reason because it means Muhammad pbuh preached Shariah and political change as part of his 10-day message. Thus modernists use the mercy displayed at Taaif to make incomplete lessons rather than use it as an example of Muhammad pbuh being confrontational and political in his preaching they use it to say "Be extra nice and non-confrontational to non-Muslims." Whereas Muhammad pbuh was nice to the people of Taaif but he was still confrontational, thus he got stoned. However the incident with Al-Husain took place in public in Mecca, long before the Taaif incident, when there were few Muslims and they were all suffering great persecution. So while persecuted in Mecca Muhammad pbuh gets asked a simple question about why he is speaking hatred against the popular gods and the idolaters when his own father had worshipped the same idols he denounces. What did Muhammad pbuh say in response? Did he apologize and say he crossed the line being unjustly disrespectful and unislamic when preaching hatred for idols and idolaters? No. Muhammad pbuh said: "*O Husain, indeed my father and your father are in the Hellfire. O Husain, how many gods do you worship?*" Al-Husain told him: "*Seven on earth and one in the heavens.*" Muhammad pbuh said, "*And when you are afflicted with harm, whom do you invoke?*" Al-Husain said, "*The One that is in the heavens.*" Muhammad pbuh said, "*And when (your) wealth is wiped out, whom do you invoke?*" Husain said, "*The One that is in the heavens.*" Muhammad pbuh said, "*He alone answers you, yet you make them His partners!*" A few minutes later Al-Husain agreed to accept Islam and become a Muslim. Yet remember what Muhammad's first response to this guy was, he said both of their fathers were in the hellfire. Now if you talk to most Muslims today they'd say you should never ever say that to a disbeliever under any circumstances, because Islam teaches kindness and mercy etc. While Islam does teach kindness and mercy, it still remains a fact that Muhammad's first sentence when responding to a disbeliever in Mecca as a persecuted minority when he was harshly confronted about cursing the gods of the people and insulting their dead disbelieving relatives, was to say that his and the other guy's dead dads were both in the hellfire. Is that offensive? Yeah, but just a few minutes later the guy became a Muslim. But that's not the only detail of importance regarding Al-Husain's reversion to Islam. Before he could even stand up after saying the Shahada his Muslim son Umraan went to his father (Al-Husain) and kissed his head, hands and feet. Thereupon Muhammad pbuh cried and said, *"I cried because of what Umraan did: When Al-Husain entered here, he was a disbeliever, and Umraan neither stood up for him nor turned in his direction; then when Al-Husain embraced Islam, Umraan fulfilled his (father's) right (over him). A feeling of warmness and mercy entered me because of that."* Thus in context we can see how Muslims treated their disbelieving relatives differently due to their disbelief and how Muhammad pbuh treated the non-Muslim parents of Muslims. Likewise I have a similar policy with my family in that I won't hug or kiss any of them as long as they are disbelievers. I even let my parents know this and politely refuse to let them hug me explaining how I don't feel its proper to display any physical affection when they disbelieve in God(Allah) and have the offensive beliefs they have about Jesus pbuh. While with other family I just don't kiss or hug and they don't really ask anyways. I can now explicitly politely reject giving or receiving physical affection from my family due to their religion, while at the same time they don't get that offended or outraged over it because I explain it with good manners and reject their hugs and kisses with kind hatred. So again don't take these examples of Muslims showing hatred or preaching hatred for disbelief/disbelievers out of context. I just stress the hatred because Muslims today tend to ignore or even deny it altogether focusing so much on kindness that they forget how the animosity expressed during the dawah in Mecca helped the dawah and pleased God. Abu Dharr al-Ghafaari is another example of how expressing hatred for disbelief and disbelievers lead to his entire tribe becoming Muslims almost immediately after he did. Yet again it's important to stress the hatred must be presented prophetically and not satanically. It's a courteous type of honesty to inform a disbeliever that the religious differences between Muslims and non-Muslims obstruct the feelings they can have or express for each other. It's not that Muslims don't want to be affectionate toward people, it's just that because we love God most we hate those who disbelieve in him to an extent that we cannot feel much more than our common biological affinity for another person until they become Muslims. When/if that happens then we shower them with love once they believe in Islam because God makes us love those he loves and hate those who he hates since Muslims are God's slaves. A Muslim's heart is not their own, it belongs to its Creator. All Muslims care deeply about disbelievers, since we are all kin via our relation to Adam pbuh, but love just doesn't enter our hearts for disbelief or disbelievers because that is not how the heart of a believer works and we cannot and dare not change it and thereby disobey, displease and disbelieve in our Creator. The kindness is there for those who aren't hostile to Islam or Muslims, but the disbelief of disbelievers breaks our heart and prevents us from loving them and instills hatred for them. While simultaneously the love for God makes us love all believers in a way which disbelievers would fight us to get if they only knew how much Muslims loved each other. Thus this love/hate relationship is a spiritual and worldly reality that unites the Muslims and separates us from disbelievers, who sometimes as a result of our hate or disavowal feel hatred towards Islam/Muslims and harm us, because the disbelievers love for the sake of Satan and hate for the sake of Satan even though they all think and claim otherwise. I even tell my parents when they say they love me that if they loved me they would love Allah, Muhammad pbuh, Jesus pbuh and be great Muslims if they truly loved me. But they don't really love me. Abraham pbuh taught the same and we wouldn't criticize Abraham's preaching abilities or messages. But of course I'm not Abraham pbuh so I must be hateful in the unprophetic manner right? Well the Quran says what means: "*Indeed there has been an excellent example for you in Abraham and those with him, __when they said__ to their people: "__Verily, we are free from you and whatever you worship besides Allâh, we have rejected you__, and there has started __between us and you, hostility and hatred for ever__, until you believe in Allâh Alone.*" so that wasn't "just Abraham" pbuh saying that, the non-prophet followers of Abraham pbuh said that then and say it now. They didn't simply say "*We just reject and hate your religion*", they included the disbelievers in the category of what they rejected and hated as well. Abraham pbuh made little distinction between idolatry and idolaters, in fact when you actually think about it the idolaters are worse than the idols themselves because most idols aren't capable of doing idolatry or any other sin. So to ever hate an idol you have to hate the idolater even more. Most idols are innocent. While the specific conversations Abraham pbuh had with his father are reported in the Quran translations to have gone as follows: "*Abraham said to his father Azar: "Do you take idols as âlihâh (gods)? Verily, I see you and your people in manifest error.*" and elsewhere "*When he said to his father: "O my father! Why do you worship that which hears not, sees not and cannot avail you in anything? "O my father! Verily! there has come to me of knowledge that which came not unto you. So follow me. I will guide you to a Straight Path. "O my father! Worship not Satan. Verily! Satan has been a rebel against the Most Gracious (Allâh) "O my father! Verily! I fear lest a torment from the Most Gracious (Allâh) should overtake you, so that you*

become a companion of Satan (in the Hell-fire)." He (the father) said:
"Do you reject my gods, O Abraham? If you stop not (this), I will indeed
stone you(to death). So get away from me safely (before I kill you)."
Now realistically was Abraham pbuh being hateful to his father?
Yes but he was polite too and expressed deep care and concern yet
still even Abraham pbuh himself had his blood relations react in a
evil manner to his hate. However Abraham pbuh was not wrong
to express this hatred. It all depends on how and why you do it,
but people getting upset with it doesn't mean it's wrong or sinful
rather sometimes it's good and obligatory to preach in such a
manner. Likewise with the Jews who wanted to kill Jesus pbuh,
nobody dares to say that, "Well if Jesus pbuh wisely preached more
love and less hate then maybe they wouldn't have wanted to kill him so
much." To express hatred for disbelief AND disbelievers is part of
the prophetic way of preaching, if you don't do it at all then one
would not be preaching the prophetic way. Yet it's important to
stress this must be done with wisdom. "With wisdom" doesn't
mean that it's not to be done as some may claim under the guise of
wisdom, but that it's best to do it smartly. You can publicly
express hatred for disbelief and disbelievers without doing it in an
overtly offensive or reckless manner. Thus my hatred comes with
lots of context and reasons, and it's polite. You don't have to use
the word hatred to express your hatred, if you have a large
vocabulary you can say very hateful things in public and have
people smile at you even when they know you are expressing
hatred because you use clean words when doing it. It's not that
hatred is offensive in itself, most of the times its vulgarity that's
offensive. You don't have to be vulgar or crude and the prophets
weren't. With most people in person I don't even explicitly state I
hate them, but imply how "There is only 1 true religion and God
would hate all who aren't following it, so if Me and You are upon
different religions then God must hate at least one of us. While if we

believe in God we must hate who God hates, thus one of us or both of us should change our religion for the true one so that God can love us both and we are both on the road to paradise. " Then I can have a genuine religious conversation with the person who knows I hate them because I think they are disbelievers, but I still care about them and want us to be on the same team to go to paradise with them, whereupon I believe Islam is God's only team and that their team is that of the devil. It also lets them know that I know they hate me for being upon a different religion, Islam, and it's expected/normal for them to hate me for that reason and they need not hide it or pretend that they don't. That's what I call hate preaching and most people have no issues with this at all and appreciate the honesty, unless they don't believe in the fundamental concept that only 1 religion is true. In that case then we can discuss/debate/prove that on the spot. So this is what I consider to be the prophetic hate preaching. The faith of equality and freedom forbid and oppose this type of hate preaching because those are false faiths which get refuted by it. So if people don't like this type of preaching it's due to their religion, and any such religion is an evil religion that will lead them to hell. It's actually a part of faith to hate as reported in a Saheeh hadith in At-Tabaraani's collection wherein Muhammad pbuh said what means: *"The strongest bonds of faith are allegiance for the sake of Allah, enmity for the sake of Allah, love for the sake of Allah and hate for the sake of Allah."* Many modern people only count the allegiance and love parts forgetting that 50% of the "strongest bonds of faith" are enmity and hatred for the sake of Allah. Meaning to have faith in itself means you have to have enmity and hate, for the sake of Allah and Allah alone. Or that's what Islam teaches, in the past, present and forever regardless of what others desire. The reason people don't like the idea of hating people due to their religion is because they believe in freedom and want all to be treated equal.

Which is why they want everybody to love everybody and say it. However the Muslim is not equal to the non-Muslim, thus we cannot say we love both because then we would be equating them with each other. So for Muslims the potential harms of using the word "love" with non-Muslims outweighs the benefits. Thus if we can only use the word "love" with one, Muslims or non-Muslims then we say we love the Muslims and we don't love non-Muslims. To say we love both would be to give them affection and equal treatment and Muslims can't do that. Since the Quran says what means in 60:1,

"O you who believe! Take not My enemies and your enemies (i.e. disbelievers, polytheists, non-Muslims) as friends, showing affection towards them, while they have disbelieved in what has come to you of the truth"

Is not saying "I love you" showing them affection? Friends don't say they love each other and friendship between Muslims and non-Muslims is forbidden, since it denotes love, leads to displays of affection and religious influence. So if Muslims can't take them as friends how then can Muslims say "I love you" to disbelievers when friends don't even say that to each other? Furthermore in the Quran verse of 4:89 it enumerates why the disbelievers yearn for the Muslims to tell them we love them:

They wish that you reject Faith, as they have rejected (Faith), and thus that you all become equal (like one another)

The salaf would say that the kings of the disbelievers would fight us for the love we have for each other if they only knew what it was like. Thus how can a Muslim ever possibly say "I love non-Muslims" when the salaf said they would fight us in order to get that love. Kafirs have not gotten that love through fighting for it. Thus why would we say we have love for them?

What have they done to get it? Say the shahada? Or do they drop bombs on the Muslims, slander Jesus pbuh, reject Muhammad pbuh, Islam and the Quran and persist in disbelief? The disbelievers in the past treated Muhammad pbuh better than they treat us today yet he didn't say he loved them, using the same word as he used for expressing his love for Muslims. In fact in the Sahih Bukhari and Sahih Muslim collections of authentic hadith they both reported on the authority of Amr ibn Al-Aas that he said: "*I heard the Prophet say publicly, not in secret.* "*Verily the family of so and so are not of my awliya-referring to one group among his relatives* (Note: awliya means: those who are close, beloved, allied with, or closely related by blood) *My awliyya are none other than Allah and the righteous believers.*" Thus Muhammad pbuh himself said publicly how his own relatives are not loved by him but only God and "the righteous believers are", note he didn't say "all Muslims are loved by me" because some Muslims sin and it's obligatory to hate sinners even if they are Muslims and such hatred cannot exist for an awliyya. Yet the point is Muhammad pbuh publicly disavowed his own family stressing that he cared about those who belonged to his religion more than his own blood relatives. So why should Muslims today say the word "love" for our attitude towards disbelievers when Muhammad pbuh explicitly publicly said he didn't have "love" for his non-Muslim relatives? Is it because it's the common thing to do? Well Muslims don't imitate disbelievers or the phrases they say to each other to express their feelings for each other. First they get us to say the word "love" on the tongue. Then they get us to show "love" in our actions. Then we have love for them in our heart. Then we follow them into the hole of a lizard, just as Muhammad pbuh prophesied Muslims would do. Then we follow them into the hellfire. Then we say if only we had listened to or understood or followed those strict Muslims preaching hatred and forbidding love for non-Muslims then we would not then have been in the hellfire. Then we beg to be sent back to earth so we can be amongst the good doers who preached intolerance, realizing that had we been amongst the Muslims in dar al islam we would not have fallen into this trap of Shaitan about loving kuffar that led us into haraam and disbelief. This is why Muhammad pbuh said how Muslims should not dwell amongst disbelievers and their campfires should not be visible to us, because he knew this type of stuff would afflict and confuse us blurring the lines. Today Muslims might not really "love" the kuffar when they say it, but what about the next generation? Will they know what was meant when the word "love" was used? Or will it be just like the statues the forefathers of Noah pbuh made that turned into idols and Satan will say *"No those Muslims really did love the disbelievers, it's not right to hate them. Everyone is human, hatred is not part of Islam even if they don't believe in your religion. God doesn't hate non-Muslims, why do you?"* For the next generation Satan will tell them *"You see even your parents knew God doesn't hate non-Muslims and everyone goes to paradise, so there is no need for offensive Jihad. Only fight against people who believe in violence."* Then for the next generation Satan will come and say *"Well the bible says you gotta be Christian or you go to hell, so to be safe you better become Christian since Islam teaches love for everybody but since the other religions don't it'd be best for you if you converted to a different religion. Afterall it's because God loves everybody that his son/himself died on the cross for your salvation."* Then the next generation of people launch a crusade against the Muslims to kill them and convert them to kufr. Sadly this happens within 1 generation in America. That is how you get Muslims who join the US army to fight in Afghanistan and kill innocent Muslims, because they started saying they "love" non-Muslims until they ended up fighting for them against Muslims despite claiming to be Muslims themselves.

While other Muslims don't shoot or kill any Muslims on behalf of non-Muslims, they merely buy the gun by paying taxes and falsely claim patriotism is part of Islam. Patriotism is forbidden in Islam. Muslims don't have "love of country" we only love what/who God loves, for God's sake. Love or hate for any country has nothing to do with you, your location, history, economics, politics, family or geography, it's all about God.

When Umar became a Muslim, Muhammad pbuh had been preaching for nearly 7 years yet after all that time, there were only 39 Muslims and Umar made it 40. Due to the animosity and persecution, that was the result of the enmity Muhammad pbuh expressed for idolatry and idolaters, the Muslims didn't even meet in public and they would go out into the desert to pray in secret so their families wouldn't catch them praying in their houses and hurt them. The persecution was so rough that 2 years before Umar became Muslim, 10 Muslim men and 4 or 5 Muslim women left Mecca to go live in Abyssinia. So although Umar is reported to have been Muslim #40, when he became a Muslim there were only about 25 Muslims in all of Mecca. Yet Umar was not the type to pray and meet in secret like the other 25, he was too bold to live as a coward and thought Muslims should preach Islam in public regardless of the consequences. To Umar since idolatry was wrong he saw nothing wrong with publicly denouncing it along with idolaters, despite having himself mercilessly tortured Muslims for years for having done that very thing in private which he now advocated doing in public. Ibn Abi Jabir reported that Jabir said Umar himself stated in regards to his desire to publicize Islam , '*My sister's time to give birth came to her at night so I went out of the house, and entered the precincts of the Ka`bah. Then the Prophet, may Allah bless him and grant him peace, came and entered the hijr (the low-walled, semi-circular area to one end of the Ka`bah) and on him there were two rough cloths. He prayed to Allah as much as Allah* *willed, then he turned away and I heard something I had not heard the like of. He went out and I followed him and he said, "Who is this?" I said, "`Umar." He said, "`Umar, will you not leave me alone, either by night or by day?" I became afraid that he might supplicate against me, so I said, "I witness that there is no god but Allah and that you are the Messenger of Allah." He said, "`Umar, keep it secret." I said, "No, by the One Who sent you with the truth, I will openly declare it just as I openly declared idolatry."'* Then as a brand new Muslim, Umar debated with Muhammad pbuh asking why they don't pray in public refuting and rebuking idolatry and the idolaters. Umar said: *"O Messenger of Allah, are we not on the truth whether we live or die? "*Muhammad pbuh said: *"Yes, by the one is whose hand my soul is you are following the truth whether you live or die."* Umar said: *"So why should we hide? By the one who sent you we should go out (and preach openly)."* After that Muhammad pbuh received revelation that it was time to stop being secretive and practice Islam in public trusting in Allah facing the persecution head-on altogether rather than trying to hide from it, since the limits of private/secretive preaching had been reached. This would happen from time to time with Umar, in that Umar would have a position that all the other Muslims might disagree with but then Allah would reveal that Umar was right. Umar wasn't always right but he did have a knack of being right when in the minority opinion and then Allah would confirm his position to be correct when people disagreed with him. Prior to this the hatred for disbelief and disbelievers was publicly expressed by Muhammad pbuh and others but many Muslims kept their faith and enmity for disbelief and disbelievers a secret to avoid persecution. The fact that even before Umar public hate preaching took place is evident by the conversation the Quraish had with Abu Talib and his subsequent request to get Muhammad pbuh to stop offending them. The Quraish had went to Muhammad's uncle Abu Talib and told him, "*Verily, your nephew has offended us both in our places of gathering and in our masjid, so prevent him from continuing to do so.*" So Abu Talib went to Muhammad pbuh and told him, "*Verily, these cousins of yours claim that you are offending them in their masjid and places of gathering so desist from harming them.*" Then it's reported that Muhammad pbuh asked Abu Talib if he could see the sun, after he said yes then Muhammad pbuh said, "*By Allah, I am not more able to abandon what I have been sent with than for someone to (reach up and) light a torch from this sun.*" Afterwhich Abu Talib declared that his nephew has never lied and told the Quraish to return because he could not and would not stop Muhammad pbuh from teaching Islam and hatred for all other faiths and disbelievers. The issue Umar brought up was not whether Muslims should or shouldn't express public enmity, it was whether all of them should do it or not. Umar thought they all should and Muhammad pbuh initially disagreed until revelation came from Allah ordering all to unite in public under Islam regardless of what happened as a result. Why didn't the Muslims maintain a "low profile" when they were hated/persecuted and there were only 25 Muslims in Mecca? Because Umar said Muslims are on the truth and cannot hide it or be afraid to publicly tell disbelievers their whole way of life is wrong and Allah confirmed that was the right approach thus showing that it is the right approach to take today. The years before that the prophet's mission was kept secret because if he failed then it would be game over forever, not because it's right to be non-confrontational. At that time, for them it was just too big of a risk when they had to start from literally 1 person. Yet once 40 Muslims existed in the world public confrontational preaching in the face of persecution was ordained by Allah himself even though most Muslims aside from Umar were averse to it. Umar knew the results such public preaching would have, experienced the results and still told the truth. Ever since then Muslim men have prayed in masjids publicly on a daily basis, except in modern day places where some Muslim men voluntarily oppress themselves by not praying in the masjids. Even though in Mecca with severe persecution the Muslims prayed their prayers in the masjid together. Prayer in the masjid gave the Muslims strength to express disavowal and do great dawah, whenever the prayer of the Muslims in the masjids declines or becomes unhealthy their disavowal declines and their dawah becomes sickly. After Muslims started practicing Islam in public without fear many may assume things got easier for them. However the persecution they suffered while "keeping a low profile" only increased after they went public. Of course, we know how it turned out in the end but when Umar suggested they go public it actually increased the persecution the Muslims suffered under and it got more intense. So the happy ending came a lot later. Due to the increased persecution after the public preaching began more Muslims from Mecca had to join the others in Abyssinia, so during the 2nd migration to Abyssinia 64 or 65 Muslim men and 18 Muslim women migrated from Mecca to Abyssinia who would not reunite with the Muslims of Mecca again until after the 98 Muslim men (25 from Mecca and 73 from Medinah) established an Islamic state in Medinah. Thus the required numbers for things are known. When the Ummah of Muhammad pbuh had 110 Muslims in one place they established a Khilafah, with 40 Muslims in the world they all preached the bold confrontational truth publicly. Yet since our Muslims today are of a different quality and worldly conditions are different, we likely need more than 110 Muslims to establish a Khilafah. However we certainly don't need more than 40 Muslims in the world to start preaching the hateful confrontational truth publicly because the prophets in the past did it with just 1. As a nation Muslims can technically only use an excuse to be secretive about Islam IF there are less than 40 Muslims in the world. Since there are more than 40 Muslims today then as a nation we should be telling the world the truth of Islam and God's love for Muslims and the falsehood of all else and God's hatred for non-Muslims. But collectively this is not being done because this truth is seen as "risky or radical", thus some spread misconceptions about religion and Islam in the name of Islam thinking and claiming they are preaching the way the prophets did when they aren't. Some are preaching the prophetic way, but the majority of individual Muslims are not, either because of fear or ignorance or inability. Now keep in mind there is a way to tell such a prophetic truth, but the prophetic truth will always be hard for non-Muslims to handle anyway you tell it. Non-Muslims didn't even like the way the prophets told them about Islam, and they were prophets who were much better at politely preaching to people than we can ever be. Therefore no matter how you tell it, you will probably get negative feedback and if you don't then either that's because Allah protected you or you diluted it. All prophets got abused for telling the truth of their faith, if Muslims today don't get persecuted or criticized then one must really wonder why. The majority of those who didn't believe in the prophets hated them, so if disbelievers don't hate Muslims today then maybe they don't really share Islam with them the prophetic way. One can never tell the truth or share Islam for any other reason than pleasing Allah. If dawah is done to make friends then it's wrong, if it's done for political reasons then it's wrong, if it's done for money then it's wrong, if done for "love" then it's definitely wrong, it can only be done to please Allah or else the intention and reward for it is spoiled. And I really do mean that you cannot preach for "love". I myself have seen Muslims go astray and I didn't tell them despite my love for them, because love is not enough to make me tell someone they

are wrong. I even decided that I'd just let my own Muslim brother
burn in hell because I could not bring myself to tell them they
were wrong, until I realized God wanted me to and that's why I
eventually corrected them not due to love but because it's what
God desires and commands one to do. Correct people in this life
or God will correct you in the next life. So the concept that people
claim to preach Islam to non-Muslims because of "love" is false, I
can't even preach Islam to Muslims because of love. Thus it's
impossible for a Muslim to preach Islam to a non-Muslim due to
care for them, they might try but it won't be sincere or pleasing to
God. Only preach due to love of God not because of care for
people. Yet modernists will quote a verse that says how Allah
told Muhammad pbuh *"You cannot guide whom you love."* But this
verse was revealed after Abu Talib died as a disbeliever and
referred to the love Muhammad pbuh had for the idea that his
uncle would become a Muslim, and the "love" is not the arabic
"wilaya" type of love but the type which is more properly
translated into english as "like". Meaning that "You can't guide
who you like." denoting that God guides or doesn't guide people
without it having to do with how much Muhammad pbuh would
like them to be guided. The prophets can only guide those who
God likes to be guided and that's all, otherwise people could be
unjustly favored due to having personal preference from the
prophets or believers, if such were the case then prophets could've
practiced nepotism with religious guidance. But they didn't and
couldn't because Allah said what means "You can't guide who you
like." Guidance is only due to the decree of the Creator. My point
is when speaking Muslims cannot be afraid of the consequences of
telling the truth as it is nor can they sinfully compromise Islamic
beliefs or systems. We don't compromise our faith or our
prophetic methodology for anybody. We don't surrender to
worldly interests we only surrender to the Creator of the world.

The example of Umar, Bilal, Abu Bakr, Abu Dharr and many others shows how the companions of Muhammad pbuh acted while brutally persecuted in Mecca, they didn't use their minority status as an excuse to be cowards or dilute their hate for kufr and kafirs. And that's the main ploy peaceful extremists use today by saying *"We're a minority in the West, so we have to be extra nice and not offend non-Muslims or push for Shariah just like how it was in Mecca."* Whereas #1 Muslims were less than 2% of the population when the Islamic State was established in Medinah, so it's actually a Sunnah to establish Shariah as a minority. Plus the Muslims eventually left Mecca, they didn't live there forever or raise their children there which is contrary to what the extremists today say about the whole "like in Mecca" minority lifestyle. Thus the minority excuse is false, also the *"Meccan dawah method"* excuse is false. If you really want to look at how Muslims preached Islam in Mecca then examine the life of Umayr bin Wahb who became a Muslim in Medinah after the battle of Badr. Umayr didn't stay in Medinah long, even though it was the Islamic State at that time, he went back to Mecca to tell every single disbeliever that he became a Muslim and that their beliefs were false, wrong and evil and that they should accept Islam as he did. He got the worst persecution because he did this in Mecca after the Muslims had left it and went to Medinah and had been victorious against the Meccans in battle. Also Umayr was hired as an assassin to kill Muhammad pbuh and he vowed to do so, thus for him to return to Mecca as a Muslim and preach Islam constituted a literal traitor coming back to preach treason. So if anyone ever uses the excuse of how being a minority in a unislamic non-Muslim land then Muslims have to "tone it down", Umayr bin Wahb did not tone it down to please the disbelievers or make life easier for himself as a minority amongst a non-Muslim majority in a non-Muslim land that was actively at war with Muhammad pbuh. Umayr bin

Wahb preached without fear publicly when he was a bigger minority than the Muslims were before the Hijra. He was almost the only Muslim in the city and he'd get beat for telling people to accept Islam, and guess what? The prophet Muhammad pbuh approved of him preaching in Mecca and gave him permission to do so even though at the time Muslims were supposed to be in Medinah AND Mecca was in a state of war with the Muslims of Medinah. Umayr even told Muhammad pbuh he planned to "hate preach" in Mecca when he said: "*O Messenger of Allah, I used to strive hard to extinguish the light of Allah and I used to inflict a great deal of harm upon the adherants of Allah's religion. I would therefore love now for you to give me permission to go to Mecca, so that I can invite it's dwellers unto Allah, His Messenger, and Islam; perhaps Allah will guide them; __otherwise I will harm them in their religion__, just as I used to harm your Companions in their religion.*" Now what does it mean when somebody says "*Maybe God will guide them to become Muslims and if not I will harm them in their religion?*" That means if they don't become Muslim he will theologically attack their false unislamic faith and make it hard for them to keep believing in it to the extent that they don't believe in their false religion even if they persist in not accepting Islam. Or as USA president Barack Obama said to Christian ministers on Easter in 2016 CE, "*the intent of the terrorists, is to weaken our faith*". Basically the true Muslim's position is as such, "*Okay if you don't want to believe in Islam, you don't have to. Nobody can force you to. But I'm not going to let you believe in a false religion. I will peacefully attack every false religion until they are all destroyed and Islam is the only faith people practice. Theologically nobody will believe in any false religion with conviction as a result of Muslims thoroughly refuting all false religions to extinction. Muslims peacefully, if given the opportunity to do so, will exterminate all false religions through sincere prophetic preaching.*" So 100% of the Muslim world was literally at war with the pagans of Mecca and

Umayr was in their midst preaching hatred for idolatry and idolaters <u>as a minority</u> IN MECCA and guess what happened as a result? Lots of people became Muslims due to Umayr bin Wahb's hate preaching in Mecca. But then some modernists may say that's a special exception and "not the rule" however it is the rule and the same dawah was done before the Hijra as well, which is a reason why the Hijra took place. For example while in Mecca with only a few Muslim men in the city, while suffering persecution, Umar bin Khattab publicly confidently told all the disbelievers, "*Do what you think fit. By Allah, if we were 300 men we would leave this city (Mecca) to you, or else you would have to leave it to us!*" Thus in Mecca while getting violently persecuted, more than Muslims had ever been before, Umar was not afraid to tell it like it was and provocatively tell disbelievers they can do what they want and if there were only a few more Muslims they would either leave their country or take over. Is that type of statement "*politically wise*"? Well the same applies today. If Umar expressed public enmity for disbelief and disbelievers along with political desires for Shariah law then under those circumstances, when Islam truly could've been wiped out if just a few Muslims got killed, then how can Muslims in the West pretend Islam teaches something different and preach otherwise today? They can't, Islamically that is, some do but they are wrong because the command to express enmity for disbelief and disbelievers is not based on demographics or politico-socio-economic conditions it is a command from Allah in the Quran in the verses revealed in Mecca. So not a single Muslim can ever say it's wrong to publicly express enmity and disassociate from kufr and kafirs because Allah ordered it, it's obligatory and actually part of the shahada itself. To say that one believes there is nothing to be worshipped except Allah (God the Creator) and that Muhammad pbuh is his messenger is a statement of hatred for all types of disbelief and disbelievers. The people of Mecca knew this was a statement of hatred because they worshipped idols and knew what Muhammad pbuh and Islam was all about. That's why disbelievers in Mecca beat people up when they heard the shahada said, as they did both to Abu Bakr and Abu Dharr when they tried to say it in public. The reason many disbelievers today see nothing wrong with the shahada is because they don't understand what it means the way the disbelievers in Mecca during the time of Muhammad pbuh did, even if they know the translation of the arabic words. The shahada is a declaration of enmity to all non-Muslims and to all things anti-islamic, unislamic and sinful. It is fundamentally a political, economic, social and theological declaration of war. Non-Muslims used to understand this and so did most Muslims. When you say the shahada you are pledging allegiance to the army of Allah to struggle against the army of Satan until you die. In fact on the battlefields before fighting in Jihad Muslims would frequently begin by saying the Athan, which is the call to prayer which contains the shahada, because just like the shahada the call to prayer is a declaration of theological warfare on all kufr. So the "tolerance" disbelievers may display towards Muslims today is mainly due to ignorance, and so is their intolerance. When the non-Muslim arabs would hear the athan they didn't say "*Oh how nice and peaceful that sounds.*" They said "*How dare they say that in public! We can't let them get away with such open intolerance for our idolatry, idols and us! We must stop Islam now!*" A perfect example of this is the athan of Urwah ibn Masood Ath-Thaqafee. Urwah was a well respected leader of Taaif and after Arabia was nearly all conquered and/or choose to embrace Islam, the city Taaif was one of the last still upon idolatry. Urwah choose to become a Muslim and after doing so when it was time to pray he called the athan from on top of his house so any Muslims in the city whom he didn't know of, since he had just recently embraced Islam, could join him for prayer and so the people of Taaif would hear him calling them to Islam since that is what the athan is. The athan is a call to become Muslim and practice Islam. Remember despite their aversion to Islam the people of Taaif loved Urwah, he was a revered leader and celebrity. Yet when Urwah called the athan his people fired arrows at him and killed him. This was how Arabs in the time of Muhammad pbuh responded to hearing the same Athan which today non-Muslims say sounds so beautiful. The difference between the non-Muslims of the past and present is that the present ones don't know as much about Islam or what it means to/for them as much as past non-Muslims did. Simply put whether a non-Muslim loves or hates Islam/Muslims they are ignorant of Islam and Muslims. Thus in regards to expressing hatred for disbelief and disbelievers, Muslims must do it and only Allah can tell us to stop, and Allah has not told us that but instead told us that Islam will never be eliminated no matter what kind of opposition we come up against. Today we have a guarantee from Allah that Islam will remain, so we have no reason to hide and shy away from hatred for kufr or kafirs as those early Muslims did who did not have that guarantee. The reason Muslims in Mecca originally kept their faith secret wasn't because of fear for hardship but because they feared Islam would cease to exist if they got crushed at that time. In our times the main problem with people is they fail to understand only 1 religion is valid and God can only possibly love the members of 1 religion and automatically hates those of all the other religions. Those few who do understand this fact think it's wrong to say because they believe hatred is wrong. I'm not going to say they think hatred is wrong because if they were thinking they would know that hatred is natural, right and unavoidable. That's why when people tell me "I think hatred is not what God wants from us." In reply I tell them "*I don't think you are thinking*". Truly they really aren't thinking intelligently but are emotionally believing satanically. Now **some** Muslims could say the way a certain individual is expressing hatred is wrong and/or overboard but the expression /disassociation must still take place. To hate is not wrong! To express hatred is not wrong! To commit a sin is wrong. To hate is an obligatory part of believing in a religion, you cannot believe in a religion without hating some things and some types of people. Those who claim they do end up hating hatred and those who hate others or preach hatred as being part of religion. Therein lies the doctrinal bigotry and hypocrisy of the anti-hate pluralistic crew, in that they hate all types of haters, this makes them a hater themselves despite claiming to be lovers of all. However the question from an Islamic perspective cannot be "should hatred be expressed for disbelief and disbelievers" but only "how/when to express hatred". Whereas the main excuse hypocrites, zindiqs and disbelievers make to say Muslims in the West shouldn't express hatred is the mythical "Mecca vs. Medinah" motto. They'll say how in Medinah things changed once Muslims had political authority, so wait until Muslims are a majority or in authority before changing tunes to hateful. Their point being that Muslims must be nice and act as though they were in Mecca, but this argument is not founded on modern reality nor past history. Now in regards to Jihad globally we are in a Meccan like pre offensive Jihad era but that applies to violent warfare and not dawah. The hate preaching was taught in Mecca more than in Medinah and Muslims were actually kinder to disbelievers in Medinah because they had political authority. That's one clue exposing the falsity of the whole "Muslims must be extra kind and never hate while they are a minority" doctrine, because those who use this usually only and always use examples of Muslim interactions in Medinah and never the Meccan examples which they claim they get their "love preaching" method from. Or if they do use examples from Mecca they take them out of context, like the famous incident of camel guts being put on Muhammad's back pbuh where they don't mention the dua/curse he made afterwards, or they mention Bilal being tortured and don't say exactly why and they conveniently ignore other dawah stories like what Hamzah did when he became a Muslim in Mecca or things that Muhammad pbuh himself said to disbelievers in Mecca or Medinah. Frequently the "preach love posse" will use fabricated hadith like the false fable about Muhammad's Jewish neighbor who threw trash on him on a daily basis, to whom he was kind and then they converted. Yet Muhammad pbuh never had a Jewish or Christian neighbor, that story of extreme kindness is a false fable. It is true that people would throw garbage on the prophet Muhammad pbuh on a routine basis and he was patient with them, but this famous conversion story has no evidence to support it. Muhammad's two neighbors in Mecca were Abu Lahab and Uqba bin Abi Mu'eet; both pagans not Jews. In fact for centuries Jews and Christians were not even allowed to enter or live in Mecca because the pagan idolaters didn't want them preaching against idolatry in Mecca, so Jews and Christians were only allowed in Mecca as slaves. This "conversion story" could never have possibly happened. Unfortunately many Muslims use this fabricated conversion story to say how Muslims living among non-Muslims should be extra kind to non-Muslims and live in loving harmony celebrating their holidays and joining them in sin. But this is wrong. Muslims are kind, but we cannot join the disbelievers in sin and disbelief or pretend that they aren't on the road to hellfire. Islam teaches Muslims to hate all those who hate their Creator and don't worship him exclusively and accept all the prophets including Muhammad pbuh. That doesn't mean Muslims aren't kind and polite to disbelievers. Just as a Christian can never possibly love a

Jew because they reject the prophethood of Jesus pbuh, a Muslim can never love someone who doesn't accept the prophet Muhammad pbuh. It is obligatory for us to hate, but hate does not mean harm, in most instances it's actually forbidden to harm non-Muslims. Unfortunately some Muslims that have been westernized are reluctant to publicly teach or even privately think that Islam teaches hate for all non-Muslims is obligatory, based on the kind treatment the prophet Muhammad pbuh displayed and they use this famous false story as a reason for their unislamic position. There are true stories of kindness leading people to embrace Islam but most aren't kind enough to be used for "love preaching" so they don't get used or they get misused. When you consider any alleged "love preaching" in Medinah, because Jihad was going on simultaneously the hateful violent Jihad against non-Muslims puts any "love preaching" in context and the context contradicts the fundamental doctrines of the inter-faith love they want preached. They can't fool anybody into thinking Muslims preached love and tolerance at the same time they were fighting non-Muslims in battle explicitly because of Islamic reasons of intolerance and hatred. The historical context of the "love" coincides with organized state sponsored religious intolerance, warfare and hatred. Therefore that "love" wasn't really "love" as modern liberals understand and preach. In Medinah there were hypocrites and in Mecca there were no hypocrites. That's the real reason why many teach "love preaching like in Mecca". In Mecca Muslims preached hate much more than "love", but the love preachers have to try to keep the mindset of their audience on Mecca so that they forget hypocrites exist. This is because with a Meccan mentality Muslims don't worry about hypocrites pretending to be Muslims teaching unislamic things, because that never happened in Mecca since nobody was a hypocrite due to all the Muslims being persecuted. As a result of that Meccan period without hypocrites, the main hope modern hypocrites have of being undetected is to get people to imagine they are living in a society similar to how the Muslim society was in Mecca when 0 hypocrites preaching unislamic things in the name of Islam existed. However that "Meccan Dawah", whatever it was/is, can never ever be done by Muslims again for the simple fact that hypocrites have existed and infiltrated the Muslim ranks ever since Muhammad pbuh entered Medinah. Muslims can never ever preach Islam the way they initially did in Mecca because now we got hypocrites in our midst pretending to be Muslims, preaching their distorted hypocrisy to the masses both Muslim and non-Muslim alike. Hypocrites today tell the Muslims living in non-Muslim majority lands to preach love and not hate "like in Mecca", despite their flimsy reasoning for unislamic love preaching coming from out of context Medinah data, because they want Muslims to treat the hypocrites as if they weren't hypocrites but Muslims; so that way the hypocrites can destroy Islam from the inside without Muslims noticing it. The "anti-hate extremists" use the examples of the Medinah period where Shariah was established to say Muslims today living in dar al-kufr without Shariah should act lovingly like that, and then they falsely claim that's how Muslims acted while in Mecca as a minority without Shariah. It's a complete deception and falsehood against the true prophetic hateful dawah method used in Mecca, which is to be done by Muslims whenever they are in dar al-kufr. As a minority group Muslims are more vocal in opposing falsehood and expressing hatred because they have to be in order to make the message of Islam known. Nobody pays attention to a love-preaching minority, but an intolerant minority gets attention. The Muslims stopped being secretive about their Islamic faith and it's doctrines in Mecca when there were 40 Muslims in the world, while within in Mecca there were only 25 Muslims when they all publicly expressed hatred for disbelief and disbelievers. Yet today we don't need 25 Muslims in one place before preaching the full undiluted message of Islam because Allah has promised to preserve Islam. So we have no good reason to hide any type of provocative controversial confrontational doctrines which Islam teaches. The mercy of Muhammad pbuh was emphasized most in Medinah, not Mecca, because in Mecca the Muslims couldn't really retaliate; so to display mercy in Mecca didn't actually mean anything. To show mercy is not to be patient under persecution but to restrain oneself when having physical power and authority to punish or harm others. You have to have power to show mercy, persecuted people cannot show mercy until they get power and the ability to persecute their former persecutors. Persecuted people can only show patience, it is only after they get power that mercy can be displayed. Basically Islam teaches Muslims to talk real tough when we are a minority and when we are the majority or in authority then we show mercy. Muslims display polite kind patience as a weak minority, and display mercy when a powerful authority. Hatred is not incompatible with kindness, politeness or mercy. To disbelievers it is incompatible because their religions don't teach God's rules on how to hate. The only good type of hatred is the Islamic hatred, any hatred a disbeliever may have is sinful because it's not for the sake of their Creator nor is it appropriately acted or not acted upon. The disbelievers can do what they think fit and we will either leave their nations or establish Shariah in their nations, but they should know disbelievers will not be running the world for long and God hates their beliefs and deeds which will lead them to hell if they don't choose Islam. Meaning Muslims believe that as long as someone lives without Islam then something is wrong with them, and if they are living without Islam as a result of their voluntary choice then Muslims would hate them because of that.

Now that previous sentence and the following two are a prime example of something a Muslim can politely say to a disbeliever to communicate hatred without any type of negative reactions. It's simply a fundamental religious doctrine to hate everyone who doesn't belong to your religion because they don't belong to your religion. If someone finds that offensive then they have a problem with religion itself and only find it offensive because their false religious beliefs teach something different. I must declare though as a important disclaimer that it is not allowed for Muslims to take senseless measures which will jeopardize the safety and security of their families, other Muslims and themselves putting the Muslim community in a position of vulnerability in front of disbelievers, by say unilaterally declaring military wars from their basements, or acting as violent vigilantes against drug traffickers, thieves, magicians, adulterers, drunks and sodomites. Yet this disclaimer for prophetic hatred also does not mean that Muslims must be accommodating or tolerant of the disbelievers' religions and customs. It's like how in a military battle you hate the enemy but use calm precision and not blind emotional fury. Muslims cannot allow their hatred for kufr or kafirs compromise their Jihad nor their Dawah. A Muslim is only rude or impolite to kafirs on the theological battlefield if it helps them to achieve victory or must be done to defend Islam and/or to separate from the enemy so as to avoid friendship with the enemy that will lead to theological vulnerability and/or sins. Always remember it is not a crime or sin to hate someone or publicly say you hate someone for religious reasons. And if it is a alleged to be a crime in the land you live in then you should move to a different land. The Muslims living in non-Muslim majority lands today should just mind their own business, and deal with all people professionally with fairness and justice for worldly matters like trade transactions with those disbelievers who are not hostile to

Muslims; and plan their move. Muslims can be nice to non-hostile disbelievers for the sake of dawah without humbling themselves before them, and they should be nice. Muslims can also express hatred without it harming their worldly affairs as Abdullah ibn Rawahah told the Jews of Khaibar when collecting Jizya from them "*My hatred for you and my love for the Prophet will not make me act unjustly towards you.*" (This statement of Abdullah's shows Muhammad pbuh approved of the public expression of "hatred" for non-Muslims because Abdullah ibn Rawahah was appointed by him to handle this transaction and he did it every year despite expressing hate. Why? Because he was just. Justice and Hatred are compatible. Anyone who claims Muslims can't hate and be just is just a fool.) Muslims should never humble themselves in front of disbelief or disbelievers, by honoring their religions and religious symbols, books, flags, logos, artifacts and festivities or pretending they aren't disbelievers hated by God and on the road to hellfire. To display public enmity is obligatory for Muslims, to have hate in the heart for disbelief and disbelievers is not enough to complete one's faith. It's an individual responsibility for every Muslim, it's not something for only the community to do, every Muslim must do it to some extent. Whereas if an individual Muslim can't do this in public then they shouldn't mix with disbelievers as isolation would be better than corruption. If one is weak in faith it is better for them to be awkwardly silent around non-Muslims than to cozy up to them and fail to express enmity and share the truth of Islam. People may disagree on my vocabulary and insistence on using the word "hate" but the fundamental concept/attitude must be publicly expressed, even if a Muslim doesn't want to use the word "hate" they must convey the meaning/message in some way and are forbidden to convey directly or indirectly, intentionally or unintentionally the meaning/message of "love" for kufr or kafirs of any type. Unless

it's due to a strategy of military warfare or literal survival, then a Muslim can let a non-Muslim think they love them or that the Muslims don't hate them due to religion. The Shahada is a verbal statement but it is lived as well as said, testifying to the truth means testifying to the distinction in disposition towards those upon the truth and those upon falsehood. If you give an impression that the truthful are equal to the liars this is not a life that is a testimony to the truth that nothing has the right to be worshipped except Allah and that Muhammad pbuh is his final messenger. Those who are truly upon the truth never let liars think they tolerate lies nor liars, even if they don't say they don't. Whenever expressing hatred for non-Muslims I'd rather have a non-Muslim think I hate them more than I actually do than for them to think I like them or love them (God forbid), unless there was a legitimate tactical benefit in letting them think otherwise. Even secular thinkers concur with the notion that "It's better to be feared than loved." Which in modern vocabulary means:
"It's better for them to think you are a crazy extremely hateful radical terrorist, than for them to think you love them." Tis safer for kafirs to persecute you than to have them pamper or be pleased with you. The belief that one can just keep their hate in their heart and never show it is a part of the heresy called Irja developed by the Murjiah, where they say the actions need not reflect the hatred and "it's what's in the heart that matters". Whereas the heart controls the rest of the body, good hearts lead to good deeds while bad hearts lead to bad deeds. Good hearts don't accompany bad deeds. Irja is such a grave misguided heresy that the one who states *"I do not take non-Muslims as enemies"*, or if they take them as enemies but don't declare them to be disbelievers, is not Muslim. It is disbelief in Islam to consider any type of non-Muslims to be believers. It's agreed upon by the consensus of all Muslim scholars and lay Muslims that to think any type of non-Muslim

(including Jews and Christians) could be a believer is to disbelieve in Islam. One cannot believe in the shahada and also think anyone can believe in God and not be a Muslim at the same time. The idea that *"Only God can judge. People can't say who goes to paradise or hell and nobody has a monopoly on salvation."* originated with the Murjiah. Originally the doctrine came about in response to the excessive Takfiri doctrine of the renegade Khwarij during the Ummayyad era. But at that time the Murjiah doctrine entailed *"All Muslims go to paradise, as long as they say the Shahada then we can't judge them or say they are disbelievers no matter what else they say or do."* The Arabic word Murjiah basically means "one who postpones" and this deviant non-Muslim unislamic sect was called the Murjiah because their doctrine was to postpone judgement on other self-proclaimed Muslims, by refusing to make takfir of hypocrites. Yet still the Murjiah, as well as all other non-Muslim unislamic sects like the Shia or Khwarij, altogether agreed that all non-Muslims go to hell. Everyone agreed, even the non-Muslim unislamic poser Muslim sects agreed that Islam teaches all of the non-Muslims go to hell. For thousands of years there was no other opinion within any Muslim or fake Muslim group. But then a doctrine of equality, freedom and tolerance started becoming popular in the world and people thought if only one type of religion is true and only it's adherents go to paradise then they can't be equal to those who have a false faith and will go to hell. Then there was a problem between religion and the doctrine of equality on which democracy and freedom relate to and base their political and social systems on. So in order for the governments to remain politically legitimate the doctrine of equality had to be reconciled with or conquer the religious inequality doctrines. Hence a new religion called Pluralism was created where the idea is that "the road to paradise is not one, but plural". Yet this religion of pluralism is not new, most of the pagans believed it.

Pluralism is the modern version of the Pagan policy towards multiple religions, yet the vast majority has no idea pluralism is a religion and an even larger majority of pluralists don't know their religion is pluralism because this dilutionary doctrine has been incorporated into many faiths due to political pragmatism. Anyways pluralists started saying "Only God can Judge" just as the Murjiah used to say. Following suit in some sects of the neo-Murjiah and Modernists or Progressives have changed doctrines and now even refrain from labeling non-Muslims as disbelievers, despite Allah saying they are such in the Quran. The popular "Only God can judge" doctrine cannot be used to postpone takfir (labeling someone a disbeliever) because God has already judged and pronounced his judgement that certain beliefs, speech and actions make one a disbeliever on earth before death. You can't say *"Well they may be worshipping a Golden Calf but "only God can judge" I can't say they're disbelievers on the road to hell and that God hates them. Only God ever knows if they are good/evil."* Few today who see someone worshipping a golden cow would see that as fine, most would condemn it but what if the idolater said *"Only God can judge me and you aren't God! How dare you think/say God hates me for worshipping a golden cow!"* it would be ridiculous because we could reply by saying God already judged that which you are guilty of and made clear his hatred of what you are doing as well as his hatred for whoever does what you are doing. It's not about being God or human, it's about not being ignorant regarding what God loves and hates, commands and forbids. Remember when the Golden Calf was being worshipped by the Israelites some people refrained and the others who committed idolatry insisted that they couldn't be judged or condemned. Today people are even more astray than those who worshiped the Golden Calf yet similarly they expect the prophetic religion and its practitioners to tolerate them and refrain from denouncing them and their blasphemy and sins. Well it was wrong then to "not judge" the Israelites who sinned and committed disbelief and it will always be wrong not to judge or condemn those who are in error. The main reason many ignorant/arrogant people will say "Only God can judge" is because they think that means they have to wait until after dying before getting labeled, and believe in equality/freedom, but contrary to their hopes God has judged the living and the dead. At this time God has judged all living creatures regarding whether they believe in him or disbelieve or if they are righteous or otherwise, this judgement can change before the final judgment is pronounced on the Day of Judgment, or they die, but at this time everyone has been judged already. There is not a person alive who hasn't been judged by God. The only catch is the test of life isn't over for everybody so we can't say what the final judgement of most of those living today will be (aside from the antichrist or yajuj and majooj). Yet we do know the categories that are available and we know that everyone is currently in one category or the other or many. So we can see where people currently are in order to judge them as God has judged and how the prophets judged and taught us to judge. The prophets came to pass judgement on mankind before God judges mankind, so that way there are no surprises. Saying that "Only God can Judge" is like a criminal saying "Only the Judge can determine whether I committed a crime or not." which is a foolish statement to make because the law determines who the criminals are. The Judge doesn't judge if you are a criminal, the judge just passes the sentence so you can be justly punished. So a better saying is "Only God can Sentence". All the prophets of God told us that God has judged X categories as disbelievers and Z category as believers and that you gotta be in Z category if you want to go to paradise since all those who die in X category go to hell. (Except for rare exceptions where the person didn't have an opportunity to join Z category, but still they will have a special test prior to entering paradise, wherein they can join Z category or X category and prove themself.) Seriously a person cannot even become a Muslim if they think Christians, Jews or non-Muslims can go to heaven after they die. God has judged and told us who he loves and who he hates and who goes to paradise and who goes to hell. We might not know all the names or the final results but we can and should judge people according to how they are today based on what we know according only to God's criteria. The Quran says how anyone who has a religion other than Islam will never have it accepted by God or enter paradise. The verses in the Quran that refer to "**Some** of the people of the Book" believing concerns Muslims who used to be Jews or Christians like Abdullah bin Salam and Salman Farsi. That's why some of the verses dealing with "believing people of the book" in context mention prostrating and believing in the Quran because a "person of the book" was a type of cultural label as well as a religious classification. The verses of the Quran in 5:83-86 explains how Muhammad himself pbuh would see Christian "people of the Book" cry when they hear the Quran recited and hear them say *"Our Lord! We believe; so write us down among the witnesses."* *"And why should we not believe in Allah and in that which has come to us of the truth And we wish that our Lord will admit us along with the righteous people."* These verses word for word describe what Muslims said to Muhammad pbuh who had previously been Christians, and subsequently Allah says they'll go to paradise, yet verse 5:86 says those who don't believe in the Quran will go to hell. The meaning is simple and easily understood during Muhammad's time to refer to a "Christian" who became Muslim and will go to paradise, everyone knew it didn't refer to any of the non-Muslims going to paradise because the verse says those who don't believe in the Quran go to hell. Likewise verses 28:52-54 explicitly have a "person of the Book" saying they considered themselves Muslims even before they heard the Quran and became Muslim but just didn't know that the name for them was Muslim. So there are 2 explicit examples of "people of the book" who were Muslims but called a "person of the book" simply because they weren't an idolater turned Muslim but a Christian turned Muslim. A "person of the book" who became a Muslim in the time of Muhammad pbuh was still sometimes classified as a "person of the book" because of their past history of being one. This was to distinguish between those Muslims who used to be worshipping idols and those who used to be Jews/Christians. Both were disbelievers before being Muslim but a Jew or Christian is a different type of non-Muslim disbeliever than a polytheistic idol worshipper. They are a better type of disbeliever despite still being on the road to eternal hellfire. Likewise Christians are a better disbeliever than Jews because they accept Jesus pbuh as a prophet and Jews don't. Yet all are still non-Muslims disqualified from paradise. The point I'm making is that Muslims in Muhammad's time were occasionally still referred to as "person of the book" because of their past despite having become a Muslim. It's like how Jews today who become Muslims are still Jews, they're Muslim Jews and I've prayed with some. So that's where not every verse in the Quran referencing Jews/Christians is about non-Muslims, most of them are but a few of them aren't. Whereas the Quran verse of 2:62 that says how *"those who believe, and those who are Jews, and the Christians, and the Sabians, whoever believes in Allah and the Last day and does good, they shall have their reward from their Lord, and there is no fear for them, nor shall they grieve."* was revealed in reference to people inquiring whether people who lived and died before Muhammad pbuh came with his message would go to hell just because they didn't accept Muhammad pbuh as a prophet; since they died before his prophethood. Specifically

Salman al-Farsi, a former Christian, had asked Muhammad pbuh about other Christians he personally knew who lived and died before the prophethood of Muhammad pbuh saying: *"They used to pray, fast, and believe in you, and testify that you would be sent as a prophet."* and it was in response to Salman's question about those specific Christians that Allah revealed the verse of the Quran in 2:62. It was a specific question from a Christian turned Muslim asking Muhammad pbuh about dead Christians who told him they believed in a future prophet and told Salman where to find him but died before Muhammad pbuh was born or began his prophethood. Obviously that was a good question about technical Muslims who were Muslims too soon to be counted officially as Muslims by Muhammad pbuh. Thus the verse 2:62 was revealed about those "Christians" or whoever was like them. Nobody ever thought the verse of 2:62 meant non-Muslims, everyone knew it was about people living before the time of Muhammad pbuh or those who never heard of Muhammad pbuh. The problem today is Muslims who don't know the Tafsir of the Quran make false conclusions. Whereas had they read the Tafsir and the curses the authors of Tafsir make upon non-Muslims they'd never have such confusions. Verse 2:62 means that those who believed in Islam, and/or/as were Jews and Christians and Sabeans who believed in God correctly as they were supposed to during their lifetime without dying upon kufr or shirk during the time before Muhammad pbuh have nothing to fear and will be rewarded for their belief. It doesn't refer to most non-Muslims today. Likewise an alternate meaning of such verses is that everyone regardless of their religion gets rewarded for their good deeds if they meet the criteria for good deeds to be good deeds and need not fear missing out on rewards for deeds they do. Even disbelievers get rewarded for their "good deeds" but their reward is only in this life and that is it, they get no credit for their "good deeds" in paradise because disbelievers' good deeds don't merit them a higher spot in paradise, since they are disqualified from paradise. However non-Muslims who do good deeds do get a better spot in hell. So while good deeds can't earn paradise, they can improve one's home in hell. Thus no matter where you are going you should still do good deeds. Those verses do not mean everyone who "believes in God and the last day" go to paradise, it explicitly says they won't have to fear missing out on any rewards due to them for doing good. The "good non-Muslims" are simply working towards a better spot in eternal hell. That's not my interpretation that's the interpretation of the Quran itself, since a verse later revealed clarified the misunderstood verse of 2:62 when Allah said in 3:85 what means "*And whoever desires a religion other than Islam, it shall not be accepted from him, and in the hereafter he shall be one of the losers.*" So anyone who claims Islam or the Quran teaches that every good religious person goes to paradise even if they don't believe in Islam, is a liar and/or ignorant. The concept of Inter-faith pluralism was explored during Prophet Muhammad's lifetime and refuted as being incompatible with Islamic doctrine by Allah. Likewise Prophet Muhammad himself pbuh also explained this in detail as related in many authentic hadiths, two of which perfectly summarize the islamic position regarding modern non-Muslims and their chances of going to paradise. In Bukhari's authentic hadith collection Abu Hurairah is reported to have heard Prophet Muhammad pbuh say what means, "*Everyone of my nation will enter Paradise except those who refuse*". He was asked: "*Who will refuse?*" He (pbuh) said, "*Whoever obeys me, shall enter Paradise, and whosoever disobeys me, refuses to (enter Paradise)*". But who did Prophet Muhammad pbuh consider to be "his nation"? Everybody who exists after he became a prophet pbuh, since in the Quran verse of 7:185 Allah explicitly tells Muhammad pbuh, "*Say: O mankind! Indeed I have been sent to you all as the Messenger of God; to Whom belongs the dominion of the heavens and the earth. None has the right to be worshipped except Him; it is He who gives life and causes death. So believe in God and His Messenger - the Prophet who can neither read nor write - who believes in God and His Words. So follow the Messenger of God so that you may be rightly-guided."* Thus when Muhammad pbuh referred to "my nation" in the hadith about those who refuse to enter paradise he referred to anyone who refuses to obey his Islamic teachings, meaning non-Muslims as well as Muslims who refuse to obey his Islamic teachings, because to blatantly refuse to obey a prophet of God is to reject that prophet. For extra clarification in an authentic hadith in Sahih Muslim, Abu Hurairah reported that he heard Muhammad pbuh say, *"By Him in whose Hand is the life of Muhammad! There is no one from this nation, be he a Jew or a Christian, who hears of me and then dies without believing in the Message that I was sent with, except that he will be one of the Companions of the Hellfire. "* Whereas faith in any prophet means affirming that which he was sent with, as well as acceptance and submission to it. Without acceptance and submission to the prophet one does not believe in them, mere affirmation of the prophetic message is not enough. So there you have it. It's not even enough for a Christian or Jew to affirm Muhammad pbuh as a prophet of God and Islam as being a true religion, they have to personally accept it as their religion and submit to it and what it teaches in totality. Just saying you believe nobody has the right to be worshipped except God and that Muhammad pbuh is a Messenger of God is not enough to be a "believer", even though that's what the shahada translates to. One must accept the message and practice the religion as well. Just affirming the shahada on the tongue does not in itself make one a Muslim if they don't know what that shahada really means and don't intend to implement what the text of the shahada means. This is why one can never force someone to become a Muslim, because verbal utterances alone do not equal belief. Islam is not a religion with lipservice salvation, belief in Islam also requires intentions and actions. Is the position of Islam towards all the non-Muslims and their chances of paradise and their chances of hellfire not clear? Someone claiming to believe in God doesn't mean anything, that's just a statement. One proves they believe in God by being a Muslim, not by saying "I believe in God but I'm not a practicing Muslim.", God says that such a statement is false. So non-Muslims who claim they believe in God are wrong. They do indeed believe in something and call that something God, but they don't believe in God as God is, they believe in a lie/falsehood concocted by themselves or others. They don't believe in God, they believe in something they call God, but God is another thing entirely which they don't believe in due to their disobedience to God via disbelief in Islam and disobedience to the rules for life taught by Allah and his prophets. Whereas whoever bears enmity to God or an ally of God such as angels or prophets is thereby theologically at war with God. Thereby whoever contradicts a prophet of God is considered a theological enemy of God. Hence to disbelieve in any prophet of God is to be an enemy of God, thus if Muhammad pbuh is a prophet of God as Muslims believe then any who don't believe in his prophethood, as Allah and Muhammad pbuh defined belief in his prophethood, are theologically enemies of God. Whereas because of love for God, Muslims express hatred for who God hates and since disbelief in God is such a great offense then Muslims express hatred for all who disbelieve in God via disbelief in Islam. This means that theologically if you aren't a Muslim then you are by default an enemy of the Muslims. You might not be an enemy militarily and many people aren't, but theologically every non-Muslim is considered an enemy by Muslims. Or at least this is what Islam teaches. Is it intolerant of other religious faiths? Yes. God is intolerant of other religious faiths he didn't ordain. Did you really think God would tolerate a false faith that lies about him? In 2006 CE some jerk in school made a false religion about me called "Gregology" to be funny and wrote a "Holy Book of Greg" and everything. I did not tolerate that false faith and hated it and all who followed and preached it. Just because I didn't kill the kid on the spot didn't mean I thought Gregology was true or that I liked him or what he was doing. So if I told people I hated that false religion about me and that if people really liked me they wouldn't preach, believe or practice Gregology then imagine how intolerant God is when people believe, practice or preach false human-made religions about God. I was not friends with people who tolerated Gregology, nor was I friends with those who tolerated those who tolerated Gregology. Yet those preaching Gregology told people they were great friends with me and loved me and the Gregologist goons actually got people, who didn't know me, to sincerely believe that they were friends with me and that I liked them despite me clearly explicitly telling them Gregologists are my enemies and that the "Book of Greg" has nothing to do with me despite it being all about me. Sadly some people fail to understand that God is intolerant of people who don't follow the 1 religion his prophets taught. The Creator of everything is religiously intolerant and made hell for disbelievers who don't practice his 1 correctly attributed religion. All of God's prophets were also religiously intolerant as well. So believers are also intolerant of other religious faiths besides Islam, but as God allows some disbelievers time to live in comfort we also allow them time to live in comfort; yet we will let them know how God and we feel about them. Does that disrupt that comfort? Sometimes. It depends on the disbeliever, as well as how the Muslim conveys the message of hate to them. Frequently though someone who doesn't believe in

God reacts in an ungodly fashion through violence or persecution, thinking that somehow such reactions will prove God doesn't hate them. The tricky part is that those who do believe in God and thereby hate who God hates, and express this hatred as is their duty, sometimes cannot handle the reactions of the enemies of God. This is part of the reason for the emigration done by some Muslims to Abyssinia, because they couldn't express the public enmity in Mecca as was required of them due to the consequences being too much for them to bear. If it were permissible for Muslims to not publicly disavow then a concession would have been made for them so they didn't have to migrate, but it wasn't. Chapter 17 verse 110 of the Quran details how the Muslims were obliged to recite the Quran out loud so that it could be heard by Muslims and those disbelievers who wanted to hear it, but not so loud that the enemies of Islam would hear it since if the hateful verses of the Quran were heard by them then it would cause danger to the Muslim reciter. Yet the hateful verses of the Quran had to be recited out loud so that disbelievers could hear it, despite the danger that resulted from doing that in Mecca. Today most people's "voice of enmity" is too low or non-existant or has even been turned into a satanic "voice of love", while the radical extremist's "voice of enmity" is too loud. So the key is to hate preach at an appropriate level, not too loud and not too soft, a detectable level. This is because obligations such as expressing hatred for disbelief and disbelievers cannot be abandoned due to fear of the consequences, one can in certain circumstances neglect doing a permissible or recommended thing but not an obligatory thing that's obligatory for every individual. The prophets never concealed their enmity for disbelief or disbelievers. However the disavowal need not be publicly expressed to every single disbeliever one meets, different types of non-Muslims deserve different types of disavowal. You can kindly politely tell someone

God hates them with concern, you shouldn't loudly shout it at them with a scary face. Islam teaches that people who are nice or indifferent to Muslims get treated with "nice polite hatred". An example of this is how the Muslims treated Abu Talib. Abu Talib was not neutral, he was actually pro-Muhammad pbuh, yet despite his kindness Muslims did not befriend him or cozy up and show him love. Rather they let him know they could never love him until he became a Muslim. Also regarding the kind protection which Abu Talib provided to Muhammad pbuh in Mecca, Muhammad pbuh never asked for his protection or help. He accepted it on his own terms after his uncle offered it to him. Muhammad pbuh never asked for aid or cooperation from Abu Talib and did not let Abu Talib influence him or his message at all, he didn't care what Abu Talib thought of his message and didn't tone it down due to his relationship with Abu Talib nor due to Abu Talib providing protection. Regarding Abu Talib, the Muslims let him know they hated him without explicitly saying it, by saying they hated idolaters; since Abu Talib was an idolater he knew where he stood in the Muslim viewpoint. Thus if say you know a Christian you don't have to say "I hate you" you could just let them know you hate Christians thereby you make it clear that if they choose to be in that category then that's how you feel about them without ever actually saying it to/about them directly, if you fear doing so. The example of Muhammad pbuh and his interactions with Abu Talib show how Muslims don't ask for protection/aid/alliances with non-Muslims. If they want to aid or protect us from the enemies of Islam then we can accept it but only as long as we don't compromise ourselves or our faith. So despite hatred for non-Muslims, Muslims and disbelievers can still cooperate as long as it's on Islamic terms. Muslims are forbidden to have a cooperation built on mutual compromise, democracy, equality or religious tolerance with non-Muslims, but we can work together for social good if non-Muslims just want to assist us in an islamically permissible manner, without causing us to neglect or relax anything our religion enjoins upon us or forbids us from. We can and will work together for good, but if we do then we are going to dictate how we work together, not the disbeliever. Sadly most of the types of Muslim and non-Muslim cooperation in the world today involves a compromise of Islamic beliefs, conduct or attitudes; particularly regarding the belief that there is only 1 true religion and that Muslims hate and express hatred for all who aren't upon Islam. Yet it is ever important to stress that with most non-Muslims you never ever actually have to say the words "I hate you until you become Muslim." One can be a "friendly theological enemy" and the non-Muslims will understand from your speech and tone that the religious differences create barriers and limits to the feelings/relationship you can have for/with them. They may not like it but they cannot argue with the concept that "If Islam is true then God hates me because I'm not Muslim and Muslims would hate me for the same reason." They may disagree with Islam, but they can't disagree with or refute the concept of hate for all non-Muslims if one believes that Islam were the only true religion. Hating all of the non-Muslims doesn't mean you aren't friendly to them, but it does mean you will never be their friend unless they change their religion to Islam. We can work together, study together or play together but we can never be friends when we don't worship the same God and pray together. There are clear boundaries which God has ordained. When interacting with a typical non-Muslim first you start with hatred for falsehood in general, then hate for their personal false doctrines subtly then openly/directly, if they persist upon falsehood after proofs have been presented to them of their falsehood then you express enmity for them as well because they are choosing falsehood. Although keep in mind that choosing falsehood doesn't necessarily mean rejecting the truth, it can include not wanting to learn the truth as well. However with disbelievers who are hostile towards Muslims and/or Islam, Muslims must hold them in maximum possible contempt and be as harsh as they possibly can while staying within the legal terms of the treaties and protocols of civil engagement. For example if I met George Bush or Barack Obama I would treat them very differently than I do my mother and would not be kind with either of them, but I wouldn't break the law or anything. Islam means justice in every aspect of life, so despite enmity and disavowal being obligatory, Muslims must never be unjust or allow their hatred to cause them to be unjust or unkind with those they are supposed to be kind to. This is because Islam teaches that Muslims have to establish justice for all and if they fail to do that then earth will have no justice at all. So while hatred and public disavowal for all types of disbelief and all types of disbelievers is an obligatory part of Islam, treating everyone (even hostile oppressive enemies of Islam) with justice is also an obligatory part of Islam. Hatred does not and must not compromise one's duty to justice. Muslims cannot be unjust just because Islam teaches them to hate all non-Muslims. Yet they cannot compromise that hatred or the public expression thereof either, even if it's compromised in the name of "Islamic kindness/mercy/justice". Why then are the majority of Muslim minorities in unislamic lands today reluctant to say as Umar bin Khattab told the disbelievers of his residence? It's not because Umar was wrong and they are wiser, Umar was better and wiser than all the Muslims today combined. The reason is that many Muslims today don't have the same type of faith that Umar or the other companions of Muhammad pbuh had and they are ignorant. So they come up with different solutions to problems which the prophet Muhammad pbuh and his companions taught us how to solve, by actually solving bigger problems in their own lifetimes. Seriously any Muslim who says "What's the solution?" is ignorant and needs knowledge. For instance for you or anybody else to solve the issues of the world 4 things are required: 1. Sincerity +Knowledge. 2. A blueprint to solve the problem. 3. The ability to follow the blueprint. 4. The means to take action and use the available abilities to fulfill the blueprint made based on the sincerity and knowledge. Fortunately God has given us the blueprint, and will give the ability and the means when it's time. The problem is people don't have the sincerity or the knowledge. The Quran and Sunnah actually contain a step by step blueprint to fix all the problems in the world today, unfortunately many Muslims don't know because they don't look at it and instead try thinking of their own blueprint. All Muslims have to do is step 1 but we don't and try going on to steps 2-4 thus causing more problems. Step 2 is already done for us and God will do step 3 and 4 if we just do step 1. The solution is literally just to do step 1. It's basic fundamental stuff. God sent Muslims his own book and it clearly details the answer, the problem is that many Muslims do know the answer but they don't know they have the answer or they don't like the answer because it's not the easy/fun answer. God never said the right answer to the test of life would be easy or fun or popular, in fact God explicitly said it would not be, yet it is best for us if we choose and implement the one right answer. What is that 1 right answer to all the problems Muslims have? Well frequently some Muslims preach the pillars of Islam in the name of Islam but the prophets preached Islam in the name of Allah because the 5 pillars are not all there is to Islam. The prophets preached the shahada to the fullest, which at the core fundamental level amounts to 1 meaning, "Total Submission" to the commands and desires of Allah as relayed by his prophet. All prophets taught people they have to become slaves of God. Slavery existed in most of those eras and people knew what a true slave who totally submitted was like in how they thought and lived. Those the prophets preached to knew of slaves who didn't have total submission and they knew of slaves who did. The human slaves may have changed the ways they submit to their human masters today, but God's slaves always submit the prophetic way according to the prophetic definition; til death.

Islam is about submitting to God as God sees fit, not as we see fit. The toughest thing to overcome is our own opinion of ourself. We tend to think that if we think God loves us then it's true or that if we think God hates us then it's true, but that's not how it works at all. Likewise the test of life isn't a numbers game about the quantity of good deeds one has, it's the quality that matters most. Another trap we tend to fall for is that we think we can continue living the way we are and march right into paradise. In reality we might have to change a few things about ourselves in order to enter paradise. The test of life is stressful but we must do whatever it takes to pass. God didn't promise mankind that passing the test of life would be easy, but he did promise that it's worth it and we can do it. What's certain, aside from our death, is that in order to enter paradise we have to believe what God wants, go where God wants us to go, stay where God wants us to stay, do what God wants us to do and don't do what God doesn't want us to do. This is how we should live every moment of every day. Every day is different and requires us to act accordingly. We should truly treat every day as a new day without thinking we have stored up any good deeds for the afterlife and treat it as though today is the only day we have in our life to do good deeds and avoid bad deeds. We don't want to get complacent or despair and let our past make us think we are either guaranteed or permanently prohibited from paradise. The past is the past, don't waste your present by dwelling on it. This would be like the person taking a test spending their time thinking about how good or bad they did on the earlier portions of the test and not proceeding to try to get more points. We'd say that's foolish regardless whether they did good or bad earlier, they should just keep going and try their best every moment. The road to paradise isn't the shortest or the easiest but it is the only one we want to finish traveling. The sinful roads seem fun in the beginning but the further you get to the end the worse it gets, and both the road to paradise and the roads to hell result in the travelers residing forever at their final destination. Allah helps those travelers who sincerely want to travel the road to paradise, because realistically we aren't going to be able to travel it without his help. We just have to take one step at a time up the incline and before we know it we'll be there God-willing. Don't look back at your previous footprints, what's important is where you put the next step. It's not about whether you think you are making progress or not, or if you think you are passing or failing and similarly it doesn't matter what you think of others. For instance you may think this book may be good or bad, but my book of deeds is what's important. It would be stupid for me to delete a good sentence, paragraph or chapter of this book but it's even dumber for me to erase good deeds from my book of deeds by doing bad deeds. Instead I should do good deeds which can cancel out the bad that I've done in the past. You have a book of deeds too, which may well be better than mine. You are writing your book of deeds at this time and will continue as long as you are alive. Regarding your book of deeds, there is only one review and opinion that matters; the opinion of the Creator of all things. Everyone is an author currently writing and revising their book of deeds before it gets published on the Day of Judgement. This is why dwelling on the past is pointless for us to do just as it would be stupid for an author to dwell on how good or bad their earlier pages were. If their book was good you'd say, "don't stop keep writing" and if it was bad you'd tell them to fix it and keep writing. But the advantage our book of deeds has over regular books is that in order to fix what we've done in the past we simply do good stuff in the present and then God will erase our mistakes or turn them into good deeds. Thus we should have very good books once they are published since we've been working on them our entire lives. However every book gets rated differently depending on who is reading it. To be rated highly an author would write according to the criteria their reader uses to judge a book. Thus for our book of deeds to be a prize winner and not tossed into the book burning pile we should write it/ live according to God's criteria, because if we live trying to please any other being, such as ourself, then we won't be getting those prizes from God which we desire. So keep your eyes on the prizes, but more importantly focus on the opinion of the Divine Judge who gives out the prizes. Although unlike worldly writing competitions, our book of deeds gets better if we help others to improve their book of deeds. So the human species is on a team. The problem is some of us are working for Satan, or for selfish interests which end up hurting our team. Also some make their book of deeds a horror story or a true crime book without realizing it and others just want to have a fun time writing an adventure book. But only a Muslim author who presents a book from the Islamic genre will get rewarded by the Creator. God will let people write whatever they want in their book of deeds, just as a teacher will let a student write whatever they want for their assignment, but what we've been told to do is clear and if we want to pass the test of life we must obey the Creator without fear of jeers from peers.

Humans have reached the sinful state we are in today as a result of being mis-educated by Satan. The solution is proper education and implementation of the teachings of the prophets. Doing this will have negative reactions, because disbelievers who are corrupt and the majority will get upset when you practice the true religion and call them to goodness, even if you do it politely. People will label a believer who practices the religion of God negatively just as the prophets were mistreated. Satan is doing everything he can to make the true religion the most unappealing thing in the world. Satan makes everything else seem fun or good except the true religion. Satan uses every person or thing he can to dissuade and intimidate someone, or cause people to doubt or fear the true religion. If you consider the prophets pbut, what do you think they would be called if they started preaching in any secular country in the world today? What would people say about Noah pbuh building an ark? What would they call Abraham pbuh when he destroys his community idols, starts circumcising and nearly sacrifices his firstborn son? What would the governments of the world say about Moses pbuh if he started telling them he got 10 commandments from God that have to become the laws of the world? What would they say about Joseph pbuh who goes to prison for not fornicating and tells the king to stockpile all food except for meager rations for 7 years, because there'll be a 7 year famine due to a dream interpretation? What would they say about Lot pbuh who told his city to stop practicing homosexuality and that it was wicked? What would they say about Jesus pbuh if he went around preaching today, taking control of temples by force, whipping those involved with interest? What do they say about Muhammad pbuh?

Due to the animosity disbelievers have for the animosity the prophets have for them they have always been declared public enemies, except for when they had political power as Moses, David and Solomon pbut had. It is for this reason that one of the first people Muhammad pbuh told he had been told by an angel that he was a prophet of God, Waraqah ibn Nawfal, after hearing what the message of Islam with which he'd been sent with was said, "*This was the same one who keeps the secrets whom Allah had sent to Moses (angel Gabriel). I wish I were young and could live up to the time when your people would turn you out.*" After hearing this Muhammad pbuh was shocked Waraqah said his own people would be hostile and turn him out and when they had nothing but love and respect for him at the time. Thereupon Waraqah replied, "*Anyone who came with something similar to what you have brought was treated with hostility; and if I should remain alive till the day when you will be turned out then I would support you strongly.*" Days later Waraqah died as a old man, but his prediction of the hostile reaction to Muhammad pbuh and "*anyone who came with something simililar to what Muhammad pbuh brought*" has proven true and will always be true, even in the "modern age" in alleged "civil tolerant societies". Except in the modern age instead of just being hostile to a religion and rejecting it, they just brand it's practitioners as crazy extremists and try to change the religion so it conforms to their own beliefs, deeds and customs. Thus the new form of religious repression is redefinition, revision and reformation. While that's the fundamental difference between the early generations of Muslims who lived amongst prophets and those alive today. During the time of Muhammad pbuh nobody was teaching something different than he was and calling it Islam saying what they were teaching was what he taught, there were no deviant sects then to deal with. Today there are deviant sects but that just means we can get more reward for dealing with them. So before it was Muslims vs. non-Muslims theologically while today it's Muslims vs. non-Muslims, hypocrites, deviants and extremists. So that's 1 group vs. 4 groups and 4 out of the 5 claim to be Muslims. The primary fundamental difference between the 4 groups claiming to be Muslim today is their treatment towards those who disbelieve or disagree. Whenever a prophet was sent to teach the religion of God, it disrupted society on nearly every level. Every person in every community was in an uproar and socially distressed that an intolerance for the ancient and popular ways of believing and living was being expressed by the followers of God's prophets. The pagan disbelievers' complaint was always the same in that, "*Everyone was getting along just fine in perfect harmony until this "prophet" starting spewing hatred for our religions and customs. They are publicly judging us as evil teaching our own flesh and blood to hate us and saying we have to accept their religion and practices or burn in hell. Personally they are very moral and pious, but polite and peaceful as they are their teachings are very offensive and intolerant. They are saying that God hates those who have a different religion than them and that their followers should hate non-members just as their God does. It makes us look and feel bad and we don't like it one bit!*" All religions thrive off of hatred. It is because of hating disbelievers that people try to convert them, because one naturally hates hating people they live and interact with. Yet if they don't hate and hate does not affect their interactions or attitudes they will not care to do what is necessary to change the religious demographic they live in. So for a religion to spread it's members must publicly espouse hatred for all who don't believe as they do. Everyone knew the prophets hated disbelief and disbelievers and that's why the disbelievers gave importance to their message of Islam, because the hate preachers demand attention. You can never hear someone saying "I hate you because of your beliefs" and then completely ignore their religion's message or doctrines. If you preach hate then people will listen and it forces the matter to be decided as either you are right or wrong, but whatever you are the matter will be known by all as important to discuss and decide upon. Hatred makes matters important. Without the public expression of hate then Islam is not important for the disbelievers to worry about. Nobody likes to be hated, if the disbelievers knew Muslims hate them for being disbelievers they will see they have an important decision to make and have motivation to make it. But if you don't preach hate then they don't care since you aren't bothering them in any way, because it's not personal. The hate must be personal to cause persons to make important personal decisions regarding their choice of religion. If it's not personal people don't think it's important. So they don't care if you hate their religion, but if they know you hate them personally then there is a potential for a serious conversation that will result in serious actions one way or the other. But remember expressing hatred must be done the prophetic way, because we aren't hating for personal reasons we are hating for God's sake. Thus we express hatred for disbelief and disbelievers publicly because God likes such public enmity for what and those he hates. So that Muslims in the West today who act worse than the Sahabah do, to interact with people who have placed less value on social ties than the Arab idolaters did means that logically we should be getting persecuted much worse than the early Muslims did. Yet we are not because most Muslims are not letting the disbelievers know we hate disbelief and disbelievers the way the early Muslims did. Honestly many Muslims don't care as much as they should that people disbelieve in God and are on the road to hellfire. They don't see it as their personal problem and neglect their duty to try to guide their fellow human being. This is why Islam is not spreading as fast as it did back then, because Muslims are afraid of having dramatic religious confrontations that disrupt social pleasantries. Many fear persecution of people more than they fear concealing the truth which God has commanded Muslims to make known, publicly to everyone in every place. (Note I did not say every time is the best time, certain times are better than others, but the place and the people don't matter.) The problem is ignorant hate preachers and extremist hate preachers give hate preaching a bad reputation. The key to being a "hate preacher" is to do it the prophetic way, otherwise it would be dangerously satanic. Such is it with most things in life, we either do it correctly the prophetic way or the satanic way. All of God's prophets were "hate preachers" but the way they did it was different than the way many today do it, yet there was public hatred there. Even the prophet Joseph pbuh spewed hatred for disbelievers when he was in prison talking to disbelievers and he even called them disbelievers to their face saying they were in great error. Even today prisons aren't places where a minority of 1 is "wise" to insult the majority, prisoners tend to get violent fast, but in Joseph's time as the only Muslim in the whole country it was even riskier to preach hatred for disbelievers in prison than it is today. Everyone knew the prophets were not pleased with those who rejected their prophethood or believed in another religion. Thus the disbelievers were not pleased with the prophets, even if they didn't combat their faith. However the prophets didn't care if anyone was pleased with them, their job and our job is to worship and please God. The prophets didn't pretend or hide their true feelings from people, they felt how God felt about them and their falsehood, said how they felt and treated them the way God said to treat them. We must do the same today. The Muslim living in non-Muslim lands actually have to be the strictest and most outspoken type of Muslims there are. This is because they are on the frontlines in the theological war against kufr/shirk. Every military strategist knows that the strongest most experienced soldiers are on the frontlines so as to quickly and effectively break the enemy lines so the rest of the soldiers who have lesser experience, wisdom and morale can follow up. The weak, meek and ignorant soldiers are in the middle or rear or even back at the home base training far away from the enemy. So that's where contrary to popular belief, the Muslims living in the non-Muslim lands should be the most intolerant towards kafirs and the most strict in their practicing of Islam because they are on the territory of the theological enemy surrounded on all sides by Satanic soldiers and traps with few Islamic footholds around. When some say how because they are in non-Muslim unislamic lands then it's harder for them to practice Islam and they have more leeway, the opposite is actually the case. Muslims have less leeway when it comes to practicing Islam in non-Muslim lands and those Muslims who dare to live amongst disbelievers in unislamic lands really do have to be more practicing than those who don't. This is because if they aren't stricter than the Muslims in Islamic lands then they won't even be practicing Islam in unislamic lands. A fool could practice Islam in Islamic lands, but a smart Muslim will end up falling into kufr, shirk, bida or sin in non-Muslim lands because it is so easy to do and difficult to avoid in dar al-kufr. Basically if a Muslim doesn't want to be extra strict they should live in Islamic lands, but if they are going to be in unislamic lands amongst the non-Muslims they must know a lot more about Islam and practice a lot more of Islam just to be Muslims than they would have to do in Islamic lands. So dare you live on the frontlines fighting Satan and his friends? It's dangerous, this theological war is no game it is a real war. Don't let Satan trap you into trying to become a hero so that you end up failing the test of life. The frontlines are the most dangerous but the whole universe is a battlefield where Satan and his soldiers will fight you even if you don't want him to. Promise me you will do what you need to do to get to the highest level of heaven by following the prophetic battleplan. I also ask you to consider whether in a world dominated by evil and falsehood where the majority of people do not believe in the truth or act according to it, will the truth be seen as moderate or extreme? Today amongst us would the religious faith, advice and lifestyles of God's prophets be labeled as extremism or not? If God told you that before you could enter paradise many people will call you an extremist while traveling the road to paradise, would you still travel the road to paradise? Hence there is the sahih hadith in Sunan Ibn Majah #3988 wherein Muhammad pbuh taught: ""*Islam began as something strange and will go back to being strange, so glad tidings(of Paradise) to the strangers.*" It was asked: "*Who are the strangers?*' He said: "*Strangers who break away from their people (for the sake of Islam).*" In another hadith graded sahih by Al-Albani reported by Abu Amr al-Dani from a hadith by Abdullah Ibn Masoud, it was asked "*Who are those strangers, O Messenger of Allah?*" He replied, "*Those that correct the people when they become corrupt.*" Another narration says the strangers were described by Muhammad pbuh as, "*Those that correct my sunnah which has been corrupted by the people after me.*" In another hadith graded as authentic by Al-Albani, Ibn Asakir reported that in response to the same question Muhammad pbuh described the strangers by saying, "*They are a small group of people among a large evil population. Those who oppose them are more than those who follow them.*" Muhammad pbuh also practiced what he preached in regards to facing dangerous criticism and violence for expressing pure correct Islamic beliefs and doctrines and refuting the foul falsehoods of disbelievers and hypocrites. On his way to Mecca for Umrah when it was still controlled by Pagans, shortly before the treaty of Hudaybiyyah was signed Muhammad pbuh was distressed at the sight of the polytheist armies of his hometown physically preparing to prevent him from worshipping God, especially after they had already fought several battles over his rights to pray, practice and preach in Medinah; since they didn't let him do that in their own country. As reported in Al Musnad Ahmad and by Ibn Ishaq both with hasan chains of narrations, reflecting on the situation Muhammad pbuh said what means:

"How unfortunate for the Quraysh. Wars destroyed them. Had they left me alone to work among the people, and, had the people embraced Islam, they would have stood to advantage. On the other hand, if the people rejected me, they could have then fought me from a position of strength. In any case, what do the Quraysh imagine? By Allah, I shall keep struggling in the cause of what Allah has sent me with until Allah gives it victory, or I die in its cause."

Also there is a hasan hadith in the collection of at-Tirmidhi which relates that Muhammad pbuh said what means:

"Whoever seeks Allah's pleasure by the people's wrath, Allah will suffice him from the people. And whoever seeks the people's pleasure by Allah's wrath, Allah will entrust him to the people."

Meaning if you do something to make Allah happy and it makes people mad and angry with you, then Allah will take care of you in every way; both in this life and the next life. But if you want to do something to please people even though it makes Allah upset, then Allah will abandon you in this life and the next so you will have nothing but people to rely upon for help. Whereas the people can't do anything for you in the next life and they can't really do much for you in this life either, since they need Allah to allow them to do whatever they want to try to do. Thus if you only care about pleasing Allah then you are set now and forever. Yet the majority of the people will get upset at you for having your Creator be the only being you desire to please. So when you live solely to make your Creator happy and they don't, they will call you a strange radical extremist; but God will be happy with you and that is all that really matters to the true believers.

Regarding the "strangers" (Ghuraba) it is reported by Al-Bukhari and Muslim that Muhammad pbuh said the following about them:

"These are the people who left mankind when they (the strangers) were in need of them the most. For, on the Day of Judgment, when all other groups will go with that which they used to worship, they will stay in their places. It will be said to them, "Will you not go as the other people have gone?" They will answer, "We had abandoned the people (in this life), and we were more in need of them then than we are today, and we will wait for our Lord whom we used to worship.""

Lastly in Sahih Bukhari 3348

Narrated Abu Sa`id Al-Khudri:

The Prophet said, "Allah will say (on the Day of Resurrection), 'O Adam.' Adam will reply, 'Labbaik wa Sa`daik', and all the good is in Your Hand.' Allah will say: 'Bring out the people of the fire.' Adam will say: 'O Allah! How many are the people of the Fire?' Allah will reply: 'From every one thousand, take out nine-hundred-and-ninety-nine.' At that time children will become hoary headed, every pregnant female will have a miscarriage, and one will see mankind as drunken, yet they will not be drunken, but dreadful will be the Wrath of Allah." The companions of the Prophet asked, "O Allah's Apostle! Who is that (excepted) one?" He said, "Rejoice with glad tidings; one person will be from you and one-thousand will be from Gog and Magog." The Prophet further said, "By Him in Whose Hands my life is, hope that you will be one-fourth of the people of Paradise." We shouted, "Allahu Akbar!" He added, "I hope that you will be one-third of the people of Paradise." We shouted, "Allahu Akbar!" He said, "I hope that you will be half of the people of Paradise." We shouted, "Allahu Akbar!" He further said, "You (Muslims) (compared with non Muslims) are like a black hair in the skin of a white ox or like a white hair in the skin of a black ox (i.e. your number is very small as compared with theirs).

As Hijra(Emigration) is a part of Hatred I shall include some information on the topic so that I will have conveyed the full message. There are 7 different types of states/lands that exist.

Dar al-Harb (The Abode of War) refers to any territory under the hegemony of disbelievers, which is on also terms of active or potential belligerency with the Domain of Islam, and presumably hostile to the Muslims living in its domain. It need not be hostile to the Muslims that reside in it's territory, just to be militarily at war with Islam or Muslims makes it Dar al-Harb. The exception is if it were a Muslim nation at war with another Muslim nation, but a non-Muslim nation that is militarily at war with Islam or Muslims anywhere on the planet belongs to the category of Dar al-Harb even if they have Muslims residents.

It's important to note that the scholar Ibn Hazm stated that: *"Whoever joins the 'land of war and disbelief', (Dar Al-Harb) of his own freewill and in defiance of whoever amongst the Muslims calls him to his side, is by virtue of this act an apostate, by all the laws of apostasy, in Islam. But whoever flees to the 'land of war' for fear of oppression, who neither opposes the Muslims in anything nor bears any malice towards them, and who was not able to find any refuge among the Muslims, is free of any guilt since he was compelled to leave."*

Dar al-kufr (The Abode of Disbelief) is any land ruled by disbelievers, in which the laws of the disbelievers are supreme and political power is in their hands. Dar al-Kufr is wherever Shariah is not the law of the land. The abode of disbelief can be of two types. One which is at war with the Muslims and/or Islam militarily which would make it **Dar al-Harb** and one which enjoys a truce with them which would be **Dar al kufr**. The determining factor is that it is ruled by the unislamic laws of the disbelievers. A land is considered to be dar al-kufr even if a large

majority of Muslims live there (as they did under the Mongols), but some places of "dar al-kufr" are better than others based on how islamic or unislamic their system/society may be.
Every Dar-al Harb is Dar-al Kufr. Two lands with Shariah can be at war, in such a case neither is Dar Al-Harb nor Dar Al-Kufr. Dar al-Kufr does not equal Dar al Harb, Dar al Harb is a type of Dar al-Kufr. There are several other types of Dar al-Kufr as well:

Dar al-Hudna (*Abode of Calm*): The land of disbelievers currently under a truce, which is a respite between wars with Muslims. A truce is bought by tribute or agreement. If either the *harbis* (inhabitants of Dar Al-Harb) break the conditions for the truce, or after ten years (whichever comes first), hostilities are resumed. In Islam a peace truce can only exist for 10 years before it expires and must be renewed if peace is to continue. Furthermore, only treaties that conform to Islamic prescriptions are valid; if these conditions are not fulfilled the treaty is void.

Dar al-'Ahd (**Abode of truce)** or **Dar al-Sulh** (**Abode of conciliation/treaty**) are terms used for territories that have a treaty of non-aggression or peace with Muslims. This term refers to those non-Muslim governments which have armistice or peace agreements with Muslim governments. The actual status of the non-Muslim country in question may vary from acknowledged equality to tributary states. This is similar to Dar al-Hudna(above) but for vassal states or nations which are on friendly terms with Muslim nations who rule by Shariah.

Dar al-Amn (**Abode of safety**) refers to the status of Muslims in non-Muslim societies. This region usually refers to countries where Muslims have the right to practice their religion. Many countries with Muslim minorities have been declared as Dar al-

Amn at different points in time. A nation can be Dar al-Amn domestically at the same time it is Dar al-Harb internationally. Or a nation could be Dar Al-Amn domestically while Dar al Ahd internationally. Or they could have a mixed status if there are mutliple Islamic nations where with some countries they could be Dar al-Amn domestically, while being Dar al Harb and Dar al Ahd. Many labels can exist if there is more than one Muslim nation or more than one nation which establishes Shariah.

Dar al-Dawa ("**Abode of Dawah**") refers to a region where the religion of Islam has recently been introduced. A good example of Dar Al-Dawa would be the area of Libya before Jihad was declared against it during the reign of Umar bin Khattab. The label Dar al-Dawa can apply to any Dar al-Kufr at any time. So Dar al-Harb could be Dar al-Dawa whether or not it allows Muslims in it's country or not. War may be preventing dawah but the land would still be considered Dar al-Dawa nonetheless.

Dar al-Islam (The Abode of Islam) is any land that is ruled by the Muslims, where the Shariah is the supreme law and the Muslims hold political power. It is *Dar ul- Islam,* even if the majority of the population are disbelievers, so long as the Muslims rule it according to the Shari'ah. Dar al Islam can also be Dar al-Dawa. The percentage of the population that is Muslim has nothing to do with being Dar al Islam, it is all about whether the Shariah is implemented and the rulers are Muslims.

Ibn Al-Qayyim said, "*The Jumhour (majority) of the 'Ulema say, 'Dar al-Islam is where the Muslims go and reside and the Islamic rules are dominant. If people (the Muslims) reside in one place and Islam becomes dominant, that is Dar al-Islam. If however, Islam does not become dominant it is not (considered) Dar al-Islam even if it is in close proximity to the state. Taa'if was so close to Makkah (at the time when Makkah was Dar al-Islam) but it did not become part of Dar al-Islam until it was conquered.'"*

Following are the 3 categories of people who live among disbelievers which the Scholar Hamad ibn Atiq listed so the reader may evaluate themselves and their situation.

<u>The first group</u>: *stays amongst the disbelievers by choice and inclination, they praise and commend them, and happily disassociate themselves from the Muslims. They help the disbelievers in their struggle against the Muslims in anyway they can, physically, morally, and financially. Such people are disbelievers, their position is actively and deliberately opposed to religion.*

<u>The second group</u>: *are those who remain amongst the disbelievers because of money, family or homeland. He does not demonstrate a strong attachment to his religion (Islam), nor does he emigrate. He does not support the disbelievers against the Muslims, whether in word or deed. His heart is not bound to them, nor does he speak on their behalf. Such a person is not considered a disbeliever merely because he continues to live among the disbelievers, but many would say that he has disobeyed Allah and His Messenger by not going to live among the Muslims, even though he may secretly hate the disbelievers.*

The third group: *are those who may remain among the disbelievers without impediment, and they are two categories:*

1. *Those who are openly able to proclaim their religion and dissociate themselves from disbelief.* ==**When they are able, they clearly disassociate themselves from the disbelievers and tell them openly that they are far from truth, and that they are wrong**==. *This is what is known as 'Izhar ad-Din' or 'assertion of Islam'.* ==This is what exonerates a person from the obligation to emigrate.== *Muhammad was commanded to tell the disbelievers of their clear disbelief and that their* religion was not the same, nor was their worship, nor what they worshipped. That _they could not be in the service of Allah, so long as they remained in the service of falsehood._ He was commanded to express his satisfaction with Islam as his religion and his denial of the faith of the disbelievers. Therefore, Whoever does this is not obliged to emigrate. _Asserting one's religion does not mean that you simply leave people to worship whatever they please without comment_, like the Christians and the Jews do. _It means that you must **clearly and plainly disapprove** of what they worship, **and show enmity** towards the disbelievers;_ failing this there is no assertion of Islam.

2. _Those who live amongst the disbelievers, and have not the means to leave nor the strength to assert themselves, have a license to remain._ Allah says, But the exemption comes after a promise to those who remain among the disbelievers. It is an exemption to those who could not devise a plan nor find any other way out.

Fatwas related to hatred

Fatwa #1 https://islamqa.info/en/answers/10213/ruling-on-the-call-to-unite-all-religions

Question

What are Ruling on the call to unite all religions?

Answer

Praise be to Allaah Alone and peace and blessings be upon the one after whom there will be no more Prophets, and upon his family and companions and whoever follows them in truth until the Day of Resurrection.

The Standing Committee on Academic Research and Issuing Fatwas (al-Lajnah al-Daa'imah li'l-Buhooth al-'Ilmiyyah wa'l-Iftaa') has examined the questions which have been submitted to it and the opinions and articles published and broadcast in the media concerning the call to unite the three religions of Islam, Judaism and Christianity; and the call which stems from that, to build a mosque, a church and a synagogue in one place, on university campuses and in public squares; and the call to print the Qur'aan, Tawraat (Torah) and Injeel (Gospel) in one volume, etc.; and the conferences, seminars and meetings on this topic which are being held in the east and in the west. After studying and pondering the matter, the Committee issues the following statement:

- *(1)One of the basic principles of belief in Islam, something which is obviously a basic principle and on which all the Muslims are agreed (ijmaa') is that there is no true religion on the face of the earth apart from Islam. It is the final religion which abrogates all religions and laws that came before it There is no religion on earth according to which Allaah is to be worshipped apart from Islam. Allaah says (interpretation of the meanings):*

"This day, I have perfected your religion for you, completed My Favour upon you, and have chosen for you Islâm as your religion" [al-Maa'idah 5:3]

"And whoever seeks a religion other than Islâm, it will never be accepted of him, and in the Hereafter he will be one of the losers" [Aal 'Imraan 3:85].

After the coming of Muhammad (peace and blessings of Allaah be upon him), Islam means what he brought, not any other religion.

- *(2)One of the basic principles of belief in Islam is that the Book of Allaah, the Qur'aan, is the last of the Books to be revealed from the Lord of the Worlds. It abrogates all the Books that came before it, the Tawraat, Zaboor, Injeel and others, and it is a Muhaymin [Muhaymin: that which testifies the truth that is therein and falsifies the falsehood that is added therein] over them. So there is no longer any revealed Book according to which Allaah may be worshipped apart from the Qur'aan. Allaah says (interpretation of the meaning):*

"And We have sent down to you (O Muhammad) the Book (this Qur'aan) in truth, confirming the Scripture that came before it and Muhaymin (trustworthy in highness and a witness) over it (old Scriptures). So judge among them by what Allaah has revealed, and follow not their vain desires, diverging away from the truth that has come to you." [al-Maa'idah 5:48]

- *(3)It is obligatory to believe that the Tawraat and Injeel have been abrogated by the Qur'aan, and that they have been altered and distorted, with things added and taken away, as Allaah tells us in the Qur'aan, for example (interpretation of the meaning):*

"So, because of their breach of their covenant, We cursed them and made their hearts grow hard. They change the words from their

(right) places and have abandoned a good part of the Message that was sent to them. And you will not cease to discover deceit in them, except a few of them" [al-Maa'idah 5:13]

"Then woe to those who write the Book with their own hands and then say, "This is from Allaah," to purchase with it a little price! Woe to them for what their hands have written and woe to them for that they earn thereby." [al-Baqarah 2:79]

"And verily, among them is a party who distort the Book with their tongues (as they read), so that you may think it is from the Book, but it is not from the Book, and they say: "This is from Allaah," but it is not from Allaah; and they speak a lie against Allaah while they know it" [Aal 'Imraan 3:78]

Hence, whatever in the previous books was correct is abrogated by Islam, and everything else is distorted and changed. It was reported that the Prophet (peace and blessings of Allaah be upon him) became angry when he saw that 'Umar had a page with something from the Tawraat written on it, and he (peace and blessings of Allaah be upon him) said: "Are you in doubt, O son of al-Khattaab? Have I not brought you something shining and pure? If my brother Moosa were alive, he would have no choice but to follow me." (Narrated by Ahmad and al-Daarimi, and others).

- *(4)One of the basic principles of belief in Islam is that our Prophet and Messenger Muhammad (peace and blessings of Allaah be upon him) is the Seal of the Prophets and Messengers, as Allaah says (interpretation of the meaning):*

"Muhammad is not the father of any of your men, but he is the Messenger of Allaah and the last (end) of the Prophets" [al-Ahzaab 33:40]

So there is no longer any Messenger whom it is obligatory to follow, apart from Muhammad (peace and blessings of Allaah be upon him). If any of the Prophets were alive, they would have no choice but to follow him, as Allaah says (interpretation of the meaning):

"And (remember) when Allaah took the Covenant of the Prophets, saying: 'Take whatever I gave you from the Book and Hikmah (understanding of the Laws of Allaah), and afterwards there will come to you a Messenger (Muhammad) confirming what is with you; you must, then, believe in him and help him.' Allaah said: 'Do you agree (to it) and will you take up My Covenant (which I conclude with you)?' They said: 'We agree.' He said: 'Then bear witness; and I am with you among the witnesses (for this).'" [Aal 'Imraan 3:81]

When the Prophet of Allaah 'Eesaa (peace be upon him) descends at the end of time, he will follow Muhammad (peace and blessings of Allaah be upon him) and he will judge according to his Sharee'ah. Allaah says (interpretation of the meaning);

"Those who follow the Messenger, the Prophet who can neither read nor write (i.e. Muhammad) whom they find written with them in the Tauraat (Torah) and the Injeel (Gospel) — he commands them for Al-Ma'roof (i.e. Islamic Monotheism and all that Islam has ordained); and forbids them from Al-Munkar (i.e. disbelief, polytheism of all kinds, and all that Islam has forbidden); he allows them as lawful At-Tayyibaat (i.e. all good and lawful as regards things, deeds, beliefs, persons and foods), and prohibits them as unlawful Al-Khabaa'ith (i.e. all evil and unlawful as regards things, deeds, beliefs, persons and foods), he releases them from their heavy burdens (of Allaah's Covenant with the children of Israel), and from the fetters (bindings) that were upon them. So those who believe in him (Muhammad), honour him, help him, and follow the light (the Qur'aan) which has been sent down with him, it is they who will be successful" [al-A'raaf 7:157]

It is also one of the basic principles of belief in Islam that the Message of Muhammad (peace and blessings of Allaah be upon him) is addressed to all of mankind. Allaah says (interpretation of the meaning):

"And We have not sent you (O Muhammad) except as a giver of glad tidings and a warner to all mankind, but most of men know not" [Saba' 34:28]

"Say (O Muhammad): "O mankind! Verily, I am sent to you all as the Messenger of Allaah" [al-A'raaf 7:158].

And there are many similar aayaat.

- (5)One of the basic principles of belief in Islam is that we must believe that every Jew, Christian or other person who does not enter Islam is a kaafir, and that those against whom proof is established must be named as kaafirs and regarded as enemies of Allaah, His Messenger and the believers, and that they are the people of Hell, as Allaah says (interpretation of the meaning):

"Those who disbelieve from among the people of the Scripture (Jews and Christians) and Al-Mushrikoon, were not going to leave (their disbelief) until there came to them clear evidence" [al-Bayyinah 98:1]

"Verily, those who disbelieve (in the religion of Islâm, the Qur'ân and Prophet Muhammad) from among the people of the Scripture (Jews and Christians) and Al-Mushrikoon will abide in the fire of Hell. They are the worst of creatures" [al-Bayyinah 98:6]

"This Qur'aan has been revealed to me that I may therewith warn you and whomsoever it may reach" [al-An'aam 6:19]

"This (Qur'aan) is a Message for mankind (and a clear proof against them), in order that they may be warned thereby" [Ibraaheem 14:52]. And there are many similar aayaat. It was reported in Saheeh Muslim that the Prophet (peace and blessings of Allaah be upon him) said: "By the One in Whose hand is my soul, no one among this nation, Jew or Christian, hears of me, then dies without having believed in that with which I was sent, but he will be one of the people of the Fire." Hence whoever does not regard the Jews and Christians as kuffaar is himself a kaafir, according to the ruling of Sharee'ah, "Whoever does not regard the kaafir as such after proof has been established against him is himself a kaafir."

- (6)In the light of these basic principles of belief and the rulings of sharee'ah, calling for the uniting of all religions, and for them to be brought close to one another and cast in the same mould, is an evil and crafty call whose aim is to mix truth with falsehood, to destroy Islam and undermine its pillars, and to tempt its followers into total apostasy. This is confirmed by the words of the Qur'aan (interpretation of the meaning):

"And they will never cease fighting you until they turn you back from your religion (Islamic Monotheism) if they can" [al-Baqarah 2:217]

"They wish that you reject Faith, as they have rejected (Faith), and thus that you all become equal (like one another)" [al-Nisaa' 4:89]

- (7)Among the effects of this evil call would be the cancelling out of the differences between Islam and kufr, truth and falsehood, good and evil. It would break down the psychological barrier that exists between the Muslims and the kaafirs, and there would be no sense of al-Walaa' wa'l-Baraa' (loyalty and friendship towards Muslims, disavowal and enmity towards kaafirs), or jihaad and fighting to make the word of Allaah supreme in the earth of Allaah. Allaah says (interpretation of the meaning):

"Fight against those who (1) believe not in Allaah, (2) nor in the Last Day, (3) nor forbid that which has been forbidden by Allaah and His Messenger(Muhammad((4) and those who acknowledge not the religion of truth (i.e. Islâm) among the people of the Scripture (Jews and

~ 209 ~

Christians), until they pay the Jizyah with willing submission, and feel themselves subdued" [al-Tawbah 9:29]

"and fight against the Mushrikoon (polytheists, pagans, idolaters, disbelievers in the Oneness of Allaah) collectively as they fight against you collectively. But know that Allaah is with those who are Al-Muttaqoon (the pious)" [al-Tawbah 9:36]

"O you who believe! Take not as (your) Bitaanah (advisors, consultants, protectors, helpers, friends) those outside your religion (pagans, Jews, Christians, and hypocrites) since they will not fail to do their best to corrupt you. They desire to harm you severely. Hatred has already appeared from their mouths, but what their breasts conceal is far worse. Indeed We have made plain to you the Ayaat (proofs, evidences, verses) if you understand" [Aal 'Imraan 3:118]

- (8) If the call to unite the religions is made by a Muslim, this considered to be blatant apostasy from the religion of Islam, because it conflicts with the basic principles of belief. It is an acceptance of disbelief in Allaah and a contradiction of the truth of the Qur'aan and its abrogation of all laws and religions that came before it. On this basis, it is an idea that should be rejected from the point of view of sharee'ah, and it is definitely haraam according to the evidence of Islam, Qur'aan, Sunnah and ijmaa' (scholarly consensus).

- (9)Based on the above:

- (i)It is not permissible for a Muslim who believes in Allaah as his Lord, Islam as his religion and Muhammad (peace and blessings of Allaah be upon him) as his Prophet and Messenger, to call people to this evil idea, to encourage it or to propagate it among the Muslims, let alone respond to it or join the conferences and gatherings held to promote it.

- (ii) It is not permissible for a Muslim to print the Tawraat and Injeel on their own, so how about printing them with the Qur'aan in one volume? Whoever does this or calls for it is far astray, because by doing so he is combining truth (the Qur'aan) with that which is either distorted or was true but has now been abrogated (the Tawraat and Injeel).

- (iii) Similarly, it is not permissible for a Muslim to respond to the call to build a mosque, church and synagogue in one place, because this involves recognizing a religion in which Allaah is worshipped other than Islam, and rejecting the idea that Islam should prevail over all other religions, and giving the idea that there are three religions and that it is OK for people to belong to any of these three. This is a kind of equality which implies that Islam does not abrogate the religions that came before it. Undoubtedly, if a person approves of this, believes it or accepts it, this is kufr and misguidance, because it clearly goes against the Qur'aan, the Sunnah and the consensus (ijmaa') of the Muslims and implies that the distortions of the Jews and Christians come from Allaah – exalted be He far above that. By the same token, it is not permitted to call churches "Houses of God" or to say that the people there are worshipping Allaah in a correct and acceptable manner, because this worship is not done according to the religion of Islam, and Allaah says (interpretation of the meaning):

"And whoever seeks a religion other than Islam, it will never be accepted of him, and in the Hereafter he will be one of the losers" [Aal 'Imraan 3:85].

On the contrary, they are houses in which disbelief (kufr) in Allaah is expressed; we seek refuge with Allaah from kufr and its people. Shaykh al-Islam Ibn Taymiyah (may Allaah have mercy on him) said in Majmoo' al-Fataawaa (22/162): "They – churches and synagogues – are not houses of Allaah; the houses of Allaah are the mosques. On the contrary, they are houses in which disbelief (kufr) in Allaah is expressed. Even if Allaah is mentioned therein, houses are the same as the people in them, and the people in these houses are kuffaar, so they are the houses of worship of the kuffaar."

- (10) It should be noted that it is obligatory on the Muslims to call the kuffaar in general, and the People of the Book in particular, to Islam through the clear texts of the Qur'aan and Sunnah. But this is only to be done by explaining to them and arguing with them in a way that is better (with good words and in a good manner) (cf. Al-'Ankaboot 29:46), not by compromising any of the beliefs of laws of Islam. This is in order to convince them about Islam and bring them into the religion, or to establish proof against them so that those who are to be destroyed (for their rejecting the Faith) might be destroyed after a clear evidence, and those who are to live (i.e. believers) might live after a clear evidence (cf. Al-Anfaal 8:42). Allaah says (interpretation of the meaning):

"Say (O Muhammad): "O people of the Scripture (Jews and Christians): Come to a word that is just between us and you, that we worship none but Allaah (Alone), and that we associate no partners with Him, and that none of us shall take others as lords besides Allaah. Then, if they turn away, say: "Bear witness that we are Muslims."
[Aal 'Imraan 3:64]

As for debating and meeting with them in order to go along with their wishes and fulfil their aims of destroying Islam bit by bit, this is falsehood which is rejected by Allaah, His Messenger and the believers, and Allaah is the One Whose help is sought against all that they ascribe to Him. Allaah says (interpretation of the meaning):

"but beware of them lest they turn you (O Muhammad) far away from some of that which Allaah has sent down to you" [al-Maa'idah 5:49]

The Committee has made the above statement to the people. We advise the Muslims in general, and people of knowledge in particular, to fear Allaah and be aware that He is always watching, to guard Islam and to protect the 'aqeedah (belief) of the Muslims from misguidance and those who promote it and from kufr and its people, and to beware of this idea.

Fatwa #2 https://islamqa.info/en/answers/6688/whoever-does-not-believe-that-the-kaafirs-are-kaafirs-is-himself-a-kaafir

Question

Is it true that anyone who does not accept that kuffaar are kuffaar is a kaafir himself, even if he prays, believes in the Qur'aan, and the Prophet Muhammad? If so, what is the proof for this? Can a person insist on believing that Jews and Christians can be believers and go to heaven after being shown clear evidence against this, and still be considered a Muslim?

Answer

Praise be to Allaah.

Yes, this is correct. Whoever is not convinced that the person who disbelieves in the religion of Allaah is a kaafir, does not believe what Allaah has told us about their being kaafirs, and he does not believe that the religion of Islam abrogates all previous religions and that all people must follow this religion no matter what their religion was before.

Allaah says (interpretation of the meaning):

And whoever seeks a religion other than Islam, it will never be accepted of him, and in the Hereafter he will be one of the losers
[Aal Imraan 3:85]

Say (O Muhammad): O mankind! Verily, I am sent to you all as the Messenger of Allaah [al-Araaf 7:158]

Al-Qaadi Ayyaad said: hence we regard as a kaafir everyone who follows a religion other than the religion of the Muslims, or who agrees with them, or who has doubts, or who says that their way is correct, even if he appears to be a Muslim and believes in Islam and that every other way is false, he is a kaafir

(Al-Shifaa bi Tareef Huqooq al-Mustafaa, 2/1071)

Shaykh Muhammad ibn Abd al-Wahhaab (may Allaah have mercy on him) said:

Know that among the greatest things that can nullify Islam are ten things:

Associating othes in worship of Allaah alone, Who has no partner or associate. The evidence of that is the aayah (interpretation of the meaning):

Verily, Allaah forgives not (the sin of) setting up partners (in worship) with Him, but He forgives whom He wills, sins other than that [al-Nisaa 4:116].

This also includes offering scarifices to other than Allaah, such as to the jinn or at graves.

Whoever regards others as intermediaries between him and Allaah and calls upon them to ask them to intercede for him, is a kaafir according to scholarly consensus.

Whoever does not regard the Mushrikeen as kaafirs or doubts that they are kaafirs or regard their way as correct, is a kaafir according to scholarly consensus.

After enumerating them, he said (may Allaah have mercy on him):

In the case of all these things that nullify Islam, there is no difference whether a person is joking or is serious or is afraid except in cases where he is forced to do something. All of them are among the things that are very dangerous and which happen very often. The Muslim has to beware of them and fear them happening to him. We seek refuge with Allaah from the things that earn His wrath and His painful prunishment, May Allaah bless Muhammad.

(Muallafaat al-Shaykh Muhammad ibn Abd al-Wahhaab, 212, 213).

Shirk and kufr are the same when it comes to the ruling (hukm)

Ibn Hazm said:

Kufra and shirk are the same; every kaafir is a mushrik and every mushrik is a kaafir. This is the view of al-Shaafa and others.

(al-Fisl, 3/124).

The Jews and Christians are kuffaar and mushrikeen. Allaah says (interpretation of the meaning):

And the Jews say: Uzair (Ezra) is the son of Allaah, and the Christians say: Messiah is the son of Allaah. That is their saying with their mouths, resembling the saying of those who disbelieved aforetime. Allaahs Curse be on them, how they are deluded away from the truth! They (Jews and Christians) took their rabbis and their monks to be their lords besides Allaah (by obeying them in things which they made lawful or unlawful according to their own desires without being ordered by Allaah), and (they also took as their Lord) Messiah, son of Maryam (Mary), while they (Jews and Christians) were commanded [in the Tauraat (Torah) and the Injeel (Gospel)] to worship none but One Ilaah (God Allaah) Laa ilaaha illa Huwa (none has the right to be worshipped but He). Praise and glory be to Him (far above is He) from having the partners they associate (with Him). [al-Tawbah 9:30-31].

It was reported from Abu Hurayrag that the Messenger of Allaah (peace and blessings of Allaah be upon him) said: By the One is Whose hand is the soul of Muhammad, not one of this nation, Jew or Christian, will hear of me and will die without having believed in that with which I have been sent, but he will be one of the dwellers of Hell fire.

(Narrated by Muslim, 153)

Whoever says that the Jews are not kaafirs is disbelieving in the words of Allaah (interpretation of the meanings):

And their hearts absorbed (the worship of) the calf because of their disbelief [al-Baqarah 2:93]

Among those who are Jews, there are some who displace words from (their) right places and say: We hear your word (O Muhammad) and disobey, and Hear and let you (O Muhammad) hear nothing. And Raaina [in Arabic it means Be careful, listen to us, and we listen to you, whereas in Hebrew, it means an insult] with a twist of their tongues and as a mockery of the religion (Islâm). And if only they had said: We hear and obey, and Do make us understand, it would have been better for them, and more proper; but Allaah has cursed them for their disbelief [al-Nisa 4:46]

Because of their breaking the covenant, and of their rejecting the Ayaat (proofs, evidences, verses, lessons, signs, revelations, etc.) of

Allaah, and of their killing the Prophets unjustly, and of their saying: Our hearts are wrapped (with coverings, i.e. we do not understand what the Messengers say) nay, Allaah has set a seal upon their hearts because of their disbelief, so they believe not but a little. And because of their (Jews) disbelief and uttering against Maryam (Mary) a grave false charge (that she has committed illegal sexual intercourse); And because of their saying (in boast), We killed Messiah Eesaa (Jesus), son of Maryam (Mary), the Messenger of Allaah, but they killed him not, nor crucified him, but it appeared so to them the resemblance of Eesaa (Jesus) was put over another man (and they killed that man)]
[al-Nisa 4:155-157]

Verily, those who disbelieve in Allaah and His Messengers and wish to make distinction between Allaah and His Messengers (by believing in Allaah and disbelieving in His Messengers) saying, We believe in some but reject others, and wish to adopt a way in between. They are in truth disbelievers. And We have prepared for the disbelievers a humiliating torment [al-Nisa 4:150-151]

Whoever says that the Christians are not kuffaar is disbelieving in the words of Allaah (interpretation of the meanings):

Surely, in disbelief are they who say that Allaah is the Messiah, son of Maryam (Mary) [al-Maaidah 5:17]

Surely, disbelievers are those who said: Allaah is the third of the three (in a Trinity). But there is no Ilaah (god) (none who has the right to be worshipped) but One Ilaah (God Allâh). And if they cease not from what they say, verily, a painful torment will befall on the disbelievers among them [al-Maaidah 5:73]

And he is disbelieving in the words of Allaah concerning the Jews and Christians who do not believe in our Prophet or follow him:

Verily, those who disbelieve in Allaah and His Messengers and wish to make distinction between Allaah and His Messengers (by believing in Allaah and disbelieving in His Messengers) saying, We believe in some but reject others, and wish to adopt a way in between. They are in truth disbelievers. And We have prepared for the disbelievers a humiliating torment [al-Nisa 4:150-151]

What is there left to say after these clear statements from Allaah, may He be exalted? We ask Allaah to guide us. May Allaah bless our Prophet Muhammad.

Fatwa #3 https://www.islamweb.net/en/fatwa/329059/

Question

Assalaamu alaykum. I saw a bunch of people claiming that we should hate the disbelievers, but some other people said that the hatred should be directed towards disbelief, and not towards the disbelievers. Which is right? I can understand hating him if he hates Islam though. Does Allaah not tell us in verse 60:8 that He does not forbid us from treating the disbelievers who are against us with kindness? He also tells us in 29:46 to treat the Jews and Christians with the 'nicest of manners'. How could we hate someone but treat him nicely at the same time? Does hatred not make the heart black and hard? I also heard that verse 60:8 was abrogated; is that true? Thank you.

Answer

All perfect praise be to Allaah, The Lord of the worlds. I testify that there is none worthy of worship except Allaah and that Muhammad sallallaahu `alayhi wa sallam (may Allaah exalt his mention) is His slave and Messenger.

It is among the requirements of the faith of a believer that he should hate the people of Kufr (disbelief) in the same manner that he hates Kufr itself. This is what is stated in religious texts, and we have already mentioned some of them in fatwa 88293.

Shaykh Ibn Taymiyyah may Allaah have mercy upon him said, "Allaah informed us that you will not find a believer who has affection for those who oppose Allaah and His Messenger since belief contradicts having affection for them in the same manner that two opposites cancel out each other. So if there is faith, it negates its opposite. Hence, if a person is an ally to the enemies of Allaah in his heart, then this is evidence that due faith does not exist in his heart."

Among the sound reasons for preventing the Muslims from having affection with the Kaafirs (disbelievers) is that this affection could lead them to consider the disbelief upon which they are as good, and hence the Muslims would be tempted by it.

At-Taahir ibn 'Aashoor said in regard to the interpretation of the verse: {O you who have believed, do not take the Jews and the Christians as allies. They are [in fact] allies of one another. And whoever is an ally to them among you - then indeed, he is [one] of them. Indeed, Allaah guides not the wrongdoing people.} [Quran 5:51] "The last part of the verse is an indication that taking the Jews and Christians as allies is a reason for apostasy, because if a group of hypocrites and those who have weak faith among the Muslims continue taking the Jews and Christians as allies, then it is feared that they will slip away from the faith."

What is forbidden here does not contradict what is permissible in the verse of Soorah Al-Mumtahanah [Quran 60], because the first is related to the inclination of the heart, whereas what is mentioned in Soorah Al-Mumtahanah is related to matters of dealing with Kaafirs.

Ibn Hajar said, "Being kind and having good contact (with them) does not require having affection for them, which has been forbidden by the verse in which Allaah says (what means): {You will not find a people who believe in Allaah and the Last Day having affection for those who oppose Allaah and His Messenger, even if they were their fathers....} [Quran 58:22]"

The same thing applies to debating with them in the best manner; because the purpose of all this is to urge them and encourage them to embrace Islam. Al-Qurtubi said in his Tafseer (Quran interpretation): "Mujaahid said, "This verse is not abrogated, so it is permissible to debate with the People of the Book in the best manner with the meaning of inviting them to Allaah and attracting their attention to His Proofs and Signs hoping that they would accept faith, and not by being harsh and rough with them..." So the verse has not been abrogated, contrary to the view of some scholars.

The same applies to the verse in Soorah Al-Mumtahanah; the most preponderant opinion is that it is not abrogated.

Ibn 'Aashoor said, "Shihaabud-Deen Al-Qaraafi clarified in the 119th difference: the difference between being kind to them and having affection for them; so you should know that this verse is not abrogated by the verse in which Allaah says (what means): {Allaah does not forbid you from those who do not fight you because of religion...} [Quran 60:8] and that each verse applies to a certain condition."

Allaah knows best.

Fatwa #4 https://www.islamweb.net/en/fatwa/88293/

Question

Is it okay to have a Christian teacher or friend? I look forward to your answer.

Answer

~ 220 ~

All perfect praise be to Allaah, The Lord of the Worlds. I testify that there is none worthy of worship except Allaah, and that Muhammad, sallallaahu 'alayhi wa sallam, is His Slave and Messenger.

The term friendship means love and affection. Therefore, it is not permissible for a Muslim to befriend a non-Muslim, whether he is a Jew, a Christian or of any other religion. Also, it is not permissible to socialize with them or befriend them because this leads to loving them and being loyal to them. Allaah Says (what means): {You (O Muhammad) will not find any people who believe in Allaah and the Last Day, making friendship with those who oppose Allaah and His Messenger (Muhammad), even though they were their fathers, or their sons, or their brothers, or their kindred (people). For such He has written Faith in their hearts, and strengthened them with Rûh (proofs, light and true guidance) from Himself. And We will admit them to Gardens (Paradise) under which rivers flow, to dwell therein (forever). Allaah is pleased with them, and they with Him. They are the Party of Allaah. Verily, it is the Party of Allaah that will be the successful.} [Quran 58:22]

The matter is even more forbidden and more serious if the friendship is between a Muslim woman and a non-Muslim man, or between a Muslim man and a non-Muslim woman, because this involves evil that leads to committing Zina (fornication and/or adultery).

Therefore, a Muslim should be very careful and cautious about this, because being friendly to non-Muslims is very serious. Allaah Says (what means): {O you who believe! Take not as intimate those outside your religion (pagans, Jews, Christians, and hypocrites) since they will not fail to do their best to corrupt you. They desire to harm you severely. Hatred has already appeared from their mouths, but what their breasts conceal is far worse. Indeed We have made plain to you the signs if you understand.} [Quran 3:118] Besides, the Prophet, sallallaahu 'alayhi wa sallam, said: "A person is upon the religion of his friend, so you have to choose whom you befriend." [Abu Daawood, At-Tirmithi and others]

However, dealing with them in fields like buying and selling, studying and so on, without taking them as friends, is permissible, but the following requirements must be met:

1-   Believing that any religion other than Islam is null and that whoever practises a religion other than Islam is a disbeliever, as Allaah Says (what means): {Truly, the religion with Allaah is Islam.} [Quran 3:19] Allaah also Says (what means): {And whoever seeks a religion other than Islam, it will never be accepted of him, and in the Hereafter he will be one of the losers.} [Quran 3:85]

2-   Not being loyal to or loving them: Allaah Says (what means): {O you who believe! Take not My enemies and your enemies (i.e. disbelievers and polytheists, etc.) as friends, showing affection towards them, while they have disbelieved in what has come to you of the truth (i.e. Islamic Monotheism, this Quran, and Muhammad)} [Quran 60:1].

3-   However, this does not mean that it is permissible for a Muslim to be unjust to them if they are not belligerent; rather, a Muslim is obliged to deal justly with them and it is forbidden for him to treat the unjustly. Allaah Says (what means):

{Allaah does not forbid you to deal justly and kindly with those who fought not against you on account of religion and did not drive you out of your homes. Verily, Allaah loves those who deal with equity.} [Quran 60:8].

{But when you finish the Ihraam (of Hajj or 'Umrah), you may hunt, and let not the hatred of some people in (once) stopping you from Al-Masjid Al-Harâm (at Makkah) lead you to transgression (and hostility on your part). Help you one another in Al-Birr and At-Taqwa (virtue, righteousness and piety); but do not help one another in sin and transgression. And fear Allaah. Verily, Allaah is Severe in punishment.} [Quran 5:2].

{O you who believe! Stand out firmly for Allaah and be just witnesses and let not the enmity and hatred of others make you avoid justice. Be just: that is nearer to piety, and fear Allaah. Verily, Allaah is Well Acquainted with what you do} [Quran 5:8]

Fatwa #5 https://www.islamweb.net/en/fatwa/230299/

Question

Assalamu Alaykum. Why does Allah tell us to be stern against the disbelievers in 48:29 and 5:54? Jazakallah Khayr

Answer

All perfect praise be to Allaah, The Lord of the Worlds. I testify that there is none worthy of worship except Allaah, and that Muhammad sallallaahu `alayhi wa sallam (may Allaah exalt his mention) is His slave and Messenger.

A requirement of loving Allaah is loving those whom Allaah loves and hating those whom Allaah hates, and being an ally of those of whom Allaah is an ally and being an enemy of those of whom Allaah is an enemy. Indeed, Allaah told us in the Quran that he does not love the disbelievers and that He is their enemy. He also said that they are His enemies and the enemies of His Messengers. Allaah says (what means): {…then indeed, Allaah does not like the disbelievers.} [Quran 3:32], {Indeed, He does not like the disbelievers.} [Quran 30:45], {…then indeed, Allaah is an enemy to the disbelievers.} [Quran 2:98]

It is not possible for sincere love of Allaah and love of Allaah's enemies or enmity to Allaah's allies to converge in the heart of a servant. It is for this reason that the Prophet sallallaahu `alayhi wa sallam (may Allaah exalt his mention) said: "The strongest bonds of faith are allegiance for the sake of Allaah, enmity for the sake of Allaah, love for *the sake of Allaah and hate for the sake of Allaah." [At-Tabaraani - Al-Albaani graded it Saheeh (sound)]*

The Prophet sallallaahu `alayhi wa sallam (may Allaah exalt his mention) also said: "Whoever loves for the sake of Allaah and hates for the sake of Allaah, he has indeed reached the level of complete faith." [Abu Dawood - Al-Albaani graded it Saheeh (sound)]

Hence, a believer in principal loves Allaah, and loving others is subsequent to it. So if we believe that Allaah loves a person, we love him even if he is of distant relation, and if we believe that Allaah hates a person, we hate him even if he is a close relative.

Here, it should be noted that this is only regarding love for the sake of religion. As for loving a disbeliever not for the sake of his religion but for the sake of kinship, marital or business relations, or for the sake of knowledge or benefit that he provides to others, this is a natural love from instinct and human nature. This kind of love is not forbidden, but it must be associated with hate and dissociation for the sake of religion.

This is in terms of the inner self or the actions of the heart. As regards manifested practical behavior, it must be governed by the guidelines of Islam. In origin, the relationship between a Muslim and non-belligerent non-Muslims is based on kindness and justice, and preaching the truth as much as possible. Hating them does not mean not being kind to them or being unjust with them. Allaah says (what means): {Allaah does not forbid you from those who do not fight you because of religion and do not expel you from your homes — from being righteous toward them and acting justly toward them. Indeed, Allaah loves those who act justly.} [Quran 60:8] For more benefit, kindly refer to Fatwa 198585.

This practical behavior does not run counter to hating them for the sake of Allaah, because they disbelieved in Him and denied His right, which is the greatest and most deserving of all rights.

It should be noted here that being stern with the disbelievers as mentioned in the two verses that you stated in the question, does not contradict being kind and just towards them, because that does not mean oppressing them or violating their legitimate rights. Rather, the way Muslims treat non-Muslims should be based on the Muslim's feeling proud of his religion and not humiliating himself before unbelievers. Dr. Abdul Kareem Zaydaan said in his book Usool Ad-Da'wah, commenting on the verse: {...powerful against the disbelievers...} [Quran 5:54]: "This is like the verse: {Muhammad is the Messenger of Allaah; and those with him are forceful against the disbelievers,...} [Quran 48:29]. That is to say that he [a Muslim] is not to be degraded, or succumb, or does not feel belittled neither in their presence nor in their absence, not outwardly and not inwardly. He is strong against them in the same manner he is gentle to the believers." [End of quote]

On the other hand, the Tafseer al-Waseet, supervised by the Islamic Research Academy in al-Azhar University, reads: "The Prophet sallallaahu `alayhi wa sallam (may Allaah exalt his mention) and his Companions may Allaah be pleased with them were described as being stern against the disbelievers in order to eliminate the disbelievers' hopes that the Prophet would flatter them or abandon or renounce some of what was revealed to him for their sake. Indeed, Allaah commanded His Prophet sallallaahu `alayhi wa sallam (may Allaah exalt his mention) in another verse to be harsh with unbelievers. Allaah says (what means): {O Prophet, strive against the disbelievers and the hypocrites and be harsh upon them...} [Quran 66:9] Allaah also described him as merciful to the believers. Allaah says (what means): {There has certainly come to you a Messenger from among yourselves. Grievous to him is what you suffer; [he is] concerned over you [i.e. your guidance] and to the believers is kind and merciful.} [Quran 9:128]...The harshness of the Prophet sallallaahu `alayhi wa sallam (may Allaah exalt his mention) and his Companions against the disbelievers is when they meet in battle, specifically that they are determined and steadfast. Allaah *promised the believers one of two good things, either martyrdom and death for the sake of Allaah, or achieving victory. As regards living with non-belligerent disbelievers, a Muslim should beware of them because they spare no efforts in plotting to harm Muslims. Indeed, Allaah said the truth us He says (what means): {O you who have believed, do not take as intimates those other than yourselves [i.e. believers], for they will not spare you [any] ruin. They wish you would have hardship...} [Quran 3:118] But this does not prevent being good neighbors with them, and being righteous and just with them."*

There is no doubt that treating non-Muslims in this way of balancing kindness and justice to them and strength and sternness may lead them to reflect on Islam and search for the truth about it. As-Sa'di said in his Tafseer: "Harshness and severity with the enemies of Allaah are matters that bring a servant closer to Allaah. He is one with his Lord in His displeasure with them. Harshness toward the enemies of Allaah does not prevent calling to the religion of Islam in the best manner. One should balance between harshness and severity with them and gentleness in calling them to Allaah. Indeed, both matters are in their interest and the benefit therefrom goes back to them."

Fatwa #6 https://islamqa.info/en/answers/154606/how-can-we-reconcile-between-the-permissibility-of-marriage-to-a-christian-or-jewish-woman-and-belief-in-al-wala-wal-bara

Question

I was having a discussion with my brother about loving the people of the Book, and I said to him that this is not permissible, and it is not permissible to take them as friends or to congratulate them on their festivals, or even initiate greetings with them, and other kinds of love. But he argued back by saying that Allah has permitted us to marry their women, and Allah has created love and compassion between spouses.

I hope that you can give us a detailed answer that will reconcile between the belief in al-wala' wa'l-bara' (love and friendship towards believers versus disavowal of disbelievers), and the notion of love for a wife from the people of the Book (i.e. a Jewish or Christian woman). What are the conditions stipulated in sharee'ah for marriage to a Jewish or Christian woman?

Answer

Praise be to Allah.

Firstly:

We have previously explained the conditions that must be met by a Jewish or Christian woman in order for it to be permissible to marry her. Please see the answers to questions no. 95572 and 2527.

Secondly:

Generally speaking, love is of two types: spiritual love (that is based on ties of faith) and natural love (that is based on human inclinations and feelings). With regard to spiritual love, some types are obligatory and some are prohibited, and some types constitute shirk (association of others with Allah) – you may find a detailed discussion of that in the answer to question no. 276.

With regard to natural love, this is that which is naturally inherent in man, such as love of cold drinks or love of wealth. That also includes love for parents, children and relatives. There is no reward for it in principle, but a person may be sinning if he goes to extremes in his love for these things at the expense of his religious commitment and going against the laws of his Lord, such as if he becomes a slave to money, or he gives precedence to obeying his father over obeying his Lord, and so on.

Ibn al-Qayyim (may Allah have mercy on him) said:

~ 227 ~

It is proven in as-Saheeh that the Prophet said: "No one of you truly believes until I am more beloved to him than his child and his father and all the people." This hadith mentions three kinds of love, for love is either based on respect and veneration, such as love for one's father; or it is based on compassion, affection and kindness, such as love for one's child; or it is love that is motivated by kindness and aspirations of attaining perfection, such as love of people for one another. No person truly believes until his love for the Messenger (blessings and peace of Allah be upon him) is greater than all these kinds of love.

End quote from Jala' al-Afhaam (1/391, 392)

Part of natural love is that which exists between spouses, which dispels the confusion mentioned in the brother's question. The existence of natural love between the spouses does not mean that one should overlook spiritual love that is based on religious ties. Therefore it is possible to dislike her in one way because she is following the wrong religion whilst loving her because she is one's wife. It is possible to differentiate between these two matters, for a person is naturally inclined to have love for fathers, mothers, children and wives, yet at the same time it is not allowed to love the disbelievers who are hostile towards Islam, no matter how close they may be to one. Allah, may He be exalted, says (interpretation of the meaning):

"You (O Muhammad (blessings and peace of Allah be upon him)) will not find any people who believe in Allah and the Last Day, making friendship with those who oppose Allah and His Messenger (Muhammad (blessings and peace of Allah be upon him)), even though they were their fathers, or their sons, or their brothers, or their kindred (people). For such He has written Faith in their hearts, and strengthened them with Rooh (proofs, light and true guidance) from Himself. And We will admit them to Gardens (Paradise) under which rivers flow, to dwell therein (forever). Allah is pleased with them, and they with Him. They

are the Party of Allah. Verily, it is the Party of Allah that will be the successful"

[al-Mujaadilah 58:22].

One of the major principles of Islam is that no soul is burdened with more than it can bear. Hence it is possible to differentiate between the two types of love, that which occurs naturally and that which is prescribed in Islam; this is within a person's capability.

Allah, may He be exalted, has told us of how Ibraaheem (peace be upon him) and the believers who were with him resented their people who were disbelievers, even though among them were their families and relatives, and there was natural love among them. Allah, may He be exalted, says (interpretation of the meaning):

"Indeed there has been an excellent example for you in Ibrahim (Abraham) and those with him, when they said to their people: 'Verily, we are free from you and whatever you worship besides Allah, we have rejected you, and there has started between us and you, hostility and hatred for ever, until you believe in Allah Alone'"

[al-Mumtahinah 60:4].

Allah, may He be exalted, approved of the love of the Prophet (blessings and peace of Allah be upon him) for his paternal uncle Abu Taalib, despite the fact that he was a disbeliever, because that was natural love that was based on ties of kinship.

Shaykh Saalih al-Fawzaan (may Allah preserve him) said:

Allah revealed concerning Abu Taalib the words (interpretation of the meaning): "Verily! You (O Muhammad (blessings and peace of Allah be upon him)) guide not whom you love" [al-Qasas 28:56]. That is, you do not have the power to guide whomever you love among your relatives or your paternal uncle. What is meant by love here is natural love, not spiritual love, for it is not permissible to have spiritual love for a mushrik even if he is the closest of people to you. "You (O Muhammad (blessings and peace of Allah be upon him)) will not find any people who believe in Allah and the Last Day, making friendship with those who oppose Allah and His Messenger (Muhammad (blessings and peace of Allah be upon him)), even though they were their fathers, or their sons, or their brothers, or their kindred (people)" [al-Mujaadilah 58:22]. So spiritual love is not permissible in this case; as for natural love, that does not have anything to do with religious matters.

I'aanah al-Mustafeed bi Sharh Kitaab at-Tawheed (1/356)

All of that was summed up by Shaykh 'Abd ar-Rahmaan al-Barraak (may Allah preserve him) in a wise answer concerning this issue. He said:

There are two types of love: natural love, such as a man's love for his wife, his child and his wealth; this is the type mentioned in the verse in which Allah, may He be exalted, says (interpretation of the meaning): "And among His Signs is this, that He created for you wives from among yourselves, that you may find repose in them, and He has put between you affection and mercy. Verily, in that are indeed signs for a people who reflect" [ar-Room 30:21]. (The other type is) spiritual love, such as love for Allah and His Messenger, and love for that which Allah and His Messenger love of deeds, words and people.

Allah, may He be exalted, says (interpretation of the meaning): "...Allah will bring a people whom He will love and they will love Him..." [al-Maa'idah 5:54]. And the Prophet (blessings and peace of Allah be upon him) said: "The likeness of the believers in their mutual love, compassion and affection is that of the body..."

There is not necessarily a connection between the two types of love, in the sense that natural love may exist alongside spiritual resentment, such as love for parents who are mushrikeen. One may resent them for the sake of Allah, but this is not contrary to love for them which is natural, because humans are created with the inclination to love their parents and relatives, as the Prophet (blessings and peace of Allah be upon him) loved his paternal uncle because he was a close relative, despite the fact that he was a disbeliever. Allah, may He be exalted, says (interpretation of the meaning): "Verily! You (O Muhammad (blessings and peace of Allah be upon him)) guide not whom you love" [al-Qasas 28:56].

Another example of this type of love is: love for a wife who is one of the People of the Book. It is obligatory to resent her in a spiritual sense because of her disbelief, but that does not rule out loving her in the sense of that love which exists between a man and his wife. So she is beloved in one way and resented in another. This is something that occurs frequently. Natural dislike or resentment may be combined with spiritual love, as in the case of jihad: it may be disliked naturally, but loved because Allah enjoins it and because of the positive consequences that result from it in this world and the hereafter. Allah, may He be exalted, says (interpretation of the meaning): "Jihad (fighting in Allah's Cause) is ordained for you (Muslims) though you dislike it, and it may be that you dislike a thing which is good for you and that you like a thing which is bad for you. Allah knows but you do not know" [al-Baqarah 2:216].

Another example of this type is the Muslim's love for his fellow Muslim who has wronged him; he loves him for the sake of Allah but he resents him because of his mistreatment of him. In fact both natural love and natural resentment may coexist, as in the case of bitter medicine: the patient hates it because it is bitter but he takes it because of the benefits he hopes to gain from it.

Similarly, spiritual love may coexist with spiritual resentment, as in the case of the Muslim who is an evildoer; he is loved for the sake of what he has of faith, but he is resented for the sin that he commits.

The wise man is the one who regulates his love and resentment in accordance with Islamic teachings and reason, far removed from whims and desires. And Allah knows best.

Fatwa #7 https://islamqa.info/en/answers/192976/we-know-the-signs-of-allahs-love-for-his-slave-what-are-the-signs-of-allahs-hatred-towards-his-slave

Question

There are many questions on your website and on the Internet in general that speak of the signs of Allah's love for His slave; what are the signs of Allah's hatred towards His slave?

Answer

Praise be to Allah.

Allah, may He be exalted, loves those who believe, hence He makes faith dear to them. And He hates those who disbelieve and disobey Him, unless they repent. If Allah helps a person to believe and makes faith dear to his heart, and makes the believers dear to him and makes him dear to them, and he lives and dies following that, then he is one of those whom Allah loves.

But if Allah makes faith and obedience hateful to a person, and He makes disobedience dear to his heart, and he makes those who are disobedient dear to him and makes him dear to them, and he lives and dies following that, then he is one of those whom Allah hates.

But we cannot be certain that any particular individual is one of those whom Allah loves, just as we cannot be certain that any particular individual is one of those whom Allah hates. It is essential to understand that Allah, may He be glorified and exalted, may hate a person at one time and love him at another time, according to his actions.

If a person commits some of the deeds that Allah hates, it cannot be ruled that he is one of those who Allah hates, for Allah may bestow His mercy upon him and he may repent before he dies and do good deeds, and Allah may forgive him; and he may have hidden righteous deeds that are unknown to people, so Allah may treat him kindly.

What we can be certain about is that Allah hates his disobedient actions and his commission of that sin.

We will highlight some signs and indications that may signal that Allah hates His slave, without stating definitively that everyone who has some of these characteristics is one of those whom Allah hates. These include the following:

·When Allah causes him to be hated and to have a bad reputation and be spoken ill of in this world, because that is usually due to a person's bad conduct and corruption.

Al-Bukhaari (3209) and Muslim (2637) narrated that Abu Hurayrah said: The Messenger of Allah (blessings and peace of Allah be upon him) said: "When Allah loves a person, He calls Jibreel and says: 'I love So and so, so love him.' So Jibreel loves him, then he calls out to the people of heaven, 'Allah loves So and so, so love him.' So the people of heaven love him and he finds acceptance on earth. If Allah hates a person, He calls Jibreel and says: 'I hate So and so, so hate him.' So Jibreel hates him, then he calls out to the people of heaven: 'Allah hates So and so, so hate him.' So they hate him and he is hated on earth."

Al-Bukhaari (1367) and Muslim (949) narrated that Anas ibn Maalik (may Allah be pleased with him) said: A funeral passed by and they spoke well of (the deceased). The Prophet (blessings and peace of Allah be upon him) said: "It has become certain." Another funeral passed by and they spoke badly of (the deceased). The Prophet (blessings and peace of Allah be upon him) said: "It has become certain." 'Umar ibn al-Khattaab (may Allah be pleased with him) said: What has become certain? He said: "For the one of whom you spoke well, Paradise has become certain, and for the one of whom you spoke badly, Hell has become certain. You are the witnesses of Allah on earth."

·He loves that which Allah, may He be exalted, hates, and he hates that which Allah loves

Allah, may He be exalted, said of the people of faith whom He loves (interpretation of the meaning):

"but Allah has endeared the Faith to you and has beautified it in your hearts, and has made disbelief, wickedness and disobedience (to Allah and His Messenger) hateful to you. These! They are the rightly guided ones" [al-Hujuraat 49:7].

·He gets carried away in sin, transgression and misguidance, moving from one sin to another, and he is not enabled to repent, and he dies in that state.

·He persists in keeping company with people of sin and avoids people of faith.

The Messenger of Allah (blessings and peace of Allah be upon him) said: "A man will follow the way of his close friend, so let one of you look at who he takes as a close friend." Narrated by Abu Dawood, 4833; classed as hasan by al-Albaani in Saheeh Abi Dawood etc.

·He does not adhere to the duties enjoined by Allah and the pillars of Islam. So you only see him neglecting the prayer, too lazy to offer it, and ignoring the rights of Allah and the rights of His slaves, not caring about the consequences of that in this world and the Hereafter.

·He hates advice and resents the one who offers it; if he is instructed to do something good or is told not to do something bad, he

takes pride in his sin. Allah, may He be exalted, says (interpretation of the meaning): "And when it is said to him, 'Fear Allah', he is led by arrogance to (more) crime. So enough for him is Hell, and worst indeed is that place to rest" [al-Baqarah 2:206].

·He is hostile towards the people of faith, and he takes the people of disobedience as friends; he loves and hates for something other than the sake of Allah, and is based on that which is not pleasing to Allah. If he loves it is not for the sake of Allah and if he hates it is not for the sake of Allah.

·He hates that which Allah loves and he loves that which Allah hates.

·He has the characteristics that Allah dislikes, such as lying, deceiving, betraying, backbiting, malicious gossip and so on, characteristics that Allah hates and He hates those who have those characteristics. If a person acquires any characteristic that Allah hates, to such an extent that it becomes second nature to him and part of his character, this is something that exposes him to the wrath and hatred of Allah, for Allah when Allah hates a characteristic, He hates for people to adopt it .

·He is one of those who show off and seek to enhance their reputation, one of those who boast, are proud and arrogant, and feel themselves to be above submitting humbly in servitude to Allah.

·His attachment to his religion is weak, and he is more attached to his whims and desires; he only strives to fulfill his desires and evil inclinations, until he becomes like one who has taken his whims and desires as his god.

·He strives hard for worldly gain, but he is heedless about matters of the Hereafter.

Allah, may He be exalted, says (interpretation of the meaning):

"Whoever wishes for the quick-passing (transitory enjoyment of this world), We readily grant him what We will for whom We like. Then, afterwards, We have appointed for him Hell, he will burn therein disgraced and rejected, (far away from Allah's Mercy)" [al-Isra' 17:18].

al-Bukhaari (6435) narrated that Abu Hurayrah (may Allah be pleased with him) said: The Messenger of Allah (blessings and peace of Allah be upon him) said: "Wretched is the slave of the dinar and dirham and fine clothing, if he is given he is pleased and if he is not given he is displeased."

·He gives in to major sins that incur the wrath and anger of Allah, such as zina, consuming riba, slandering chaste women and the like, then he is not enabled to repent.

·He is foul mouthed, evil, a slanderer and evildoer; people avoid him because of his rudeness, bad ways, wrongdoing and transgression of the limits set by Allah.

The Messenger of Allah (blessings and peace of Allah be upon him) said: "The worst of people in status before Allaah on the Day of Resurrection will be those whom the people leave alone for fear of their evil." Narrated by al-Bukhaari, 6032; Muslim, 2591.

·He imitates the disbelievers and evildoers, and hates to resemble the people of faith.

·He commits shirk and falls into it, then he is not enabled to repent from it. Shirk is the worst characteristic a person may have and it exposes him to the wrath and anger of Allah.

To sum up, if a person has the characteristic of obedience to Allah and to His Messenger, then he may be one of those whom Allah loves; if a person persists in disobedience to Allah and His Messenger, then he deserves to incur the hatred and wrath of Allah.

By the same token, it cannot be said of any particular individual that Allah loves this person or that Allah hates this person.

Al-Bukhaari (3332) and Muslim (2643) narrated from Ibn Mas'ood (may Allah be pleased with him) that the Messenger of Allah (blessings and peace of Allah be upon him) said: "A man may do the deeds of the people of Hell until there is nothing between him and it but a cubit, then the decree overtakes him and he does a deed of the people of Paradise, and thus enters Paradise. And a man may do the deeds of the people of Paradise until there is nothing between him and it but a cubit, then the decree overtakes him and he does a deed of the people of Hell and thus enters Hell."

For more information, please see the answer to question no. 23425

And Allah knows best.

https://islamqa.info/en/answers/2179/clarification-of-the-important-rule-it-is-haraam-to-take-kaafirs-as-close-friends-and-protectors

Question

We hope that you will be able to explain, with examples, what is meant by the phrase, "Taking kaafirs as close friends and protectors is haraam."

Answer

Praise be to Allaah.

Yes, examples will certainly explain and clarify what is meant, so we will move straight on to quoting some of the most important points that the scholars and leaders of da'wah have said about different ways of showing friendship towards kaafirs.

Accepting their kufr and doubting that it is kufr at all, or refraining from labelling them as kaafirs, or praising their religion. Allaah says about the kufr of the one who accepts them (interpretation of the meaning): "... but such as open their breasts to disbelief..." [al-Nahl 16:106]. Allaah says, making it obligatory to label the kaafirs as such (interpretation of the meaning): "... Whoever disbelieves in Taaghoot [false deities] and believes in Allaah, then he has grasped the most trustworthy handhold that will never break..." [al-Baqarah 2:256]. Allaah says about the munaafiqoon (hypocrites) who prefer the kuffaar to the Muslims (interpretation of the meaning) "... [they] say to the disbelievers that they are better guided as regards the way than the believers (Muslims)." [al-Nisa' 4:51].

Referring to them for judgement. Allaah says (interpretation of the meaning): "... they wish to got for judgement (in their disputes) to the Taaghoot (false judges, etc.) while they have been ordered to reject them..." [al-Nisa' 4:60]

Befriending and liking them. Allaah says (interpretation of the meaning): "You will not find any people who believe in Allaah and the Last Day, making friendship with those who oppose Allaah and His Messenger..." [al-Mujaadilah 58:22]

Inclining towards them, relying upon them and taking them as a support. Allaah says (interpretation of the meaning): "And incline not towards those who do wrong, lest the Fire should touch you..." [Hood 11:113]

Helping and supporting them against the Muslims. Allaah says (interpretation of the meaning): "The believers, men and women, are awliya' (helpers, supporters, friends, protectors) of one another…" [al-Tawbah 9:71]. He also says of the kuffaar that they are " but awliya' (helpers, supporters, friends, protectors) to one another…" [al-Maa'idah 5:51]. And He says (interpretation of the meaning): "…And if any amongst you takes them as awliya', then surely he is one of them." [al-Maa'idah 5:51].

Becoming members of their societies, joining their parties, increasing their numbers, taking their nationalities (except in cases of necessity), serving in their armies or helping to develop their weapons.

Bringing their laws and rules to the Muslim countries. Allaah says (interpretation of the meaning): "Do they then seek the judgement of the Days of Ignorance?…" [al-Maa'idah 5:50]

Taking them as friends in general terms, taking them as helpers and supporters, and throwing in one's lot with them. Allaah forbids all this, as He says (interpretation of the meaning): "O you who believe! Take not the Jews and the Christians as awliya' (friends, protectors, helpers, etc.), they are but awliya' to one another…" [al-Maa'idah 5:51].

Compromising with them and being nice to them at the expense of one's religion. Allaah says (interpretation of the meaning): "They wish that you should compromise (in religion out of courtesy) with them, so that they (too) would compromise with you." [al-Qalam 68:9]. This includes sitting with them and entering upon them at the time when they are making fun of the Signs of Allaah. Allaah says (interpretation of the meaning): "And it has already been revealed to you in the Book that when you hear the Verses of Allaah being denied and mocked at, then sit not with them, until they engage in a talk other than that; (but if you stayed with them), certainly in that case you would be like them…" [al-Nisa' 4:140]

Trusting them and taking them as advisors and consultants instead of the believers. Allaah says (interpretation of the meaning): "O you who believe! Take not as (your) bitaanah (advisors, consultants, protectors, helpers, friends, etc.) those outside your religion (pagans, Jews, Christians, and hypocrites) since they will not fail to do their best to corrupt you. They desire to harm you severely. Hatred has already appeared from their mouths, but what their breasts conceal is far worse. Indeed We have made clear to you the aayaat (proofs, evidence, verses), if you understand. Lo! You are the ones who love them but they love you not, and you believe in all the Scriptures [i.e., you believe in the Tawraat and the Injeel, while they disbelieve in your Book (the Qur'aan)]. And when they meet you, they say, 'We believe.' But when they are alone, they bite the tips of their fingers at you in rage. Say: 'Perish in your rage. Certainly Allaah knows what is in the breasts (all the secrets).' If a good befalls you, it grieves them, but some evil overtakes you, they rejoice at it..." [Aal 'Imran 3:118-120].

Imaam Ahmad and Muslim reported that the Prophet (peace and blessings of Allaah be upon him) went out to (the battle of) Badr, and a man from among the mushrikeen followed him and caught up with him at al-Harrah. He said, "I wanted to follow you and join you, and have some of the war-booty with you." (The Prophet (peace and blessings of Allaah be upon him)) said: "Do you believe in Allaah and His Messenger?" He said, "No." He said, "Go back, I do not need help from a mushrik."

From these texts it is clear that we are forbidden to appoint kaafirs to positions whereby they could find out the secrets of the Muslims and plot against them by trying to do all kinds of harm.

Putting them in administrative positions where they are bosses of Muslims and can humiliate them, run their affairs and prevent them from practising their religion. Allaah says (interpretation of the meaning): "... and never will Allaah grant to the disbelievers a way (to

triumph) over the believers." [al-Nisa' 4:141]. Imaam Ahmad reported that Abu Moosa al-Ash'ari (may Allaah be pleased with him) said: "I said to 'Umar (may Allaah be pleased with him). 'I have a Christian scribe.' He said, 'What is wrong with you, may Allaah strike you dead! Have you not heard the words of Allaah (interpretation of the meaning),
"O you who believe! Take not the Jews and the Christians as awliya' (friends, protectors, helpers, etc.), they are but awliya' to one another..." [al-Maa'idah 5:51]"? Why do you not employ a haneef [i.e., a Muslim]?' I said, 'O Ameer al-Mu'mineen, I benefit from his work and he keeps his religion to himself.' He said, 'I will never honour them when Allaah has humiliated them, and I will never bring them close to me when Allaah has expelled them from His mercy.'"

Similarly, we should not employ them in Muslim homes where they can see our private matters and they bring our children up as kaafirs. This is what is happening nowadays when kaafirs are brought to Muslim countries as workers, drivers, servants and nannies in Muslim homes and families.

Neither should we send our children to kaafir schools, missionary institutions and evil colleges and universities, or make them live with kaafir families.

Imitating the kaafirs in dress, appearance, speech, etc., because this indicates love of the person or people imitated. The Prophet (peace and blessings of Allaah be upon him) said: 'Whoever imitates a people is one of them."

It is forbidden to imitate the kaafirs in customs, habits and matters of outward appearance and conduct that are characteristic of them. This includes shaving the beard, letting the moustache grow long, and speaking their languages, except when necessary, as well as matters of clothing, food and drink, etc.

Staying in their countries when there is no need to do so. Allaah forbade the weak and oppressed Muslims to stay among the kaafirs if they are able to migrate. He says (interpretation of the meaning): "Verily! As for those whom the angels take (in death) while they are wronging themselves (as they stayed among the disbelievers even though emigration was obligatory for them), they (angels) say (to them): 'In what (condition) were you?' They reply, 'We were weak and oppressed on earth.' They (angels) say: 'Was not the earth of Allaah spacious enough for you to emigrate therein?' Such men will find their abode in Hell –what an evil destination! Except the weak ones among men, women and children, who cannot devise a plan, nor are the able to direct their way." [al-Nisa' 4:97-98].

Nobody will be excused for staying in a kaafir country except for those who are truly weak and oppressed and cannot migrate, or those who stay among them for a valid religious purpose such as da'wah and spreading Islam in their countries.

It is forbidden to live among them when there is no need to do so. The Prophet (peace and blessings of Allaah be upon him) said: "I disown the one who stays among the mushrikeen."

Travelling to their countries for vacations and leisure purposes. But going there for a legitimate reason – such as medical treatment, trade, and learning specialized skills that cannot be obtained in any other way – is permitted in cases of need, and when the need has been fulfilled, it is obligatory to return to the Muslim world.

This permission is also given under the condition that the would-be traveller has sufficient knowledge to dispel his doubts, to control his physical desires, to demonstrate his religion, to be proud of being Muslim, to keep away from evil places, and to be aware and cautious of the plots of his enemies. It is also permissible, and even obligatory, to travel to their lands for the sake of da'wah and spreading Islam.

Praising them and their civilization and culture, defending them, and admiring their behaviour and skills, without taking note of their false ideology and corrupt religion. Allaah says (interpretation of the meaning): "And strain not your eyes in longing for the things We have given for enjoyment to various groups of them (disbelievers), the splendour of the life of this world that We may test them thereby. But the provision (good reward in the Hereafter) of your Lord is better and more lasting." [Ta-Ha 20:131]. It is also forbidden to honour them, give them titles of respect, initiate greetings to them, give them the best seats in gatherings, and give way to them in the street. The Prophet (peace and blessings of Allaah be upon him) said: "Do not be the first to greet a Jew or a Christian (do not initiate the greeting), and if you meet one of them in the street, then push him to the narrowest part of the way."

Forsaking the Islamic calendar and using their calendar, especially since it reflects their rituals and festivals, as is the case with the Gregorian (Western) calendar, which is connected to the supposed date of the birth of the Messiah (peace be upon him), which is an innovation that they have fabricated and that has nothing to do with the religion of 'Eesa (Jesus). Using this calendar implies approval of their festivals and symbols.

In order to avoid all of that, when the Sahaabah (may Allaah be pleased with them) established a calendar for the Muslims during the time of 'Umar (may Allaah be pleased with him), they ignored all the systems of the kuffaar and created a new calendar starting from the date of the Prophet's Hijrah. This indicates that it is obligatory to differ from the kuffaar in this matter and others where it is the matter of distinct characteristics. And Allaah is the Source of Help.

Taking part in their holidays and festivals, helping them to celebrate them, congratulating them on these occasions or attending places where such celebrations are held. The phrase al-zoor [falsehood] in the aayah (interpretation of the meaning) "And those who do not witness falsehood..." [al-Furqaan 25:72] was interpreted as meaning the festivals of the kuffaar.

Using their names that have bad meanings. The Prophet (peace and blessings of Allaah be upon him) changed names whose meanings involved shirk, such as 'Abd al-'Uzza and 'Abd al-Ka'bah.

Seeking forgiveness for them and asking Allaah for mercy for them. Allaah says (interpretation of the meaning): "It is not (proper) for the Prophet and those who believe to ask Allaah's forgiveness for the mushrikeen, even though they be of kin, after it has become clear to them that they are the dwellers of the Fire (because they died in s state of disbelief)." [al-Tawbah 9:113]

These examples should give a clear picture of what is meant by the prohibition of forming close friendships with the kaafirs. We ask Allaah to keep our belief sound and our faith strong. And Allaah is the Source of Help.

Fatwa #8 https://www.madeenah.com/boycotting-the-people-of-innovation-and-sins/

Question: When is it permitted to cut off (i.e. boycott) from an Innovator? When is it permitted to hate for the sake of Allaah? Is boycotting effective in this era?

Response: The believer looks at these situations from the angle of Imaan and the Sharee'ah, free from desires. If boycotting the innovator and being distant from him does not lead to a greater evil then boycotting him is correct, and the least level it reaches is that it is Sunnah (i.e. recommended but not obligatory). Similar to this is boycotting a person

~ 244 ~

whose disobedience is public, and makes it apparent – the least level it reaches is that it is Sunnah (i.e. recommended but not obligatory).

However, if not boycotting [such people] is better for their rectification – because a person considers it more effective to give Da'wah to the innovators, direct them to the Sunnah, teach them what Allaah has obligated upon them and wanting [good] for them – then one should not be hasty in boycotting them.

Despite this, a person should hate them for the sake of Allaah; hate the disbeliever for the sake of Allaah and also hate the disobedient people for the sake of Allaah. [He should hate these people] according to their level of sin and according to their level of innovation. One's hate for the disbeliever is more severe; and the hate towards an innovator is according to his innovation. If his innovation is not an innovation of disbelief then to this level; and the sinner according to his level of sinning. Also, he is loved for the sake of Allaah according to his level of Islaam.

As for boycotting, [the issue] contains some detail. Ibn Abdil Qawiyy (may Allaah have mercy upon him) said in his famous poem,

It is said that if [boycotting] restrains him, it is obligatory and more emphasised

and boycotting a person who openly shows his sins is recommended

Greet him with a gloomy face…

And it is said [boycotting] is obligatory as long as he [sins] in open

In summary, the most correct and better opinion is that a person considers what is more beneficial [in boycotting or not boycotting].

The Prophet (sal Allaahu alayhi wa sallam) boycotted a group of people, but did not do so with another group of people. [He did this] considering the Islamic legislated benefit. He boycotted Ka'b Ibn Maalik and his two companions (may Allaah be pleased with them) when they stayed behind in the Battle of Tabuk without any valid excuse. He boycotted them fifty nights until they repented, and Allaah forgave them.

However he did not boycott Abdullah ibn Ubay ibn Salool and a group of others who were accused of hypocrisy. This was due to certain legislated reasons that necessitated [not boycotting]. So a believer has to consider what is of more benefit.

This however does not negate hating the disbeliever for the sake of Allaah; hating the innovator for the sake of Allah; hating a sinner for the sake of Allaah; [whilst at the same time] loving a Muslim for the sake of Allaah, loving a sinner according to the level of his Islaam and loving an innovator as long as his innovation has not caused him to become a disbeliever – [the innovator is loved] according to his level of Islaam.

As for boycotting them, one should consider the potential benefit: If by boycotting them, some goodness is hoped and it is hoped they will repent to Allaah from their sin, then [in this case] the recommendation is to boycott. A group of scholars considered it to be an obligation in this situation, they said it is an obligation.

If in boycotting them or not boycotting them, the expected outcome is the same, i.e. there is no evil nor good, then it is better to boycott them, implementing this legislated act, and also making clear the obligation of forbidding an evil. In such a case, boycotting them is better and safer, and also to teach the people their sin and mistake.

The second situation is where boycotting them leads to a disadvantage, a greater evil. In this situation, a person should not boycott them. If by boycotting this innovator, his evil upon the people *will increase, and he will advance further in spreading his message to innovations, and his innovations and evil will increase*

He will exploit the boycotting in calling the people to falsehood. [In such an instance] he is not to be boycotted, rather debated, and the people are to be warned against him. The people should not be too distant from him so they can observe his actions, so they can prevent him expanding his innovations and so they can warn the people from him. They should constantly give him Da'wah. Perhaps Allaah will guide him and people can be safe from his evil.

Similar to this is a person who sins in public, if by leaving and boycotting him will result in his evil becoming widespread and he will gain some influence over the people then he is not to be boycotted. Rather he should always be debated and disputed; people should be constantly warned against his evil so they can be safe from it and so trials and tribulations do not occur due to his sins. We ask Allaah for safety.

Fatwa #9
https://www.islamweb.net/en/fatwa/85074/hating-a-muslim-for-his-bad-behaviour

Question

Is hate permitted? Is there a difference between hating the behavior of someone or the person himself?

Answer

Praise be to Allah, the Lord of the World; and may His blessings and peace be upon our Prophet Muhammad and upon all his Family and Companions.

To have a pure creed, Muslims are required to hate disbelievers. This, in fact, constitutes the creed of al-Baraa (i.e. to hate disbelievers and to avoid helping them).

Allah Says (interpretation of meaning): {Indeed there has been an excellent example for you in Ibrâhim (Abraham) and those with him, when they said to their people: "Verily, we are free from you and whatever you worship besides Allâh, we have rejected you, and there has started between us and you, hostility and hatred for ever, until you believe in Allâh Alone," ...} [60: 4].

Thus, it becomes clear that our father, the Prophet Ibrahim (Alaihi As-Salaam), and believers with him declared freedom from all obligations towards disbelievers and showed them hate.

Therefore, every Muslim is required to do and be so. In simple words, a Muslim has to hate disbelievers from the depths of his heart unless they embrace Islam and become true Muslims.

The Prophet (Sallallahu Alaihi wa Sallam) said: "The strongest bond of faith lies in loving and hating for Allah's sake" [al-Bazzar].
As for a Muslim, we - Muslims - are required to love him to the extent he demonstrates good and piety, and hate him and his disobedience and misdeeds likewise. Then, our love to him increases by his better obedience and good deeds. Allah knows best.

https://islamqa.info/en/answers/189207/an-atheist-is-asking-why-do-you-hate-me

Question

I came across this site some time ago and have been intrigued but also felt a little uncomfortable and what has been written. As a non muslim i am well aware that you hate me, you have stated plenty of times when answering questions posed by others that non believers are to be hated and that you cannot understand why anyone would care about them or love them. In my opinion you view me as a lower form of life that is to be hated, why? what have i ever done to you? i feel insulted that you would blame me for actions i did not make or offences i did not give. i do not speak for others i speak only for myself. why should i convert if i will be surrounded by evil people who hate me.

Answer

Praise be to Allah.

We appreciate your frankness and your courage in sending this question, and we are very happy to answer it. Our hearts and the heart of every Muslim are filled with mercy and compassion towards all of creation, believers and disbelievers, male and female, young and old, white and black. All of them are the children of Adam, and Adam was created from dust. So the humanity that unites us reminds us Muslims that our father Adam (peace be upon him) was expelled from Paradise as a result of his sin, and that results in trials for his progeny so long as this world remains. The one who adheres to the innate, sound human nature of monotheism, to which Adam (peace be upon him) adhered, will be victorious and will be saved, and he will return to his original home which is eternal Paradise with the Lord of the Worlds. But those of the progeny of Adam who are diverted by whims and desires and other distractions will suffer true loss and will be deprived of returning to the eternal Paradise from which our father Adam (peace be upon him) was expelled.

Our Prophet (blessings and peace of Allah be upon him) said:

"O people, Your Lord is One and your father is one. There is no superiority of an Arab over a non-Arab, or of a non-Arab over an Arab, or of a white man over a black man, or of a black man over a white man, except in terms of taqwa (piety, God-consciousness)."

~ 249 ~

A saheeh (sound) hadeeth, narrated by Ahmad in his Musnad, no. 23489.

It is from this point that our relationship with you begins, and it is with this philosophy that the Muslim is required to look at all of creation, that they are prisoners of their own evil inclinations and the Shaytaan (Satan), who are their real enemies, and it is essential to help all of them to escape from these bonds by means of believing in Allah, the One and Only, the Unique, the Eternal, Absolute, Who begets not, nor was He begotten, and there is none like unto Him. This is the way to freedom, and this is the message of all of His noble Prophets.

This is how our Prophet Muhammad (blessings and peace of Allah be upon him) was; he shed tears and his heart was broken out of compassion and sorrow for those who did not believe in him and did not join his caravan that would take them back to their original home for which they were created and from which they were expelled, which is Paradise. That great compassion that filled the heart of the Prophet (blessings and peace of Allah be upon him) deserved to be recorded by Allah in the Qur'an, where He said (interpretation of the meaning): "Perhaps you would kill yourself (O Muhammad) in grief, over them (for their turning away from you), because they believe not in this narration (the Quran)" [al-Kahf 18:6] i.e., perhaps your grief for them would destroy you.

See Tafseer al-Qur'an al-'Azeem, 5/137

We do not hate you personally. How could we hate you when we do not know you and have never met you; we could never despise you for your colour, your race or your family. All of that is forbidden to us, to love or hate people because of their colour, lineage or forebears. Rather our hatred and enmity is directed towards the disbelief and atheism that you carry in your heart and will soon destroy you and lead you to the eternal punishment of Allah, and that will bring upon you misery in this world and in the hereafter. We feel very sorry for you because of this misery and we are striving to save you from it; we wish that we could do that!

It was narrated from Abu Hurayrah (may Allah be pleased with him) that he said: The Messenger of Allah (blessings and peace of Allah be upon him) said: "Allah has taken away your pride of Jaahiliyyah (ignorance) and your boasting about your forefathers. One is only a righteous believer or a doomed evildoer. You are the sons of Adam and Adam was created from dust. Men should stop boasting about their forefathers, who are no more than the coal of Hell, or they will certainly be more insignificant before Allah than the beetle that rolls dung with its nose." A saheeh (sound) hadeeth, narrated by Abu Dawood (5116) et al.

We think that you will agree with us that all humans are free to believe in and to love or hate any idea or belief. This is one of the freedoms that are guaranteed by modern constitutions. But no human being has the right to mistreat those who differ from him in belief by wronging them, annoying them or betraying them, or trying to cause them harm, just because of the differences in belief between them.

If you were living among Muslims who truly adhere to Islam, you would be living a good and happy life, and you would have the rights brought by Islamic law over fourteen hundred years ago, which are not surpassed by the rights brought by modern civil societies. At that time the earth was filled with oppression and tyranny that trampled upon human dignity. The first of these rights is the right to follow the beliefs that you choose, as is the view of many of the jurists and scholars. Ibn al-'Arabi (may Allah have mercy on him) said: All of our scholars said that the jizyah (a form of tax paid by non-Muslims in return which they are granted protection and freedom of worship by the Islamic state) is to be taken from every disbeliever, and this is the correct view. End quote from

Ahkaam al-Qur'an, 1/156; there is a similar remark in Tafseer al-Qurtubi (8/110). If your belief is Judaism or Christianity or Zoroastrianism, then you have complete freedom according to the consensus of the jurists. Allah, may He be exalted, says (interpretation of the meaning): "There is no compulsion in religion" [al-Baqarah 2:256].

If you lived among Muslims, you would be safe from any harm by any means. The Prophet of Islam Muhammad (blessings and peace of Allah be upon him) said: "Whoever kills a mu'aahad (non-Muslim living under Islamic rule) will never smell the fragrance of Paradise, although its fragrance may be detected from a distance of forty years."

Narrated by al-Bukhaari, no. 6914.

If you lived among Muslims, you and all of your property would be safe against any transgression. The Prophet of Islam Muhammad (blessings and peace of Allah be upon him) disavowed anyone who transgresses against non-Muslims.

If you lived among Muslims and you fell sick or were stricken by harm or calamity, they would hasten to visit you and they would support you in the hope of reward from Allah, may He be glorified and exalted. They would always be eager to save you from the Fire even if you were on your deathbed, at which time you would have no power to cause them harm or bring them benefit. In such a situation they would not hope for anything from you except what they would hope for you now when you are healthy, which is that Allah should save you from the Fire.

Have you not heard the report from the Prophet Muhammad (blessings and peace of Allah be upon him) that he had a Jewish servant who served him and he treated him kindly? He (the Jewish boy) fell sick, so the Prophet (blessings and peace of Allah be upon him) came to visit him. He sat by his head and said to him: "Become Muslim." (The boy) looked at his father, who was there with him, and he said to him: Obey Abu'l-Qaasim [i.e., the Prophet] (blessings and peace of Allah be upon him). So he became Muslim, and the Prophet (blessings and peace of Allah be upon him) left, saying: "Praise be to Allah Who has saved him from the Fire." Narrated by al-Bukhaari, no.1356

If you lived among Muslims, society would allocate to you a monthly stipend to help you with living costs. In the covenant that Khaalid ibn al-Waleed wrote for the people of al-Heerah in Iraq, who were Christians, it says: "I allocate to them: for any old man who is incapable of working or who has been stricken by calamity, or who was independent of means and then became poor and his coreligionists start giving charity to him, the jizyah is waived and a stipend is to be given to him and his dependents from the bayt al-maal (treasury) of the Muslims."

End quote from al-Kharaaj by Abu Yoosuf, p. 144.

The title that may be given to the mission of our Prophet Muhammad (blessings and peace of Allah be upon him) in brief is: mercy. Allah, may He be exalted, says (interpretation of the meaning): "And We have sent you (O Muhammad) not but as a mercy for the worlds" [al-Anbiya' 21:107]. And Allah knows best.

And our Prophet Muhammad (blessings and peace of Allah be upon him) said of himself: "O people, I am but a mercy that has been bestowed." Narrated by ad-Daarimi, 15; classed as saheeh by al-Albaani.

If we were to quote examples of Islamic tolerance throughout the history of the Islamic state, that would fill dozens of pages. If you would like to read and study further, you could read the book by Prof. 'Umar ibn 'Abd al-'Azeez entitled Samaahat al-Islam (Islamic Tolerance), published by al-Maktabah adh-Dhahabiyyah and Maktabat al-Adeeb.

We ask Allah, may He be glorified and exalted, to guide you and open your heart.

https://www.thesunniway.com/articles/item/263-calling-a-kafir-a-kafir

Question

Respected Mufti Sahib, Someone that says that we mustn't call a kaafir as a kaafir as because what if he died whilst reciting the Shahadah. As we know on the same token a Muslim may be a Muslim but we don't know how he will die

Please enlighten us with the proper Islamic ruling

Answer

Only an ignorant person can make such a comment. All throughout the history of Islam, the magnificent scholars have unanimously agreed that it is a part of Imaan (faith) to know a kafir as a kafir and a Muslim as a Muslim. This is the reason why in their books they have a section named Baab Al-Murtad. All the books of Aqaa'id (Beliefs) and Fiqh (Jurisprudence) have included this section and clearly clarified that whoever did such and such or said such and such is a 'kafir'.

In Bahare Shariat, it says:

"To regard a Muslim a Muslim and a kafir a kafir is from the necessities of faith."

Sadr Al-Shariah further writes:

"Although we cannot say with certainty regarding a specific individual that he died as a Muslim or (may Allah protect) as a kafir until the state of his death is proven by Shar'i evidence; however, this *does not mean that one may doubt the kufr of someone who has clearly committed kufr, because doubting the kufr of a clear kafir makes the person a kafir."*

He further writes:

"Judgement in the hereafter will be based on the state at the time of death, but the hukm (rule) of Shariah is based on the apparent. For example, if a kafir such as a Jew, Christian or idol worshipper died, it cannot be said with certainty that he died as a kafir; but it is the command of Allah and His Messenger (peace and blessings be upon him) for us to regard him as a kafir. We must deal with all his matters in his life and after his death as we deal with the matters of every kafir such as: the matters of association; marriage; Salah Al-Janazah; shroud (kafan for the deceased); and burial. When he has committed kufr, then it is an obligation that we know him as a kafir and leave his state of death to Allah (whether he died a kafir or a believer); in the same way as a person who is an apparent Muslim and has not made any statement or committed any action against Imaan (faith), it is an obligation that we must know him as a Muslim, even though we do not know the state he died in."

The tremendous Scholar Qadi Iyad in his Shifaa' writes:

"There is a unanimous consensus upon the kufr of he who does not regard the Jews, Christians or anyone who separates from the religion of the Muslims as a kafir; or he who hesitates in calling them kafir; or he who doubts in this matter. Qadi Abu Bakr (Al-Baaqalani) said: This is because the tawqeef (Shar'i evidence from the Quran and Sunnah upon which none can speak with their own opinion like the number of units in Salah) and the consensus (of the Ummah) both agree upon their kufr; therefore, whoever hesitates or has a doubt in calling them kafir, has rejected the evidence and the tawqeef. Only a kafir would reject or doubt in such a matter."

From the above, one can understand how ignorant a person must be to feel so confident that he is prepared to dispute and differ from not only all the giant scholars all throughout the Islamic history, but also against the unanimous agreement of the Ummah. Yet, he does not wish to stop there; he takes this dispute against Allah and the Messenger of Allah (peace and blessings be upon him) that he will not call a kafir a kafir.

Qadi Iyad further writes in his Shifaa':

"He is a kafir who does not regard those who believe in other than Islam as kafir; or he who hesitates or has doubt in this matter; or he deems their religion correct, even if he himself claims to be a Muslim and apparently deems the rest of the false religions incorrect; he is a kafir for making apparent what he made apparent against that."

Is it not clear that black is black, white is white, water is water, fire is fire, a book is a book, a pen is a pen, a man is a man, a woman is a woman, a child is a child, a Jew is a Jew, a Christian is a Christian, a Buddhist is a Buddhist and a Muslim is a Muslim? Of course it is! Then why is a kafir not a kafir?

If you look in the Quran and Sunnah, you will find that Allah and His beloved Messenger (peace and blessings be upon him) rendered many nominal Muslims kafir. These were people who swore that they were Muslims, performed Salah behind the Prophet Muhammed (peace and blessings be upon him) and even took part in Jihad side by side with the Sahaabah (Allah is pleased with them); but because they uttered a sentence of kufr, Allah and His Messenger (peace and blessings be upon him) rendered them kafir. It is mentioned in Musannaf Ibn Abi Shaybah, Ibn Munzir, the Tafseer of Sheikh Addi Bin Abi Haatim and recorded in Al-Durr Al-Manthoor, by Imam Jalal Al-Deen Al-Suyooti, regarding a man who lost his female camel and came to ask the Messenger of Allah (peace and blessings be upon him) for help. The Messenger of Allah *(peace and blessings be upon him) advised him to go to such and such a place and that he would find his camel there. Upon this some people said:*

"Muhammad says that such and such a person's camel is in such and such a place; what does he know of the gayb (unseen)?"

These were people who had declared that there is none worthy of worship but Allah Muhammad is the Messenger of Allah; they performed Salah behind the Prophet (peace and blessings be upon him); and they fought in the battlefields under the banner of Allah. When the Prophet (peace and blessings be upon him) was informed of their statement, he called for them and enquired why they said such. They replied:

"We were only joking and playing."

Allah, the Almighty and Wise, revealed a verse of the Quran upon this; this is the sixty fifth verse of Surah Al-Tawbah:

"Say O Beloved: Are you joking with Allah, His verses and His Messenger? Do not make excuses, you have become kafir after your Imaan (faith)."

There are several other verses in which Allah has declared some who accepted Islam and became Muslims as kafir, due to an act or a statement. Even in the Hadith, the Messenger of Allah (peace and blessings be upon him) foretold us of people who will be nominal Muslims, yet will not be Muslims. This Hadith in Bukhari Shareef is an eye opener, and one should read it again and again. Sayyiduna Ali (Allah is pleased with him) narrated that the Messenger of Allah (peace and blessings be upon him) said:

"A time will come upon the people in which nothing from Islam will remain but its name; nothing from the Quran will remain but its written form; their Masaajid will be full but empty from guidance; fitnah (corruption) will be released from them and in them, it will return."

In the time of Sayyiduna Ali (Allah is pleased with him), he regarded the khawaarij as kafir and went to war against them; and then there were those who said Ali is worthy of worship. Thus, Sayyiduna Ali regarded them as kafir and ordered for them to be burnt in fire.

This continued all throughout the history of Islam where the Ulema regarded groups who deviated as either misguided or kafir based upon their actions, statements and beliefs. The Messenger of Allah said:

"When fitnah or innovation becomes apparent and the Scholar does not express his knowledge, then the curse of Allah and the Angels and all the people is upon him."

If we were to follow the ideology of this person, where we do not call a kafir a kafir, because we do not know what is in his heart or in what state he will die, then this would mean that we must not call a Muslim a Muslim, because we do not know what is in his heart or in what state he will die. This would also mean that he cannot call his own father a Muslim or even the Sahabah (Allah is pleased with them) cannot be called Muslims and the pious predecessors, like Imam Abu Hanifah and Imam Shafa'i and Sheikh Abd Al-Qadir Al-Jeelaani, cannot be regarded a Muslim anymore. In the same way, Khumeni cannot be called a kafir, nor can we call Salman Rushdie or George Bush a kafir.

May Allah protect us from such ignorance and keep us firm on the path of the pious predecessors.

Allah knows best and He is most Wise.

www.ingramcontent.com/pod-product-compliance
Lightning Source LLC
Chambersburg PA
CBHW070917120626
46546CB00001B/302